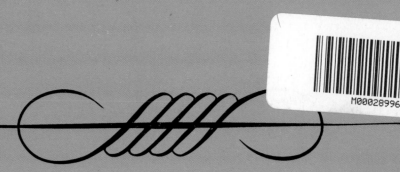

SODA

ADVERTISING

OPENERS

Donald A. Bull and John R. Stanley

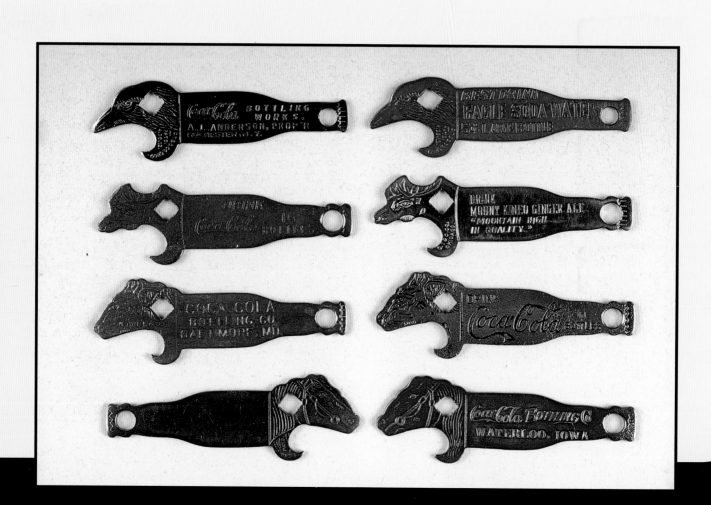

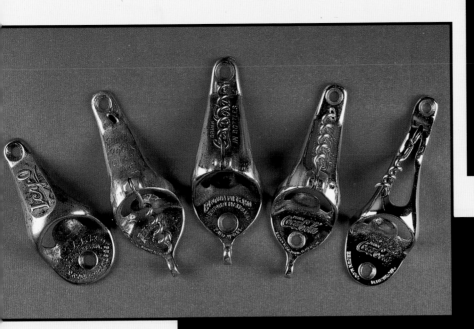

SODA
ADVERTISING
OPENERS

Donald A. Bull and John R. Stanley

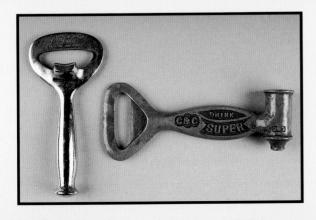

4880 Lower Valley Road, Atglen, PA 19310 USA

DEDICATION

To Harry L. Vaughan

Copyright © 2000 by Donald A. Bull & John R. Stanley
Library of Congress Catalog Card Number: 99-68313

Cover design by Bruce Waters
Book design by Blair Loughrey
Type set in Americana XBd BT/ZapfHumnst BT

ISBN: 0-7643-1056-9
Printed in China
1 2 3 4

Published by Schiffer Publishing Ltd.
4880 Lower Valley Road
Atglen, PA 19310
Phone: (610) 593-1777; Fax: (610) 593-2002
E-mail: Schifferbk@aol.com
Please visit our web site catalog at
www.schifferbooks.com

This book may be purchased from the publisher.
Include $3.95 for shipping.
Please try your bookstore first.

We are interested in hearing from authors with book ideas on related subjects.
You may write for a free catalog.

In Europe, Schiffer books are distributed by
Bushwood Books
6 Marksbury Ave.
Kew Gardens
Surrey TW9 4JF England
Phone: 44 (0)208 392-8585; Fax: 44 (0)208 392-9876
E-mail: Bushwd@aol.com
Free postage in the UK. Europe: air mail at cost.
Try your bookstore first.

CONTENTS

ACKNOWLEDGMENTS

Since its formation in 1978, *Just For Openers (JFO)* has been the guiding light for soda and beer advertising opener and corkscrew collectors. The organization is thriving and this book is a collective result of their research and efforts over the years.

As with any endeavor of this kind, special thanks must be given to a number of individuals for their contributions. Many of the openers pictured in this book were loaned by these collectors. A special thanks to these contributors: John Archer, Murray Atkinson, Kurt Bachmann, Larry Biehl, John Bitterman, Linwood Blalock, Dick Britton, John Burrus III, John Cartwright, Gary Comer, Gary Deachman, Dale Deckert, Clayton Denny, Sandra Emme, William Ennis, John Fisher, Jack Ford, Paul Gauvin, Joe Gormally, Janet Goss, Eldon Gregg, John Hall, Ray Hanson, Ollie Hibbeler, Ben Hoffman, David Hoffman, Ardea Horn (wife of the late John Horn), Harry Horn, Roger Jarrell, Judy Jay, Art Johnson, Art Johnson, Jr., Vic Keown, Dave Lendy, Elvira McKienzie (wife of the late Bill McKienzie), Gerry McLellan, John Minges, John Mlady, Fred Mosrie, Larry Moter, Jim Osborn, Dave Pinney, Harold Queen, Carl Rees, Mike Rose, Art Santen, Ed Schaefer, Ray Schmeisser, Don Sherman, Bob Stahly, Henry Stawarz, Stan Summers, Lou Sutton, Thom Thompson, Verne Vollrath, Paul Wagner, Jack Westall, Don Whelan, and Joe Young. We must also extend a very special thank you to Thom Thompson who generously loaned half of his Coca-Cola opener collection. Without his contributions this book would be missing many of the known opener types. Another major contributor who has since sold his collection was William Ennis. His early efforts provided a major portion of the listings section of this book.

The willingness of so many collectors to contribute openers from their collections was greatly appreciated. Sharing information has always been one of the core focal points of *JFO*. The results in this book are due to four years of gathering information from the above collectors.

The knowledge shared by the above collectors will hopefully be passed on through this book to future generations of collectors. The authors hope that many new collectors will be convinced that opener collecting is a viable and interesting hobby. One would not think that such small objects have had such a major impact on the twentieth-century world as have openers and corkscrews. The advent of pop top cans and screw-off top bottles has eliminated the need for bottle openers. Preserving the history of these little gems for future generations is the scope of this book.

A special thank you is reserved for Ollie Hibbeler, who convinced John Stanley, who in turn convinced Don Bull that *Soda Advertising Openers* would be a worthwhile endeavor. Hopefully readers will agree. And another special thank you to Bonnie Bull for her assistance with the photographs.

IN THE BEGINNING

In 1978, *Beer Advertising Openers, A Pictorial Guide* by Donald Bull was published. This book pictured over 200 types of American beer advertising openers and classified them by type and category. A catalog of known American advertising pieces by type was included in the book. In the following year, Bull founded *Just For Openers* with the introduction of a quarterly newsletter. The purpose of the newsletter was to give advertising opener collectors a vehicle to broaden their collections and to keep a running catalog of new finds by type and by advertising. In less than a year membership had reached 200, a convention was held, and plans were underway for a meeting in the next year. Along the way many soda openers collectors have joined and become an integral part of *JFO*.

More books by Bull followed along with twenty *JFO* conventions. Ed Kaye was *JFO* editor from 1984 to 1988, followed by Art Santen from 1989 to 1993. In 1994 John Stanley took over as editor of *JFO*. By then many members were interested in soda openers. Most beer opener collectors were more than willing to trade soda openers for beer openers. But the passing years have certainly proven that interest in soda openers far surpasses beer openers. This is reflected especially in prices. While major soda brands such as Coca-Cola, Pepsi-Cola, and Dr. Pepper lead the way, many minor brands have faired well in the collecting market.

In 1995 John Stanley was persuaded by *JFO* member Ollie Hibbeler that it was time to produce a book on soda openers. With Schiffer's publication of *Just For*

Openers by Bull and Stanley, *Soda Advertising Openers* was the logical next step. Who knows what might come next, Whiskey Advertising Openers? or maybe even Dairy Advertising Openers? After four years of work, a soda opener book is now offered.

PLOTTING

The idea for *Soda Advertising Openers* began with Ollie Hibbeler offering his 200 different soda openers as a start for the book in 1995. The groundwork was laid and through *JFO*, hundreds of listings and types were sent to Stanley. William Ennis alone contributed about two hundred types and a thousand listings. A decision was made by Stanley early in the process to list only United States distributed openers with either soda or bottling advertising. He believed that most bottlers have at one time or another bottled some brand of soda. This book certainly contains several Canadian openers and even some English patented openers. The authors assume they were given out by American companies and these pieces add to the variety and scope of the book.

By 1997 Stanley had a fairly comprehensive list of soda openers. After a trip to photograph Thom Thompson's collection, his plan was to publish a small book on soda openers. Unfortunately he was missing many of the types needed in the book as William Ennis had given his collection to his son Roy. Through 1997 and much of 1998 Stanley worked with Roy Ennis in selling his father's collection and he was able to gather many of the types needed for the book. By this time Bull and Stanley were working on *Just For Openers* and after some conversa-

tion Bull was convinced to help complete *Soda Advertising Openers*.

With the considerable help of Thom Thompson, Bull and Stanley were able to gather the types shown and to photograph and complete *Soda Advertising Openers*. The final product will hopefully meet expectations of soda collectors everywhere.

RESULTS

The following guidebook is now presented for your enjoyment. We should make some clarifications. Don Bull originally set up the alphanumeric system used for this book in 1978. Over the years close to 900 beer types have been listed. Not wanting to change this system, we chose to use the same type numbers whenever possible. But many soda types did not have a corresponding beer alphanumeric listing. Stanley decided to start non-corresponding beer types with 501, 502, and so on whenever needed. Many beer types are not represented in soda openers resulting in many gaps in the numbering system. Please refer to *Just For Openers* if you would like to see any missing types.

Stanley also decided to only present pre-1970 openers and corkscrews. Some exceptions may be in the book and arguments could be made either way as to what year some openers and corkscrews were made. A chapter has been added to deal with some of the post-1970 openers and corkscrews. Within categories, we have grouped similar types together while maintaining the original assigned alphanumeric designation. To help locate types by alphanumeric designation, there is a type index included in the back of this book. Each chapter contains an

Alpha type, e.g., Flat Figural Openers are type A; Key Shape Openers are type B; etc.

This book first presents the known types followed by an information chapter and finally a chapter of listings which includes all of the advertising openers known by brand name for that opener type. The listings section is alphabetized by brand and in many cases even if the brand is not listed first on the opener it is shown first to help readability.

The history of the openers and corkscrews is best told through the bits of information in the chapter introductions, some facts included in captions, and the American Patent chronological list in Part 2. Notable advertisement and highlights from some openers are included in the captions in *italics*.

In *Just For Openers* we included a value range for each type. With soda openers many of the types have a wide value range so values were assigned to each opener in the "Catalog of Openers" Section. Please use the following guidelines when using values in this book:

> Value ranges are based on past sales both public and private, prices advertised in the media and at shows, prices realized on Internet sales, and gut feelings. In cases where prior sale information is not readily available, value is based upon relative scarcity versus known values.
>
> Condition: Values are for openers in at least excellent condition. Exceptions to this rule would be rare openers where only a few are even just one are known. The condition of a rare opener would be what is acceptable to the buyer and usually that is an opener in at least good condition. (See "Grading Openers" in the information section.)
>
> Scarcity: The highest values are generally the hardest to find especially in nice condition. Several types have few examples known and this is reflected in the value.
>
> Demand: Bottling companies and little known brands are usually at the low end. Major brands such as Coca-Cola, Pepsi-Cola, and Dr. Pepper usually bring the highest value. Also brands names with local towns and cities almost always bring more than openers with just generic advertising. From time to time, a discovery of a hoard of openers will affect the values. For example, the G-13 Coca-Cola and the H-5 Pepsi=Cola have been found in large numbers. The G-13 was found about 15 years ago and the price has remained $15-20, while the H-5 was found more recently and prices are now about $10 each (previously they were valued $20-25).

Neither the authors nor the publisher will be responsible for any gain or loss experienced by using the value guidelines.

If you would like to join *Just For Openers*, have questions about openers, or want to add to the catalog listings of soda openers, contact:

John R. Stanley
P. O. Box 64
Chapel Hill, NC 27514

If you would like further information on corkscrews, contact:

Donald A. Bull
P. O. Box 596
Wirtz, VA 24184

Part 1
SODA ADVERTISING OPENERS

FLAT FIGURAL OPENERS

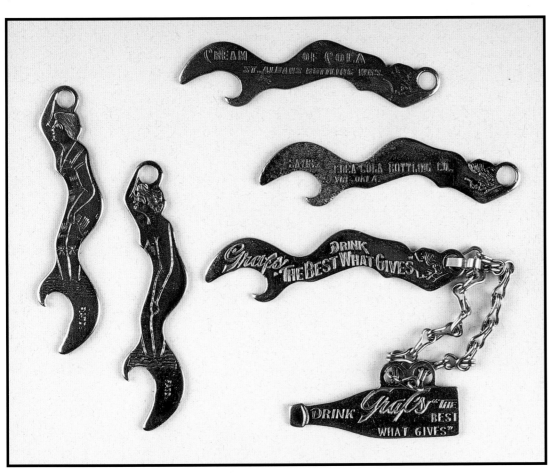

Openers in the shapes of bathing beauties, nudes, legs, automobiles, swords, bridges, hands, fish, various animals, and bottles have been used extensively for advertising. In some cases, the designs were actually patented. Many of the shapes are found with a Prest-O-Lite key added. This is a square hole that was used to turn the valve on gas tanks of old cars for lighting the car lamps. (Note: the key has been frequently misidentified as a skate key.) Manufacturers include Crown Throat and Opener Company, Chicago (later Vaughan Company); Louis F. Dow Co., St. Paul, Minnesota; J. L. Sommer Manufacturing Company, New Jersey; and Indestro Manufacturing Company, Chicago.

A-1 Bathing girl, mermaid, or surf-girl. Found in clothed and nude versions. Marked C. T. & O. CO. PATD. CHICAGO or PATD (C. T. & O. CO. is the abbreviation for Crown Throat & Opener Company—the first name for Vaughan Novelty). American design patent 46,762 issued to Harry L. Vaughan, December 8, 1914. 2 7/8". Prices in a 1922 Vaughan catalog were $6.50 for 250 to $15.00 per thousand in 10,000 quantity.

Right:
Left two: A-3 Girl in bathing suit and cap. 3 1/8". *Produced by Indestro Manufacturing Company of Chicago.*
Right two: A-508. Clothed lady. *Only found with "Drink Concord Grape Soda" advertising.* 3".

Below:
Top four: A-4 Girl clothed (calendar) and nude (Early Morn). Marked C. T. & O. CO. PAT'D. CHICAGO or PATD. American design patent 44,226 issued to Harry L. Vaughan, June 17, 1913. 2 3/4".
Bottom two: A-5 Girl in clothed (calendar) and nude (Early Morn) versions. Marked C. T. & O. CO. PAT'D. CHICAGO or MADE IN U. S. A. PAT'D. American design patent 44,226 issued to Harry L. Vaughan, June 17, 1913. 2 3/4".

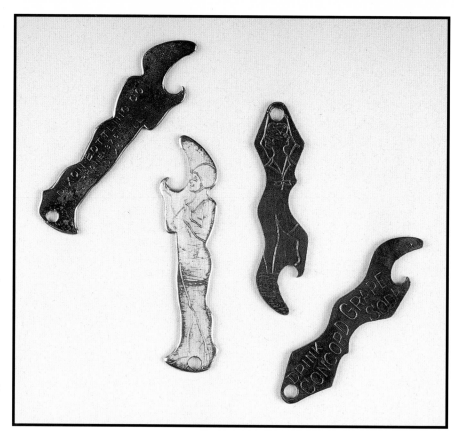

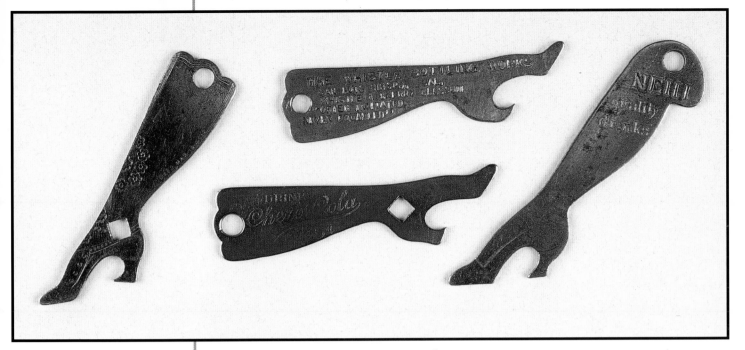

Top center: A-7 Lady's fancy boot. American design patent 42,306 issued to John L. Sommer, March 12, 1912. 3 1/8".
Left and bottom center: A-35 Lady's fancy boot. Prest-O-Lite key. Marked PATD MAR 12-1912. American design patent 42,306 issued to John L. Sommer, March 12, 1912. 3 1/8". *The award for most appropriate advertising for the design goes to: "You won't kick if you drink Wineberg's beverages."*
Right: A-509 Large lady's leg. 3 1/2".

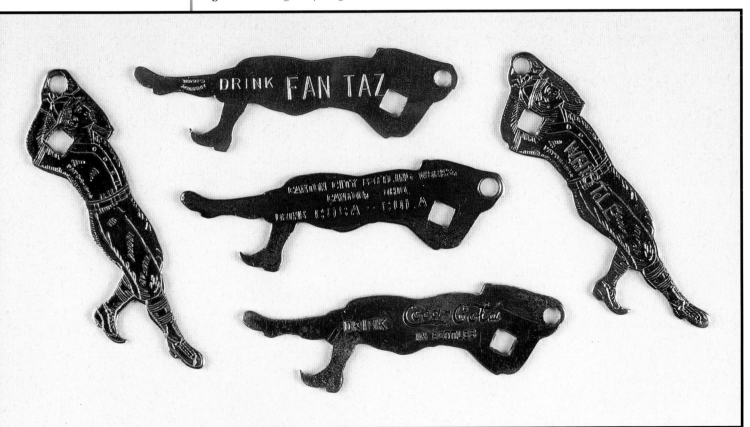

A-9 Baseball player in pitching position. Prest-O-Lite key. Marked PATD-8-18-14. One example is marked ADV. NOV. CO. CHICAGO. American design patent 46,298 issued to John L. Sommer, August 18, 1914. 3 1/8".

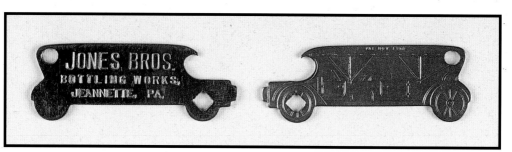

A-13 Automobile. Prest-O-Lite key. American design patent
41,895 issued to John L. Sommer, November 7, 1911. 2 7/8".

Pairs from top to bottom:
A-15 Eagle Head & Bottle. With and without Prest-O-Lite key. Various marks include
C. T. & O. CO., CHICAGO, PAT.APPLD.FOR., C. T.& O. CO., CHICAGO
PAT.APPLD.FOR/PATENTED, and C. T. & O. CO. CHGO. PATD 4.30.12. 2 7/8".
A-16 Elk or Moose head and bottle. Prest-O-Lite key. Marks include C. T. & O. CO.,
CHICAGO, PAT APPLD FOR and C. T. & O. CO., CHICAGO PATENTED. 2 7/8".
A-17 Lion head and bottle. Prest-O-Lite key. Marks include PATENTED, PAT APPLD,
PAT APPL FOR or PAT. APR.30.12 CROWN T. & O. CO., CHICAGO, ILL. 2 7/8".
A-43 Horse head and bottle. Prest-O-Lite key. Marked C. T. & O. CO. PATD. 2 7/8".

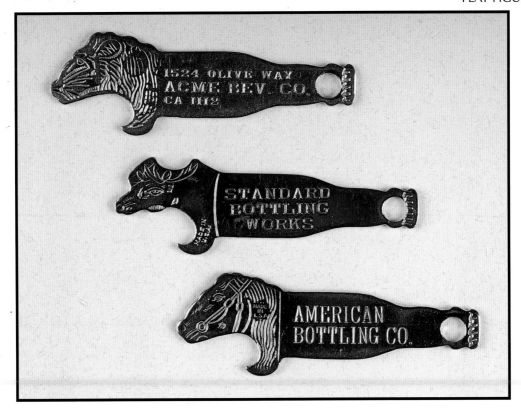

Top to bottom:
A-44 Lion head and bottle. Marked PATENTED MADE BY C. T. & O. CO.,
CHICAGO. 2 7/8".
A-46 Elk head and bottle. Marked C. T.& O. CO., CHICAGO, PAT APPLD FOR
or C. T. & O. CO., CHICAGO, PATENTED. 2 7/8".
A-57 Horse head and bottle. Marked C. T. & O. CO. MADE IN U. S. A. 2 7/8".

Left three: A-21 Hand Spinner. Usually marked SPIN TO SEE WHO PAYS, MADE BY
BROWN & BIGELOW CO., ST. PAUL, MINN. 3 1/4". *And this company told you how
you lose:* "Lyons Bottling Co. Phone 105—you lose if you do not use our mixers."
Right two: A-33 Fish, large. Spinner made by L. F. Dow Co., St. Paul, Minnesota. 3 1/4".

Top: *A-12 Sword. 2 7/8". One of these was made for a special event with this advertising: "Shasta Water from Shasta Springs 'Naturally Better'—Shrine Victory Convention July 1946 San Francisco."*

Center: *A-34 Powder Horn, Fancy. Prest-O-Lite key. Marked PAT. AP'D. FOR or PATD. 4-28-14. American design patent 45,678 issued to John L. Sommer, April 28, 1914. 3 1/8".*

Bottom: **Left and center:** *A-30 Dancer legs. Called "Dancer" or "Tango." Marked C. T. & O. CO. CHICAGO PATD or PATD. American design patent 44,945 issued to Harry L. Vaughan, November 25, 1913. 2 3/4".*
Right: *A-53 Dancer legs. Prest-O-Lite key. Called "Dancer" or "Tango." Marked C. T. & O. CO. CHICAGO PATD or PATD. American design patent 44,945 issued to Harry L. Vaughan, November 25, 1913. 2 3/4".*

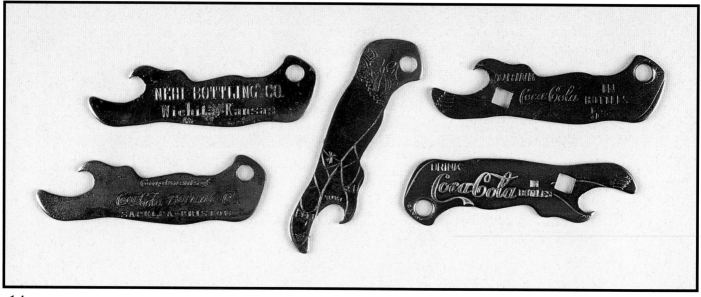

Left two: A-20 Fish Spinner. There is a knob punched in the center. The opener spins on the knob and whomever it points to, pays for the drinks. 3 1/8".
Right: A-42 Fish. Prest-O-Lite key. Marked PAT. NOV. 7, 1911. American design patent 41,894 issued to John L. Sommer, November 7, 1911. 3 1/8". *"Don't be a fish drink Ingleside Ginger Ale, Ingallis Bros. Portland, Me."* was a strange bit of advertising on this type.

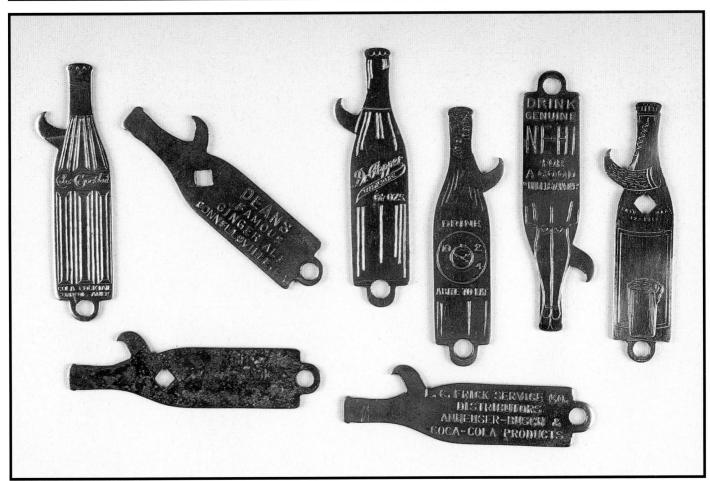

Middle left two and far right: A-28 Bottle. Pictures a stag handle corkscrew. Some show a glass of beer. Prest-O-Lite key. Marked PATD. MAR. 12-1912 or PAT APD FOR. American design patent 42,305 issued to John L. Sommer, March 12, 1912. 3 1/4".
Far left and middle right four: A-29 Bottle. Some picture a stag handle corkscrew. Some show a glass of beer. Marked PATD. MAR. 12-1912 or PAT APD FOR. American design patent 42,305 issued to John L. Sommer, March 12, 1912. 3 1/4".

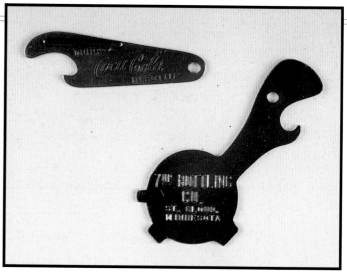

Left: A-23 Stainless steel opener made by Louis F. Dow Co., St. Paul, Minnesota. Marked on reverse DOW ST. PAUL STAINLESS. 2 1/2".
Right: A-39 Turtle with three screwdrivers. Marked PATD 161,321 B&B U. S. A. Made by Brown & Bigelow, St. Paul, Minnesota. American design patent 161,321 issued to Le Emmette V. De Fee, December 16, 1950. 3".

Above: **Top left:** A-24 Outline of Nu-Grape bottle. 2 5/8".
Top right: A-502 Outline of Try-Me bottle. 3 1/8".
Bottom: A-503 Outline of Coca-Cola bottle. 3 1/4".

Right: **Left:** A-59 Hand holding Chero-Cola bottle. 3 1/8".
Middle pair: A-505 Bottle with swing-out opener. 2 7/8". *Only found with "Clicquot Club Ginger Ale/(Eskimo) Clicquot Club Pale Dry Ginger Ale" advertising.*
Right pair: A-504 Outline of "Orange Crushy Man" and Orange Crush bottle. 2 5/8".

A-39 Turtles.
1970s
productions.

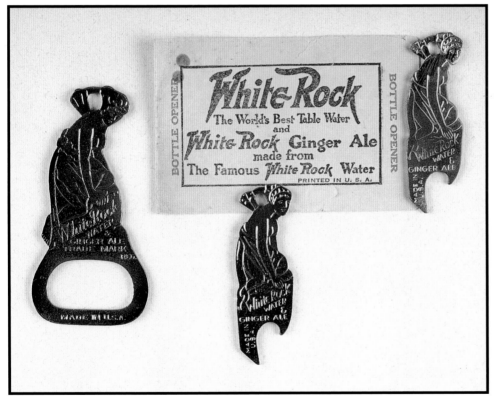

Above:
Left: A-506 Large "White Rock Lady". 3".
Right: A-507 Small "White Rock Lady". Shown with original package. 2 5/16".

Right:
A-501 Arrowhead. *Only found with "Open a bottle of Arrowhead Pale Dry Ginger Ale" advertising.* 2 1/2".

KEY SHAPE OPENERS

Although very few of the openers in this chapter look like a key, they all have a hole or other provision for adding to a key chain. And they are the "key" to opening a bottle. Advertising frequently includes the words "Key to" before the brand name. Some have been found in leather cases in which the opener and keys swivel out on a pin for use. An interesting notice was included by one advertising specialty company on this type: "Finder rewarded if keys are returned or drop in any mail box. L. F. Grammes & Sons, Allentown, Pa." The owner's registration number was engraved on the opener. Most of the types were produced and used prior to the 1919-1933 Prohibition period.

Top: B-1 Brass or steel enameled cap lifter. 2 1/2". *Found with advertising for the manufacturer: "Electro Chemical Engraving Co., Suite 511, 90 West St., New York City, Highest Quality."*
Middle: B-2 Brass or steel enameled cap lifter. Prest-O-Lite key. 3 1/8".
Bottom: B-27 Brass enameled cap lifter. 2 1/2". *Maker J. K. Aldrich, 1098 Brook Avenue, New York used this type to advertise "Bottle Openers."*

Top: B-5 Combination cap lifter, cigar box opener, nail puller, and key holder. Marked PAT APL'D FOR. 3 1/8". *Manufactured by National Selling Co. of Allentown, Pa.*
Bottom two: B-42 Combination cap lifter with cigar box opener, nail puller, key holder, and Prest-O-Lite key. Marked PAT APL'D FOR. 3 1/8".

Top and left: B-6 Combination cap lifter, screwdriver, and key holder. Some marked PAT. JAN. 27, 03. Made by Whitehead & Hoag Co., Newark, New Jersey. 2 7/8".
Bottom and right: B-7 Combination cap lifter, key holder, button hook, and ruler. Marked PATENTED NOV. 28, 1905 and sometimes including HANDY POCKET COMPANION. American patent 805,486 issued to Julius T. Rosenheimer, November 28, 1905. 3 1/8".

The Handy Pocket Companion had eighteen uses: bottle cap opener, key ring, ruler, lifting and pulling carpet tacks, lifting pots or kettles from fire or stove, glove buttoner, cigar box opener, pulling rusty pens from holder, winding or tightening window shade springs, shoe buttoner, pulling wire from bottles, watch case opener, nail file and cleaner, basting thread puller, paint can opener, and wide mouth bottle opener. What more could you ask for?

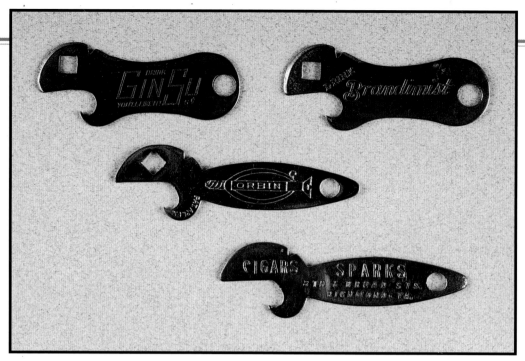

Top pair: B-8 Combination cap lifter, Prest-O-Lite key, cigar box opener, and nail puller. Made by L. F. Grammes & Sons of Allentown, Pennsylvania. 2 3/8".
Middle: B-9 Combination cap lifter, Prest-O-Lite key, cigar box opener, and nail puller. Cigar shape. Marked C.T.&O. CO. PATD. CHICAGO or PAT.APL FOR. 2 7/8".
Bottom: B-65 Cap lifter with cigar box opener and nail puller. Cigar shape. 2 7/8".

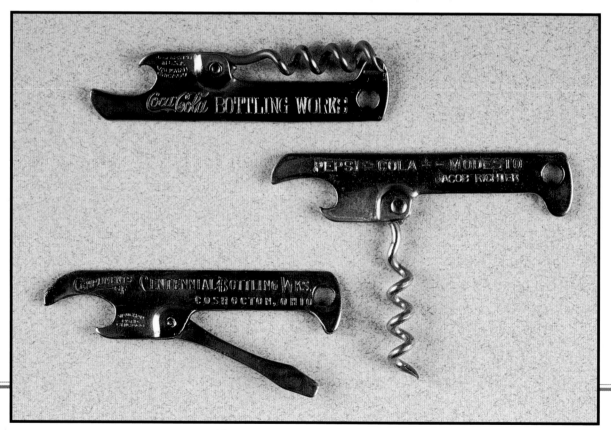

Top two: B-13 Cap lifter with folding corkscrew known as the "Nifty." Marked MADE & PAT'D IN U. S. A. VAUGHAN, CHICAGO. Double steel body. American patent 1,207,100 issued to Harry L. Vaughan, December 5, 1916. 2 7/8". *"Drink Sunny Kid Pale Dry Ginger Ale Made Famous by the Public"* – so now we know!
Bottom: B-48 Cap lifter with folding screwdriver. Double steel body. 2 7/8".

Nifty Bottle Opener and Cork
Screw on original packaging.

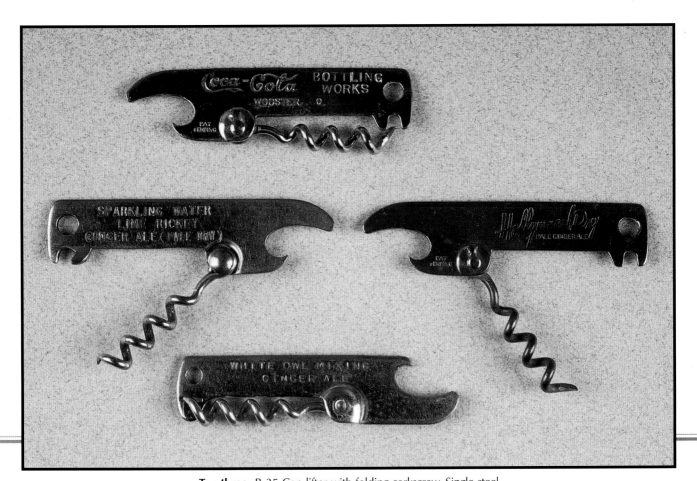

Top three: B-35 Cap lifter with folding corkscrew. Single steel body. Some marked PAT. NO. 1680291. Made by John L. Sommer Manufacturing Co. American patent 1,680,291 issued to Thomas Harding, August 14, 1928. 2 7/8".
Bottom: B-36 Cap lifter with folding corkscrew. Single steel body. Cap lifter and corkscrew are on opposite sides. 2 7/8".

Top two: B-14 Vaughan's "Special Pocket Bottle Opener." 2 5/8". *Here's a good reason for keeping openers: "Eskimo Pop a pal for your palate/Eskimo Syrup Co. Pittsburgh, Pa. one dollar reward for return of these keys 1904."*
Bottom: B-41 Cap lifter. 2 3/4". *Found with advertising from the manufacturer: "Louis F. Dow Co., St. Paul, Minn., No. 100 Bottle Opener."*

Top: B-15 Cap lifter. 2 1/2".
Bottom: B-16 Cap lifter with Prest-O-Lite key. 2 1/2".

Top: B-17 Cap lifter with oval key chain hole. Marked THE GREENDUCK CO., CHICAGO. 3".
Bottom: B-34 Cap lifter with oval key chain hole. Prest-O-Lite key. Marked THE GREENDUCK CO., CHICAGO. 3". *Only found with "'Everybody's Drinken It' Lemon-Kola" advertising.*

B-18 Cap lifter with double punched key chain hole. Stephens design patent of 1901. 3".

B-19 Cap lifter with double punched key chain hole. Diamond Prest-O-Lite key. Stephens design patent of 1901. 3".

Top two: B-21 Cap lifter with Prest-O-Lite key and key-ring hole. Stephens design patent of 1901. 3".

Bottom: B-501 Cap lifter with Prest-O-Lite key, but no key-ring hole. Stephens design patent of 1901. 3". *Only found with "Buffalo Rock Ginger Ale" advertising.*

Top two: B-22 Cap lifter with Prest-O-Lite key. Vaughan's pre-prohibition "Outing" key type pocket bottle opener. 2 7/8".

Bottom two: B-23 Cap lifter. Vaughan's post-prohibition "Outing" key type pocket bottle opener. 2 7/8".

Top two: B-24 Vaughan's "Never Slip" bottle opener. American patent 2,018,083 issue by James A. Murdock, October 22, 1935. 3 1/8". *Vaughan proclaimed on one of these "World's largest manufacturers of bottle openers. Item No. 3. Compliments of Vaughan Novelty Mfg. Co., Chicago, Ill."* **Bottom:** B-25 Cap lifter with Prest-O-Lite key. 3 1/4".

Top two: B-29 Cap lifter with Prest-O-Lite key. 3". *This was Williamson Company's catalog number 108 advertised as "Prest-O-Lite tank key & crown opener."* **Bottom two:** B-31 Cap lifter with Prest-O-Lite key. Screwdriver tip. Extra thick steel. 3 1/4". *This was Williamson Company's catalog number 110 advertised as "Prest-O-Lite tank key, crown opener, screw driver."*

Top:
Top two: B-30 Cap lifter with double punched key chain hole. Stamping with formed end. 2 3/4".
Bottom three: B-40 Cap lifter. Bottle shape stamping with formed end. Made by Emro Manufacturing Co. of St. Louis, Missouri. 2 7/8".

Bottom:
Top: B-49 Cap lifter with cigar box opener and nail puller. Stamping with formed end. 2 1/4".
Middle two: B-504 Cap lifter with formed end to act as a bottle cap. Marked PAT. PEND. Top and side views shown. 3 1/2". *Only found with "Original 'Manitou' Sparkling Water And Pale Dry Ginger Ale" advertising.*
Bottom: B-505 Cap lifter. Two points to grip cap. Steel version of type D-11. 3 5/8". *Only found with "Apollinaris" advertising.*

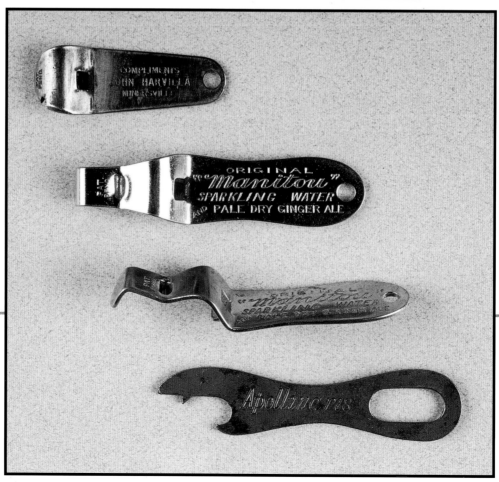

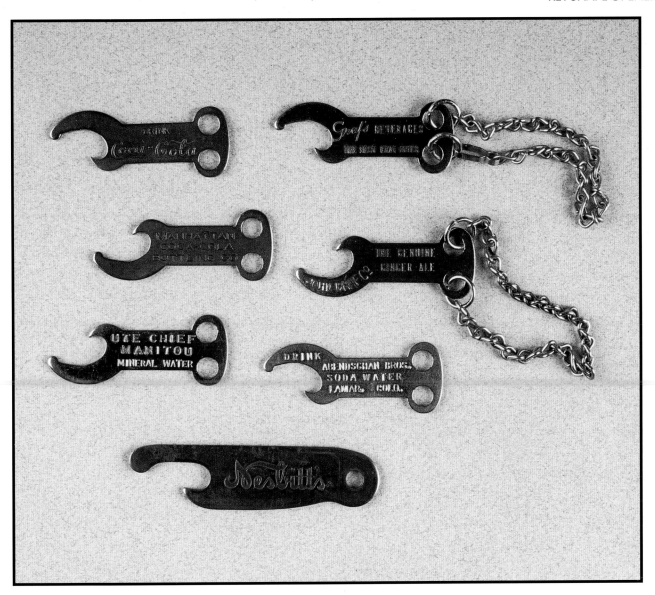

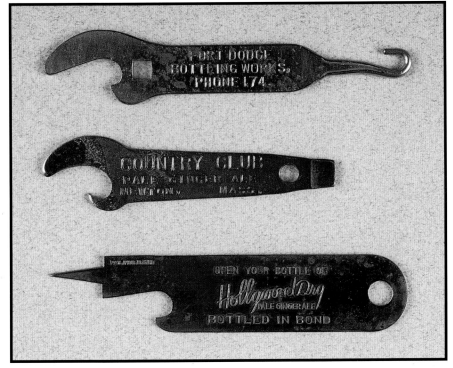

Above: **Top six:** B-32 Cap lifter with two key chain holes. 2".
Bottom: B-502 Cap lifter. 2 13/16". *Only found with "Nesbitt's" advertising.*

Left:
Top: B-53 Cap lifter with Prest-O-Lite key and button hook. 3 3/4".
Middle: B-75 Cap lifter with screwdriver tip. 3 1/16".
Bottom: B-503 Cap lifter and milk bottle opener. Marked PAT. PEND. B&B (Brown & Bigelow). 3 7/8".

FLAT METAL CAP LIFTERS

This type of opener is usually a metal stamping with a large hole that has a tab to engage the underside of a crown cap. The handle is lifted up to remove the cap. In some instances a second tab is found at the top of the opening enabling the user to remove the cap by engaging the lip opposite the handle. The cap is removed by pushing the handle down. They are found with vertical and horizontal advertising. The horizontal advertising is most commonly for right-handers and, less frequently, for left-handers. When placed in the right-hand to open a bottle, the advertising on a left-hand model will be upside down (and vice-versa).

Top: C-3 Cap lifter with Prest-O-Lite key (diamond pattern). 2 3/4".
Bottom: C-5 Cap lifter with screwdriver tip. 3 1/4".

Left: C-6 Cap lifter. Rounded top. 3 1/8".
Right: C-7 Cap lifter. Squared top. 3 1/4".

Top: C-9 Cap lifter. Tab in base. Handle 3/8" wide at narrowest point. 3 1/8".
Bottom: C-10 Cap lifter. Tab in base. Handle 1/2" wide at narrowest point. 3 1/8".

Top two: C-11 Cap lifter. Tab above base. B.P.O.E. example is marked DRINK COCA-COLA IN BOTTLES on reverse side. Probably given out as a souvenir for an Elks Convention. 3 1/8".
Bottom: C-27 Cap lifter. Opener end bent 45 degrees. 2 7/8". Note: Type is like the C-11 type. However, anyone can bend the opener end, therefore, this may not be a legitimate type.

Top: C-12 Cap lifter. Tab in base. 3 1/8". *Most unusual advertising on this style is "Coca-Cola (Script) drink of the 'Fans' (in ball bat) League (in baseball)".*
Middle three: C-13 Cap lifter. Tab above base. 3 1/8".
Bottom: C-14 Cap lifter. Tab above base. 3 1/4".

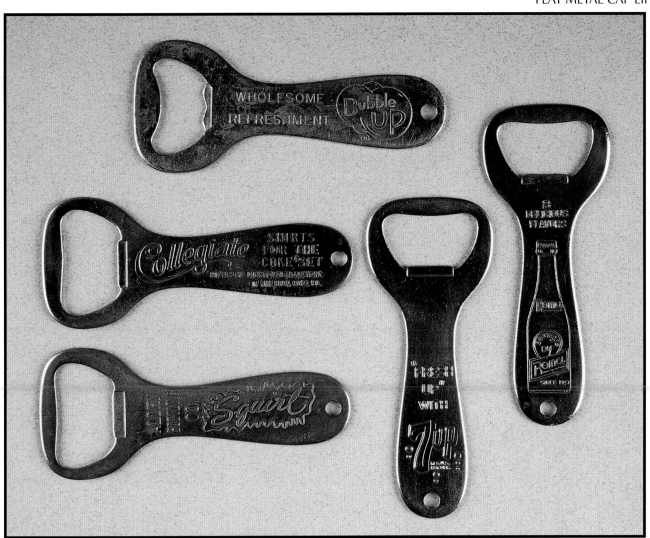

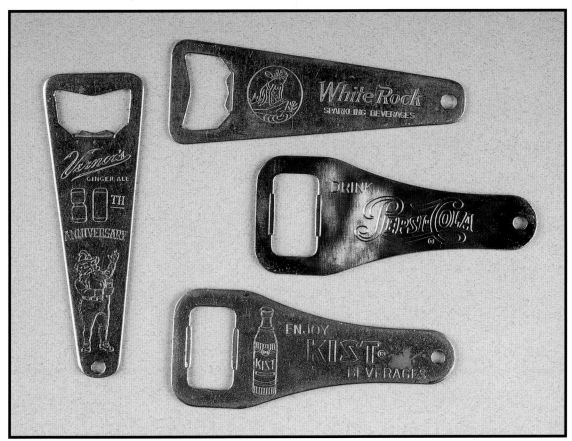

Above:
Top: C-16 Cap lifter. Double pointed tab above base. 3 3/4″.
Bottom four: C-17 Cap lifter. Straight tab in base. 3 3/4″.

Left:
Left and top: C-18 Cap lifter. Tab above base. 4 1/4″.
Bottom right two: C-19 Cap lifter. Tabs in base and top. 4″.

Above:
Top: C-28 Cap lifter with Prest-O-Lite key. 3 1/4".
Bottom: C-36 Cap lifter. 3 1/4".

Right:
Top: C-39 Cap lifter. Marked PAT. FEB. 6 1894. 3 1/4".
Bottom: C-41 Cap lifter. 3 1/4".

Below:
Top left: C-31 Cap lifter with cigar box opener and nail puller. 3 1/8".
Bottom left: C-34 Cap lifter. Marked EKCO, CHICAGO. 3 1/2".
Right: C-501 Cap lifter. Bottle shape. 3 3/4".

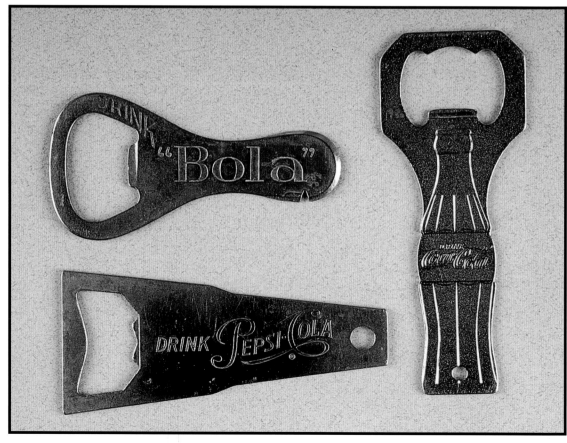

CAST IRON CAP LIFTERS

Cast iron openers were among the first cap lifters produced in the late 1800s when the crown cap was introduced. An opener similar to type D-6 appears in the drawings of Patent No. 514,200 issued to William Painter, Baltimore, Maryland, February 6, 1894. The patent claims "a capped bottle opener consisting of a suitable handle with a cap engaging lip adapted to underlie a portion of an applied bottle sealing cap, and also having a centering gage affording gauging contact with the side of the cap adjacent to the engaging lip, and still further affording fulcrum contact for enabling bearing engagement with the upper portion or top of the cap" (in other words—it removes a bottle cap!).

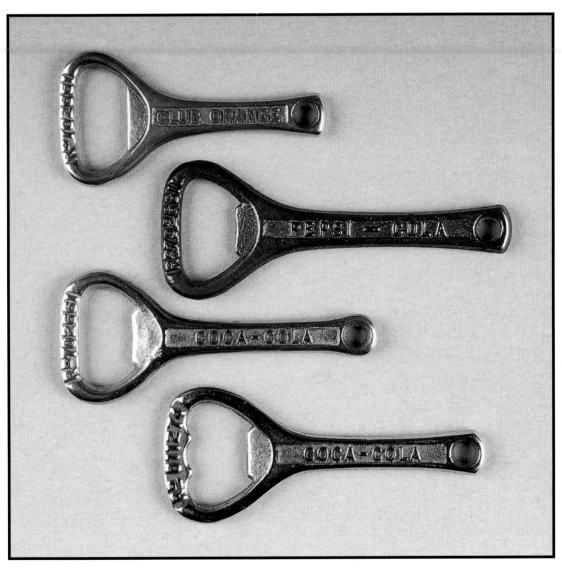

Top: D-503 Cap lifter. Raised letters. English registered design number 702661 (1923). 3".
Middle two: D-504 Cap lifter. Raised letters. English registered design number 702668 (1923). 3 1/2" – 3 7/8".
Bottom: D-505 Cap lifter. Raised letters. English registered design number 811274 (1936). 3 5/8".

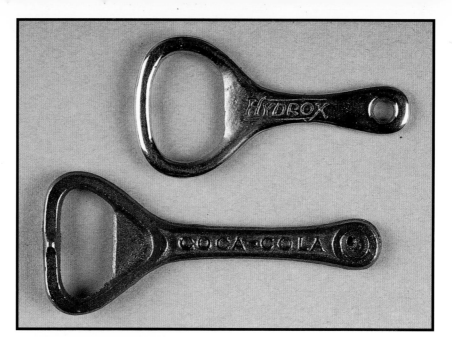

Above:
Top: D-1 Cap lifter with wire breaker. Made with recessed letters. 2 7/8".
Bottom: D-3 Cap lifter. Raised letters. 3 3/8".

Left:
Left: D-6 Cap lifter with bottle stopper. American patent 514,200 issued to William Painter, February 6, 1894. 3 1/4".
Right: D-501 Cap lifter with bottle stopper and bottle cap handle. 3 1/2".

Below:
Top: D-11 Cap lifter. Two points to grip cap. 3 7/8".
Bottom: D-502 Aluminum (has a cast iron look) cap lifter with wide mouth for milk bottles. 3 3/4".

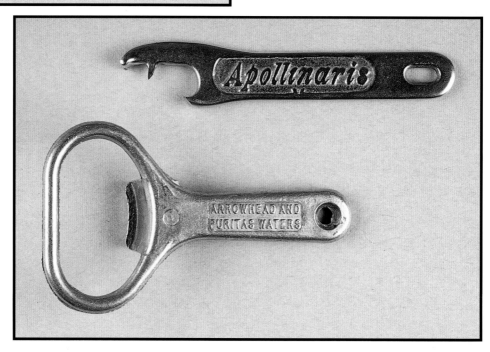

WIRE FORMED OPENERS

In 1915, renowned corkscrew inventor Edwin Walker of Erie, Pennsylvania, was granted an American patent (No. 1,150,083) for a wire formed cap lifter. The application for the patent was made in 1909 and claimed "as a new article of manufacture, a bottle cap lifter comprising a loop bent from a wire rod, and a plurality of lips swaged from the metal of the loop and extending inwardly from the inner contour of the loop." It was cheap to produce and, therefore, an extremely popular means of advertising a soda bottler's product. One manufacturer from Oakville, Connecticut, claimed "We make the best and cheapest crown openers."

The "lips" referred to in the previous paragraph are called "frets" in the following descriptions. These "frets" were what actually touched the bottle cap and provided leverage when opening the bottle.

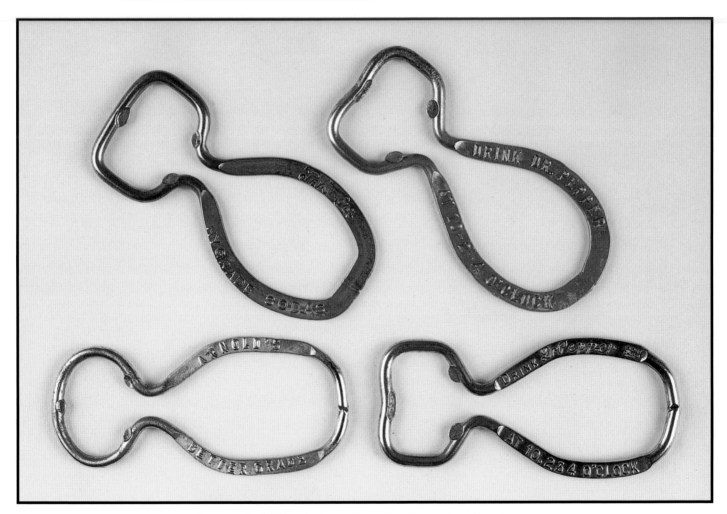

Top two: E-1 Wide wire hoop. Three frets. Squared or dipped top. Flattened handle at base. 3 1/2".
Bottom left: E-2 Wide wire hoop. Three frets. Rounded top. 3 1/2".
Bottom right: E-3 Wide wire hoop. Three frets. Squared or dipped top. Rounded handle at base. 3 1/2".

Left: E-18 Wide wire hoop. Squared top. Flat handle at base. Two frets. 3 1/2".
Right: E-22 Wide wire hoop bowed for better leverage. Rounded top. Flat handle. One fret. 3 1/4".

Top: E-6 Single wire loop. Squared, dipped, or rounded top with flat base. Three frets. 3 1/2" to 3 3/4". *This advertisement is for the not so sane: "Dr. Nut, World Bottling Co."*
Bottom three: E-7 Single wire loop. Flat top and flat base. 3 1/2".

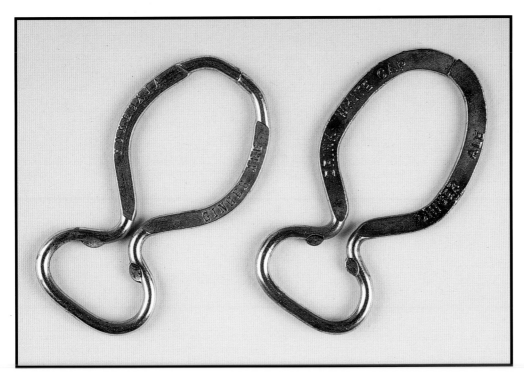

Left: E-21 Wide wire hoop. Flat top. Rounded base. Two Frets. 3 1/4″.
Right: E-31 Wide wire hoop. Flat top. Flat base. Two frets. 3 3/8″.

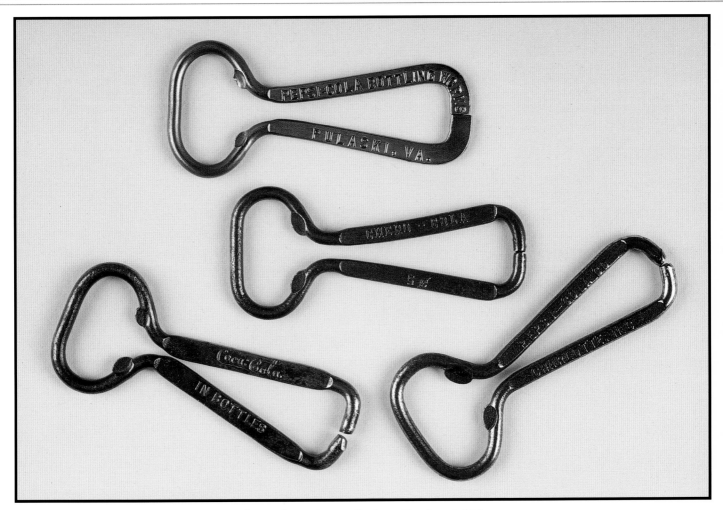

Top: E-25 Single wire loop. Flat top. Flat base. Two frets. 3 1/8″.
Bottom three: E-8 Single wire loop. Flat top and rounded base. American patent 1,150,083 issued to Edwin Walker, August 17, 1915. 3 1/8″.

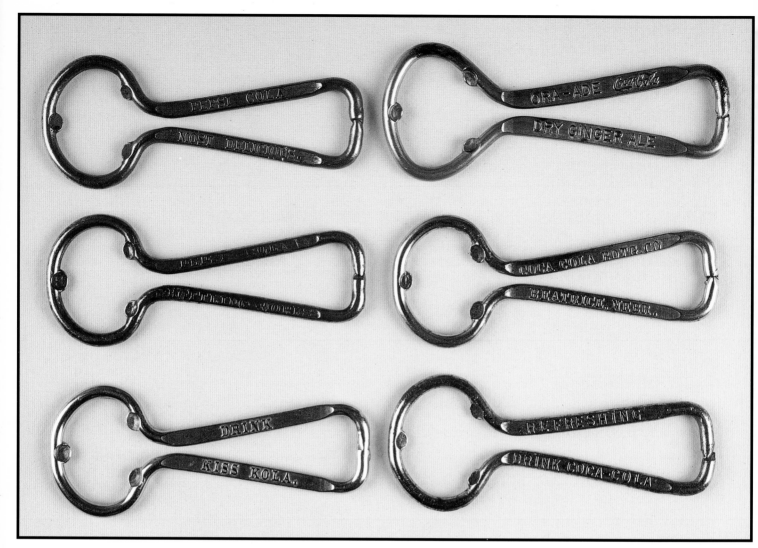

Above:
E-9 Single wire loop. Rounded top. Three frets. Some marked MADE IN U. S. A. 3 1/4" to 3 3/4".

Right:
E-11 Parallel stem handle. Squared or dipped top. Three frets. 4 5/8".

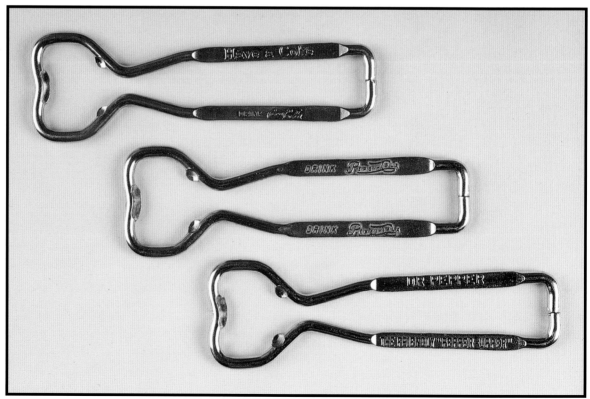

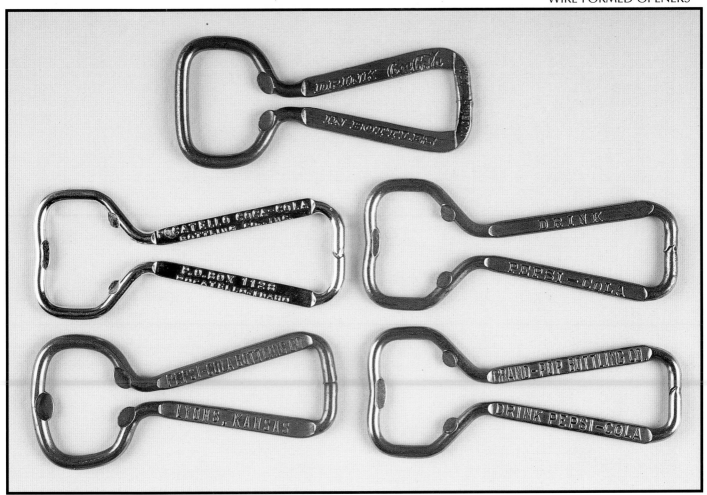

Top: E-13 Single wire loop. Squared or dipped top. Two frets. 3 1/2" to 3 3/4".
Bottom four: E-14 Single wire loop. Squared or dipped top. Three frets. 3 1/4" to 3 3/4". Six variations are shown. Almost 200 different sodas and variations have been reported for this type. *Some of the great slogans on this type include: a)"More zip in every sip"; b)"It's the real thing"; c)"Drink a bite to eat"; d)"Thirsty or not?"; e)"Every drop pure"; f)"Taste that beats the others cold"; g)"Best by taste test"; h)"You'll like it, it likes you"; i)"Never an after thirst"; j)"Deliciously different". Do you know the sodas? a) B-1 Lemon-Lime; b) Coca-Cola; c) Dr. Pepper; d) Grapette; e) Hydrox, f) Pepsi; g) Royal Crown Cola; h) Seven-Up; i) Squirt; j) Vernor's Ginger Ale.*

Top: E-16 Single wire loop. Rounded top. Flat base. One fret. 3 1/2". *A most interesting example is found with "Champagne Fizz. The Drink. What Is Celery tonic." advertising.*
Bottom: E-17 Figure eight single wire loop. Flat top. Two frets. 2 1/2".

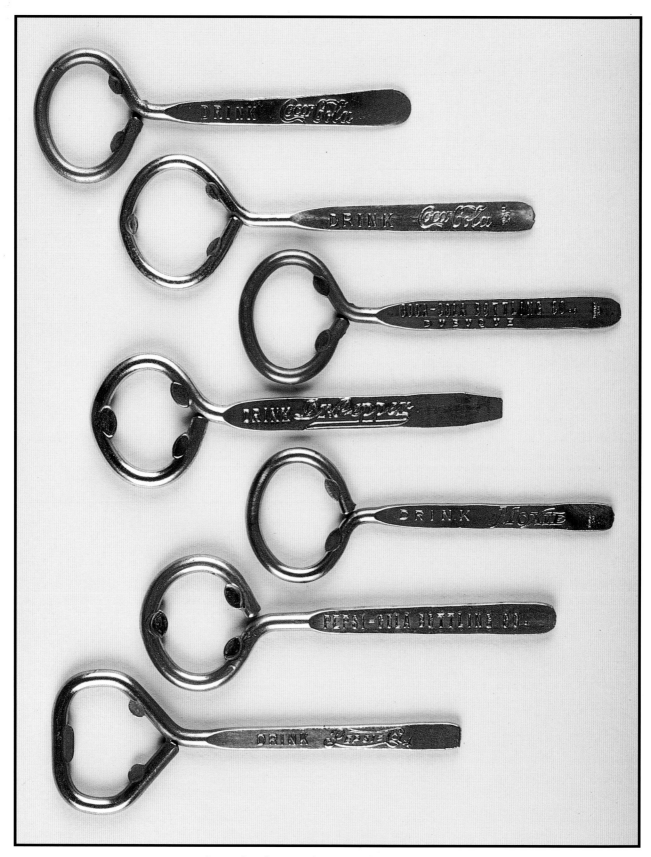

E-4 Single wire handle. Some have screwdriver tips. One, two, or three frets. Rounded, squared, or dipped tops. 4 1/4" to 4 3/4". *Most interesting advertising: "Drink Orange Crush it's real orange juice/Say it by it's full name to avoid substitutions".*

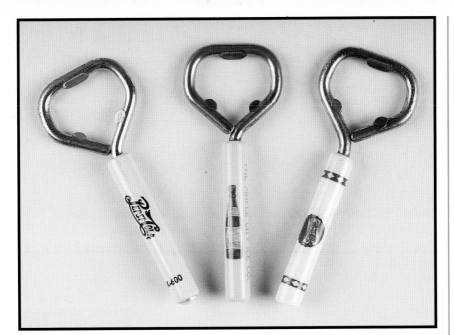

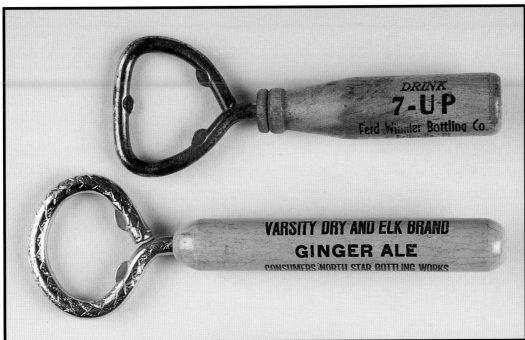

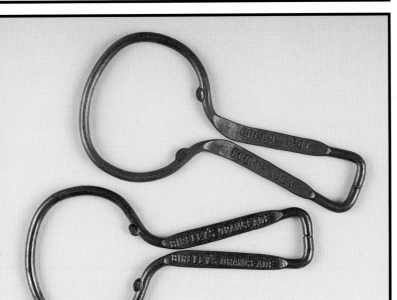

Top:
E-5 Celluloid handle. Various colors. 4 1/4″.

Center:
Top: E-19 Bottle shape wood handle with loop. Rounded or squared top. Two or three frets. 4″.
Bottom: E-24 Wood handle with wire loop. Two frets. 5 1/2″.

Bottom: E-501 Wide wire hoop for milk bottles. Two frets. Rounded top and rounded handle at base. 4 3/8″.

MULTI-PURPOSE OPENERS

The advertising salesman who could sell a combination cake turner and bottle cap lifter to a soda bottler for advertising purposes deserves special recognition in the lore of openers. That unknown salesman evidently convinced Becker Products in Utah to buy this advertising gimmick. And he's probably the same guy that sold a Coca-Cola bottler on a cap lifter with spatula and the same bottler on a cap lifter and measuring spoon. Were the cocktail spoons with soda advertising for mixing up ice cream floats? The ice picks seem to make the most sense—ready for a good ice cold bottle of soda?

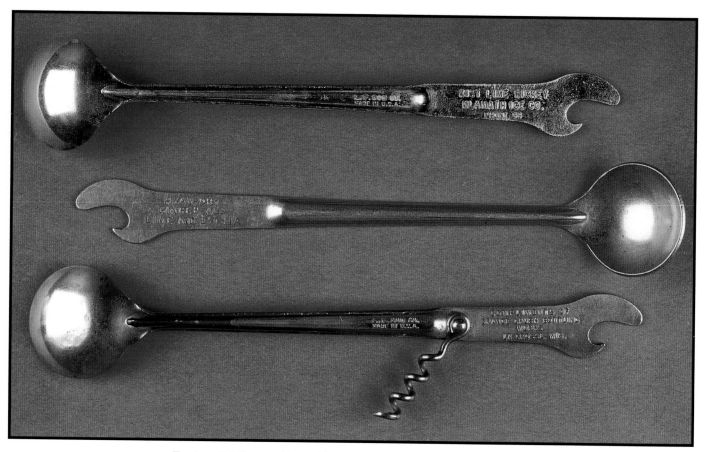

Top two: F-1 Spoon with cap lifter. Made by L. F. Dow Company. 7 7/8".
Bottom: F-501 Spoon with cap lifter and folding corkscrew. Made by L. F. Dow Company. 7 7/8".

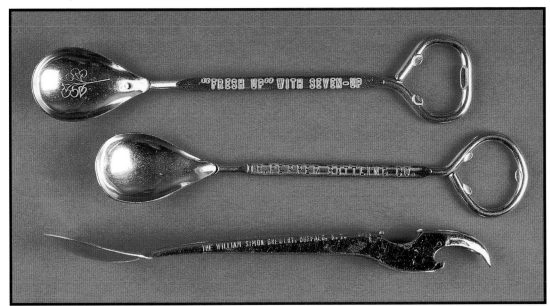

Top two: F-2 Spoon with cap lifter. American design patent 85,178 issued to Thomas Harding, September 22, 1931. The patent was assigned to the John L. Sommer Manufacturing Company. A 1937 Vaughan catalog says this is "The handiest combination of all for mixing drinks. Ideal for room service." 7 3/4".
Bottom: F-3 Spoon with cap lifter and can piercer. American design patent 160,1950 issue by Le Emmette V. De Fee, October 31, 1950. Manufactured by Brown & Bigelow, St. Paul, Minnesota. Packaging for this names it "Spoonopener." Side view only. 8".

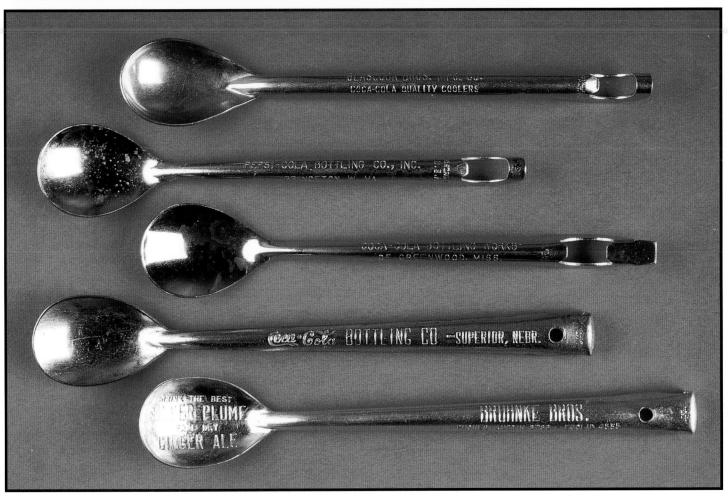

Top two: F-4 Spoon with cap lifter. Curved or straight handles. Made by Brown & Bigelow. 7 1/4". *An appropriate advertisement on this one was: "Gold Seal Soda Fischer Bros. A Good Stirrer for a Good Mixer."*
Middle: F-15 Spoon with cap lifter and screwdriver tip. 7 1/2".
Bottom two: F-29 Spoon with over-the-top type cap lifter. Marked PAT APL FOR, BOTTLE OPENER. 8 1/8".

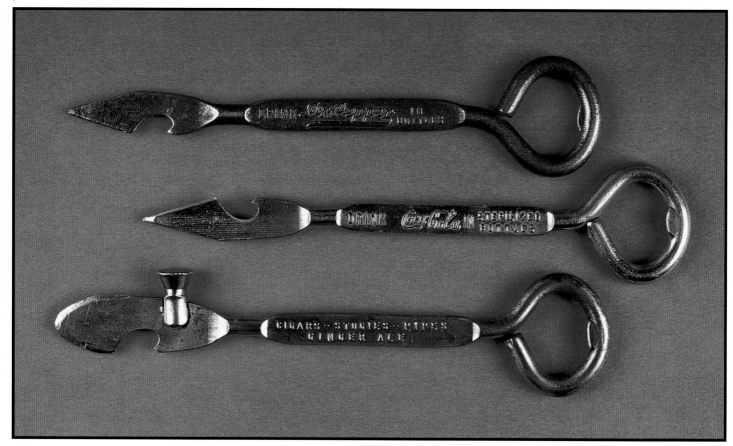

Top two: F-5 Two cap lifters and ice pick. 7 3/4".
Bottom: F-505 Two cap lifters, cigar box opener, and cigar box hammer. 7 7/8".

Top: F-8 Cap lifter with ice pick. Wood handle. 10".
Bottom: F-24 Cap lifter with ice pick. Wood handle.
Produced with square top and round top. 10 3/4".

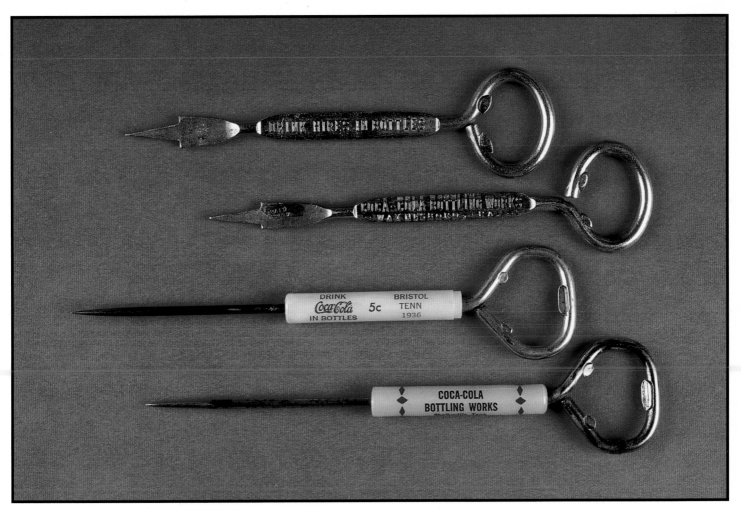

Top two: F-6 "Four in 1 Handy Tool." Bottle opener, friction cover opener, ice pick, and milk bottle cap lifter. One, two, or three frets. American design patent 43,278 issued to Thomas Harding, November 26, 1912. 6 1/4".
Bottom two: F-7 Cap lifter with ice pick. Celluloid handle. Various colors. 7 1/4".

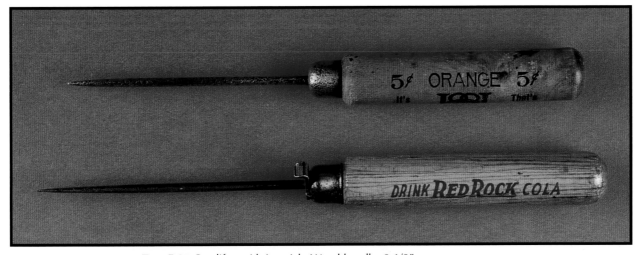

Top: F-25 Cap lifter with ice pick. Wood handle. 9 1/8".
Bottom: F-504 Cap lifter with ice pick. Three-sided wood handle. 9 1/4".

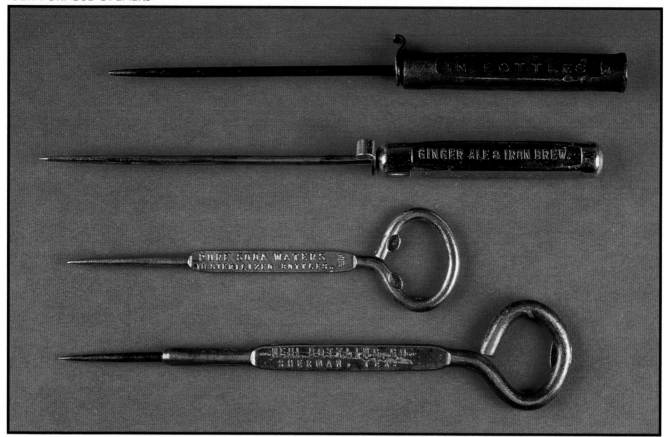

Top two: F-9 Cap lifter with ice pick. Heavy (4 oz.) steel 4-sided handle. 8 1/8" – 9".
Middle: F-18 Cap lifter with ice pick. One piece construction. American design
patent 46,311 issued to Thomas Harding, August 25, 1914. 8 1/4".
Bottom: F-27 Cap lifter with ice pick. Two piece construction. 8 1/2".

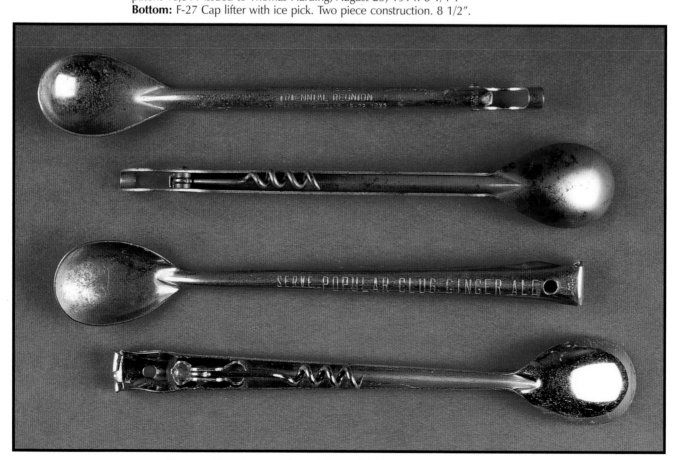

Top two: F-21 Spoon with cap lifter and folding corkscrew. 7 1/2".
Bottom two: F-23 Spoon with over-the-top type cap lifter and folding
corkscrew. Marked PAT. APL'D FOR, BOTTLE OPENER. 8 5/8".

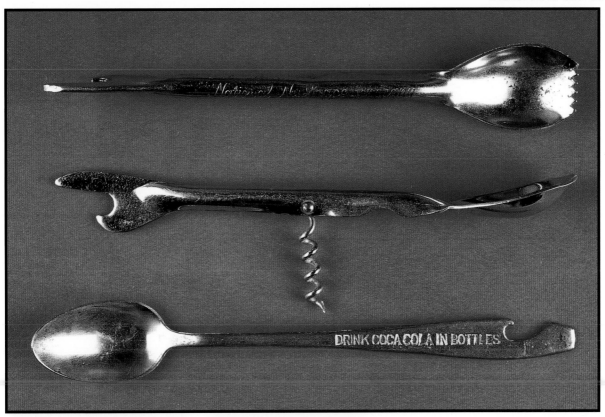

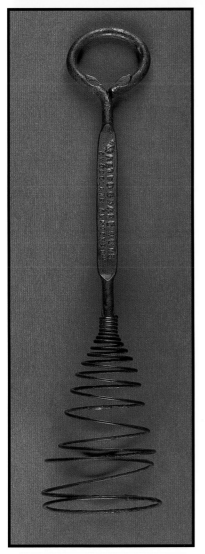

Above:
Top two: F-502 Ice chip spoon with cap lifter cut into handle and folding corkscrew. 7 3/4".
Bottom: F-508 Spoon with cap lifter cut into handle. 7 7/8".

Far left: F-503 Cap lifter and "French Whisk". 8 3/4".

Left:
F-509 Cap lifter with four-point ice chopper. 9 1/2".

Right:
F-506 Cap lifter and measuring spoon ladle. 10 1/2".

Below:
F-507 Cap lifter and large spatula. 11 1/2".

Bottom:
F-13 Cap lifter and cake turner. American design patent 46,702 issued to John L. Sommer and Thomas Harding, November 24, 1914. 11 5/8".

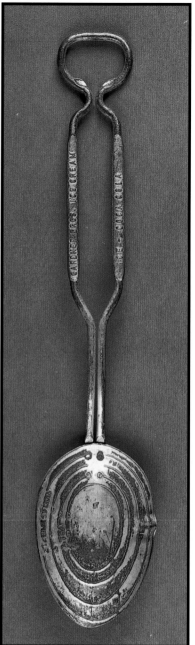

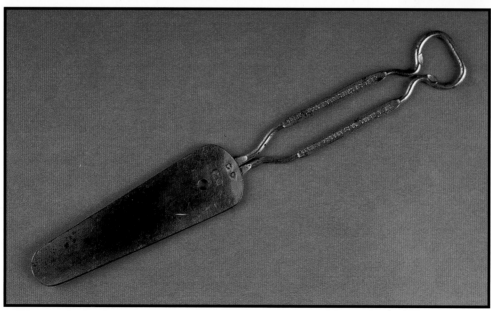

FORMED CAP LIFTERS

This section contains cap lifters that have a three-dimensional look and feel. Some of the earliest cataloged examples were stampings with formed sides. The surfaces left plenty of room to carry the advertisers' messages. With a stretch of the imagination, one realizes that they can be easier to spot in a drawer and, by all means, easier to pick up than the flat types—ready for action. Harry Edlund patented the G-9 type in 1933 adding a wood handle and giving the advertisers a colorful opener for display of their message that was imprinted with a hot foil process. Later G types were cast with company logos and names and sold more often as souvenirs than as advertising openers.

G-1 Formed metal cap lifter. Bottle shape.
Marked VAUGHAN CHICAGO. 4".

Top left: G-2 Cap lifter with curved handle. 3 5/8".
Bottom left: G-34 Cap lifter. Curved handle. 3 1/4".
Right: G-502 Cap lifter. Curved handle. Marked
TRADE-MARK PATD. 2 3/16".

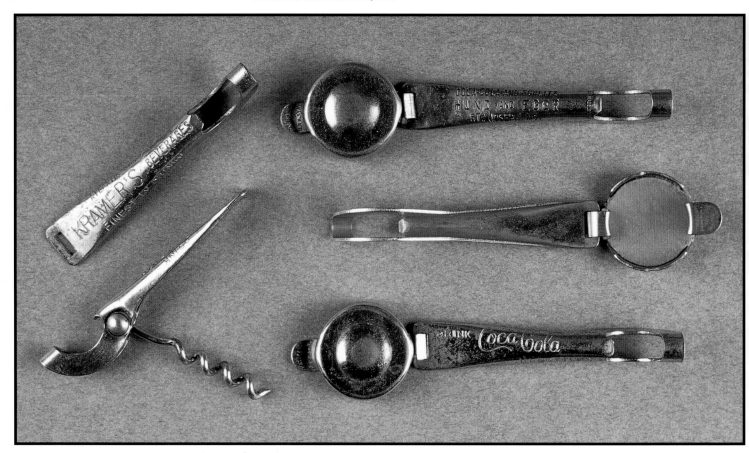

Top left: G-3 Cap lifter. Made by Brown & Bigelow (B & B) of St. Paul, Minnesota.
3 5/8". And they advertised "Adlerika superior to laxatives"!
Bottom left: G-53 Cap lifter with folding corkscrew. Made by Brown & Bigelow
(B & B) of St. Paul, Minnesota. 3 5/8".
Right three: G-25 Cap lifter with recapper. Marked PAT.PEND. B&B ST.P. 4 5/8".

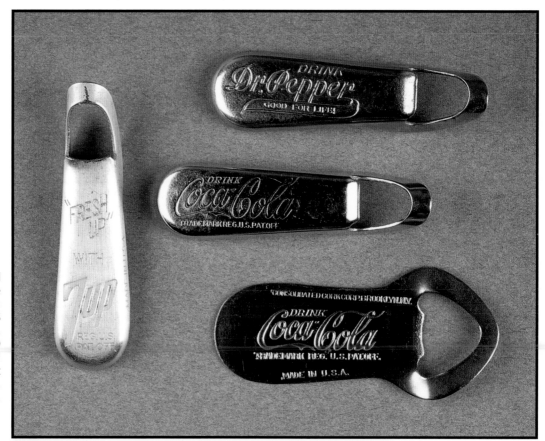

G-4 Cap lifter with curved handle. On some these marks have been noted: CAPITOL STAMPINGS CORP. MILWAUKEE, WIS. and CONSOLIDATED CORK CORP. BROOKLYN N. Y. Note: Coca Cola at bottom right not formed. 3 1/4".

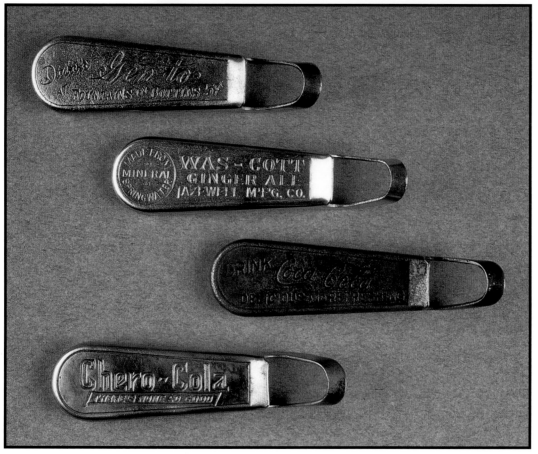

G-5 Cap lifter with flat handle. On some these marks have been noted: SEALTITE, 115 MAIDEN LANE, NEW YORK CITY PAT'D JULY 13, 1909, MF'D BY RYEDE SPECIALTY WORKS, PATENTS PENDING, MF'D BY RYEDE SPECIALTY WORKS, 137 MAIN ST., W., ROCHESTER, N. Y., PATENTED, and N. Y. SPECIALTY BY 'SESCO' PAT. JULY 13, 1909. American patent 928,156 issued to Adolph Rydquist, July 13, 1909. 3 1/4".

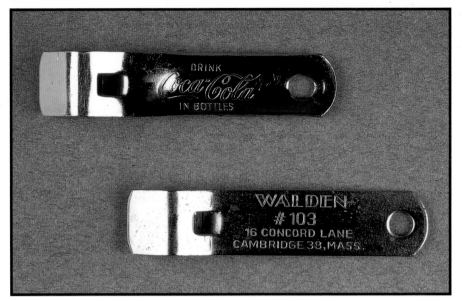

Top: G-6 Cap lifter with curved handle.
Marked WALDEN, CAMBRIDGE, MASS. 3".
Bottom: G-7 Cap lifter with flat handle.
Marked WALDEN, CAMBRIDGE, MASS. 3".

Above & opposite:
Top: G-8 Cap lifter with flat handle. Marked VAUGHAN
MADE IN U. S. A. 4" to 4 1/8" long, 3/4" wide.
Bottom: G-501 Cap lifter with curved handle. Made by the
Anchor Cap & Closure Corporation of Long Island, N. Y.
Originally sold for five cents each. 4 1/4".

ANCHOR OPENER
Anchor Cap & Closure Corporation
LONG ISLAND CITY, N.Y.
5 cents

INSIST ON Anchor VACUUM CAPS
YOUR BEST PROTECTION

Anchor Vacuum Caps

ARE TIGHT SEALS
CANNOT BE TAMPERED WITH
INSURES CONTENTS
ARE EASY TO REMOVE

SEALING RING OUTSIDE JAR
DOES NOT TOUCH FOOD
COVER CAN BE USED AGAIN
TO PROTECT CONTENTS

DIRECTIONS:—TO REMOVE CAP WITHOUT DESTROYING,
HOLD PACKAGE FIRMLY ON TABLE, APPLY ANCHOR OPENER,
RAISING CAP SLIGHTLY IN TWO OR THREE PLACES.
WILL REMOVE METAL CAPS FROM TUMBLERS, JARS AND BOTTLES.

G-503 Two views of a Coca Cola opener like type G-9 but with squared handle. Manufactured by the Edlund Company of Burlington, Vermont. 4 1/2".

Left: G-9 Cap lifter with wood handle. Colors: black, blue, gold, green, natural, red, and yellow. American patent 1,934,594 issued to Harry G. Edlund, November 7, 1933. Manufactured by the Edlund Company of Burlington, Vermont. Please note that all of the soda G-9s listed are probably made by The Newell Mfg. Co, Limited of Prescott, Ontario Canada. Newell handles are rectangular shaped while Edlund handles are tapered from back to front. 4 1/2".

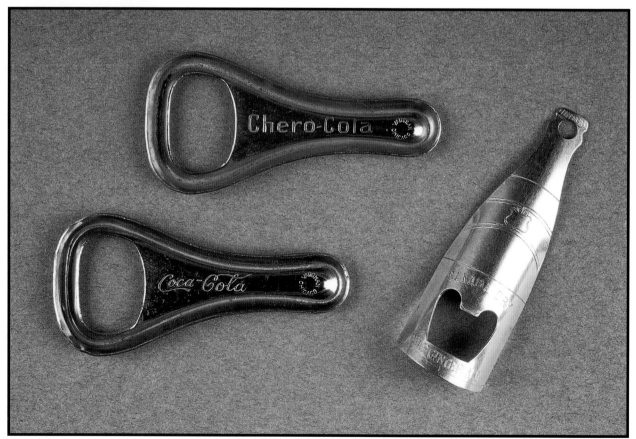

Left pair: G-13 "Perfection" cap lifter. Marked VAUGHAN CHICAGO. 3 3/8".
Right: G-21 Cap lifter. Curved bottle shape. The Canada Dry Pale Ginger Ale advertising opener was designed at Scovill Manufacturing Company., Waterbury, Connecticut, October 7, 1927. 4 3/8".

OVER-THE-TOP TYPE CAP LIFTERS

In 1924, Harry L. Vaughan of Chicago, Illinois, was granted Patent No. 1,490,149 for the invention of the over-the-top type opener. The patent application was filed in 1921 and was assigned to the Vaughan Novelty Manufacturing Company. The cap lifter goes over-the-top of the cap and fits under the far edge of the crown. In a 1922 Vaughan catalog, the opener is presented with these comments: "A slight downward pressure and off comes the cap in the hand. Everybody says—The best Bottle Opener ever invented." Prices ranged from $7.50 each for 250 to $17.00 per thousand in 10,000 quantity. Vaughan advertised this type with one stamped "Over the top bottle opener manufactured by Vaughan Novelty Mfg. Co., Inc., Chicago, Illinois, Trade Mark, Made in U. S. A."

The Mergott Company of Newark, New Jersey, imitated the over-the-top type with a folding corkscrew added on the underside per William Hiering's 1928 and 1929 patents. This was followed by the production of a colorful bottle shape over-the-top version lithographed by the Muth Company in Buffalo, New York.

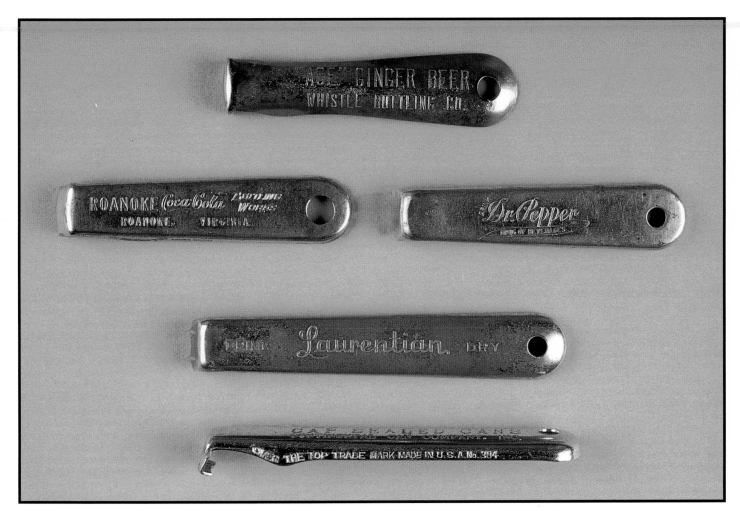

Top: H-1 Over-the-top cap lifter. Widening contoured handle. American design patent 1,490,149 issued to Harry L. Vaughan, April 15, 1924. 3 1/2".
Middle two: H-2 Over-the-top cap lifter. It has a pair of curvilinear rounded points or sharp points, bearing edges that engage top surface of bottle cap. Marked VAUGHAN NOV. MFG CO.

CHICAGO PAT.PEND. or VAUGHAN CHICAGO. American patent 1,490,149 issued to Harry L. Vaughan, April 15, 1924. 3 3/8".
Bottom two: H-3 Over-the-top cap lifter. It has a pair of curvilinear rounded points or sharp points, bearing edges that engage top surface of bottle cap. Marked VAUGHAN CHICAGO. American patent 1,490,149 issued to Harry L. Vaughan, April 15, 1924. 4 1/4".

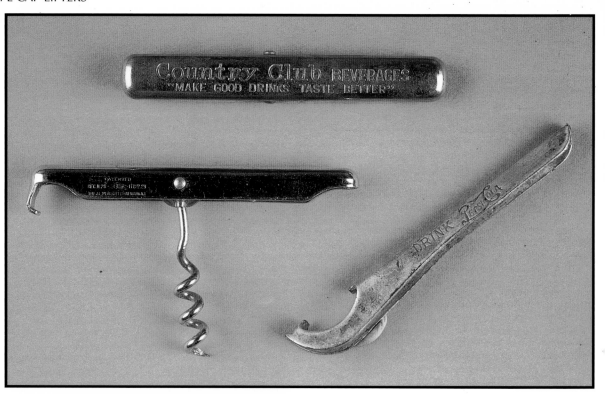

Top two: H-4 Over-the-top cap lifter with folding corkscrew. Marked PATENTED DEC.11.28 FEB.12.29 (JEM CO IN LOGO) THE J. E. MERGOTT CO. NEWARK, N. J. American patents 1,695,098 and 1,701,950 issued to William Hiering, December 11, 1928, and February 12, 1929. 3 3/4".
Bottom: H-5 Combination over-the-top cap lifter and conventional opener. 4".

Top: H-7 Over-the-top cap lifter. Two dimples. 4 1/8".
Bottom: H-11 Over-the-top cap lifter. One dimple. 4 1/8".

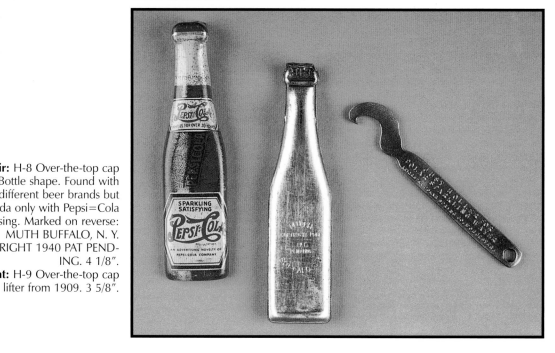

Left pair: H-8 Over-the-top cap lifter. Bottle shape. Found with many different beer brands but in soda only with Pepsi=Cola advertising. Marked on reverse: MUTH BUFFALO, N. Y. COPYRIGHT 1940 PAT PENDING. 4 1/8".
Right: H-9 Over-the-top cap lifter from 1909. 3 5/8".

COMBINATION CAP LIFTERS/CAN PIERCERS

On January 24, 1935, the first beer in cans was produced. The beer was from the Krueger Brewing Company, Newark, New Jersey. The can was manufactured by the American Can Company. The can piercer had already been invented in 1932 for opening other containers with liquid but the demand now was significantly increased. Can piercers became a necessity of life and were given away by the millions by vendors of soda and beer drinks in cans. Initially American Can Company manufactured openers in Newark, New Jersey. During the period of 1935-1936, they licensed Vaughan Manufacturing to produce openers as well. During the ensuing boom years for the can opener, Vaughan was by far the largest producer. Others included Handy Walden, Ekco, Emro, Mira, Crown, and Greene.

Basic types of cap lifter/can piercer combinations are shown in this category. Variations of the types include: slight differences in length and width; presence of "ears" designed to prevent dropping the opener into a bottle; bottle and can ends in opposite planes; presence or absence of a hanging hole; and presence or absence of strengthening ribs. Other variations include manufacturer's names, manufacturing years, patent dates, and patent numbers. Some of the openers are copper, nickel, cadmium, chromate, or brass plated.

Product names for this type include Quick and Easy, Can Tapper, Safe-Edge Can Piercer, Tu-way, Easi-Ope, and Por Ezy. An early American Can Company opener advises "Don't throw me out! I'm the quickest and best opener for all liquid foods."

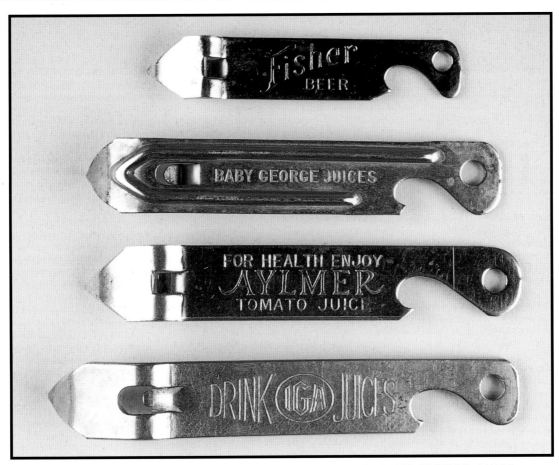

Top to bottom:
I-1 Cap lifter/can piercer. 3 1/4".
I-4 Cap lifter/can piercer. American design patent 143,327 issued to Michael J. LaForte, December 25, 1945. 4 1/8".
I-6 Cap lifter/can piercer. 4 1/2" to 4 5/8".
I-7 The original cap lifter/can piercer. Marked FOR BEER IN CANS MARKED KEGLINED CANCO PATENT 1,996,550 TRADE MARK AM. CAN CO. or PAT. NO. 1,996,550 VAUGHAN CHICAGO MADE IN USA or QUICK & EASY OPENER CANCO PATENT 1,996,550 MADE IN U. S. A. American patent 1,996,550 issued to Dewitt F. Sampson and John M. Hothersall, April 2, 1935. 4 3/4".

Above: **Top two:** I-11 Cap lifter/can piercer. 3 1/4" to 3 3/8".
Third: I-12 Cap lifter/can piercer. 3 5/8" to 3 3/4".
Bottom: I-13 Cap lifter/can piercer. 3 7/8" to 4 1/8".

Right: **Top:** I-16 Cap lifter/can piercer. Ribbed. 3 7/8" to 4".
Bottom two: I-17 Cap lifter/can piercer. Ribbed. Some marked
VAUGHAN PATENT 1,996,550. 4 1/4" to 4 3/8". Bottom opener
made by Handy Walden, Inc. using their RO-LOC LOGO IN COLOR
PROCESS (painted metal plate is wrapped around the handle).

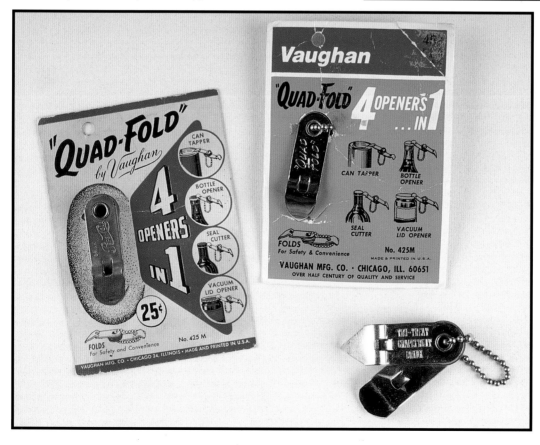

Left: I-19 Cap lifter/can piercer. Quad-fold. 3 1/2". Sales cards from Vaughan, Chicago, describe this as "4 openers in 1. Can tapper, bottle opener, seal cutter, and vacuum lid opener."
Right: I-20 Cap lifter/can piercer. Quad-fold. American design patent 168,053 issued to Michael J. LaForte, October 28, 1952. 3 7/8".

I-27 Cap lifter/can piercer. Quad-fold. Steel
swivel ring (I-19 & I-20 have plastic). 3 3/4".

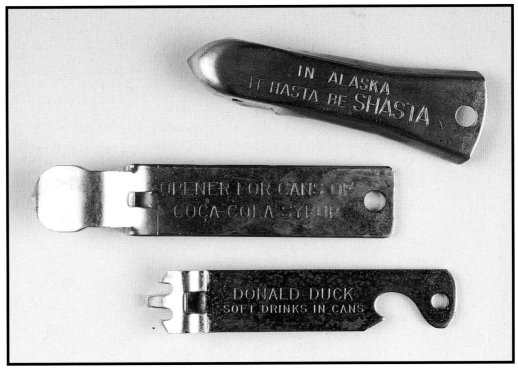

Top: I-23 "Easi-Ope" cap lifter/can piercer. American design patent
164,448 (September 4, 1951) and mechanical patent 2,517,443 (August
1, 1950) issued to Harland R. Ransom. 3 3/4".
Middle: I-501 Cap lifter/three-prong can piercer. Marked EMRO MFG.
CO. ST.L. MO. SAFETY CAN OPENER PAT.PEND. 4".
Bottom: I-502 Cap lifter/can piercer. Two ribs at can piercer end. 4 1/4".

Pat Stanley best describes these types as "If you know the 'I' type, you know what these look like. They are one-half of an 'I'."

J-11 Can piercer. Vaughan Company's "O-G Junior Can Tapper." Top example is made out of aluminum. 2 7/8" long and 9/16" wide.

Top: J-5 Can piercer. Ribbed can piercer end. Made by Vaughan, Chicago. 4".
Bottom: J-6 Can piercer. Whole opener ribbed. Marked PAT. 143,327; 1,996,550, OTHERS PENDING, VAUGHAN, CHICAGO, MADE IN U. S. A. 4".

J-9 Can piercer with tubular handle. American design patent 155,314 issued to Joseph G. Pessina, September 20, 1949. 4".

CAN AND BOTTLE SHAPE OPENERS

The earliest bottle shape openers were corkscrews. The worm was stored inside of a two-part bottle, which served as the pulling handle to remove the cork. Tablets were attached to these bottles to promote products. But what better way for a bottler to promote his soda, than by replicating the whole can or bottle in miniature form? These free-standing, three-dimensional bottles and cans add a lot of color and character to any collection of openers.

Two at left: L-1 Retractable can piercer. The piercer is released by pushing a button on the top of the can. Made in West Germany. 1 3/4". *The only known soda advertising example of this type is "Pepsi-Cola."*

Below: L-2 Mini bottle roundlet corkscrew. Round or square shoulders on bottle. American patent 583,561 issued to William A. Williamson, June 1, 1897, for his invention of a corkscrew, which is concealed inside a small bottle or bullet shape roundlet. The ends thread together and when unscrewed, a helix pivots at an angle to the base. The two pieces are then screwed back together to form the handle. Advertising plaques were applied to some bottles and bullets. American patent 657,421 issued to Ralph W. Jorres, September 4, 1900, for his version of this corkscrew. Jorres attached the helix to the top of the bottle instead of the base. Bottles were produced by the Williamson Company in nickel plated brass. Some bottles have Stanhopes in the top. The top is held up to the light and a small magnifier (Stanhope) contains a photograph. Unfortunately, the photo was delicate and finding one complete is rare. 2 3/4".

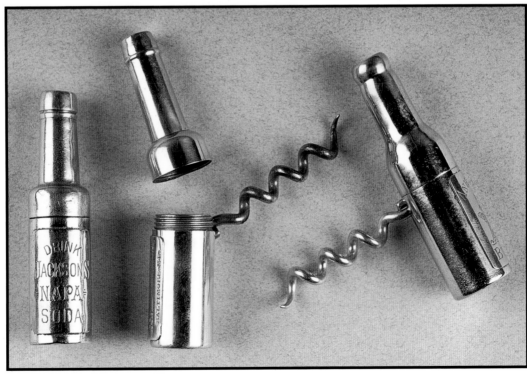

MISCELLANEOUS OPENERS

When the classification system for openers was presented in the 1978 book *Beer Advertising Openers*, there were 28 openers that didn't seem to fit any of the other categories. There were bell shapes, cast iron openers, openers with stag handles, star shape, bullet shape, and even a couple with corkscrews. The "Miscellaneous" category became sort of a "dumping ground" for those perplexing pieces that raised the question "Where the heck do I put this?" Now there are many openers here and although one could argue for classifications for tableware, bone handles, and many others, we've opted to just leave the lot in this dumping ground. We invite the reader to call them whatever they like!

Left: M-1 Lithographed cap lifter. Rounded base. Made by H. D. Beach Company of Coshocton, Ohio. Some marked with patent date, Sept. 11, 1911. American design patent 41,807 issued to Harry L. Beach, September 11, 1911. Front side curves in. Back side curves out. 3 1/2".
Right: M-2 Lithographed cap lifter. Squared base. Made by H. D. Beach Company of Coshocton, Ohio. Some marked with patent date, Sept. 11, 1911. Front side curves in. Back side curves out. 3 1/4".

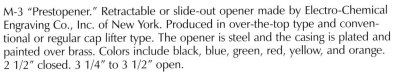

M-3 "Prestopener." Retractable or slide-out opener made by Electro-Chemical Engraving Co., Inc. of New York. Produced in over-the-top type and conventional or regular cap lifter type. The opener is steel and the casing is plated and painted over brass. Colors include black, blue, green, red, yellow, and orange. 2 1/2" closed. 3 1/4" to 3 1/2" open.

M-6 Cap lifter with bell. Marked PAT. PENDING. 3 1/8".

Left: M-120 Hook cap lifter and muddler. 5 1/8".
Right: M-509 Cap lifter and cone top can muddler. 6".

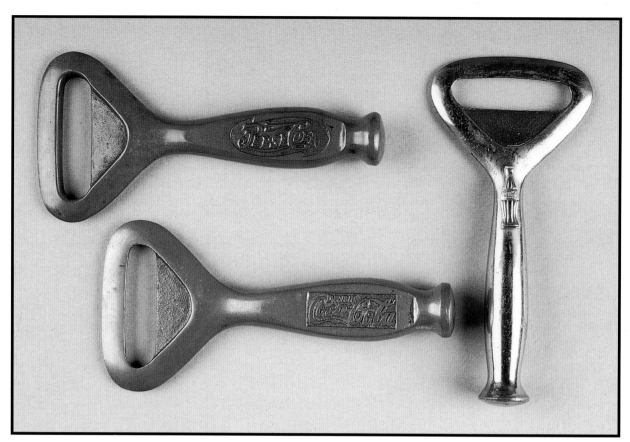

M-19 Cap lifter and muddler. American design patent 148,535
issued to Frank E. Hamilton, February 3, 1948. 5 1/4".

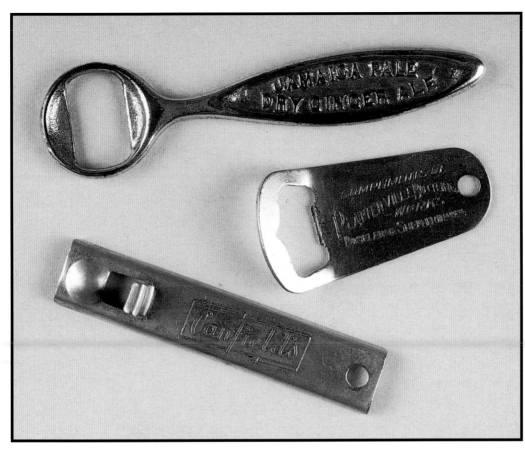

Top: M-45 Cast iron cap lifter. 5 1/4".
Middle: M-508 Cap lifter with opener end curved upward 45 degrees. 2 3/4".
Bottom: M-507 Cap lifter. Steel handle. Marked KRAG CHGO 12, ILL. PAT.PEND. 4".

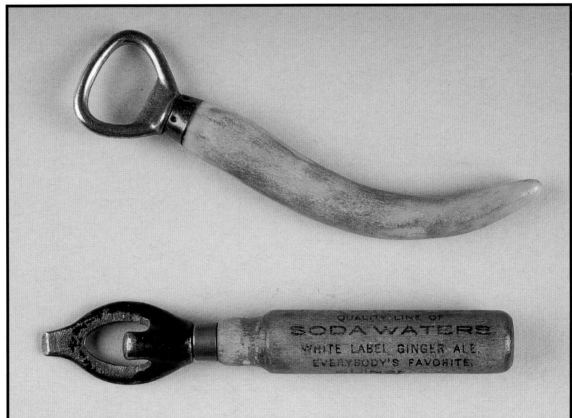

Top: M-21 Cap lifter and loop seal remover with bone handle. Various lengths. *Found with collar marked PUREOXIA and STERLING.*
Bottom: M-20 Cap lifter with wood handle. 6".

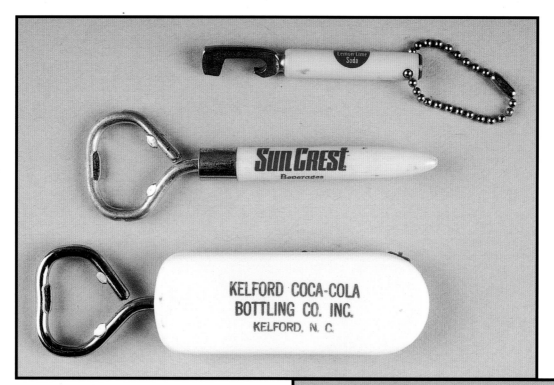

Above & right:
Top: M-60 Cap lifter. Plastic handle. 3 1/4".
Middle: M-51 Cap lifter with plastic handle. Made by Newton Mfg. Co. of Newton, Iowa. 5".
Bottom: M-100 Cap lifter. Plastic handle. Two sizes of plastic bottle recappers on reverse. Marked PAT.PENDING. 5 3/4".

Below: **Left:** M-9 Cap lifter and can piercer with plastic handle. Made by Vaughan Company. 5".
Middle: M-33 Cap lifter and can piercer with wood handle. Marked EDLUND CO. INC. BURLINGTON, VT. U. S. A. 6".
Right: M-54 Cap lifter and can piercer. Plastic handle. Marked JAPAN. 5 5/8".

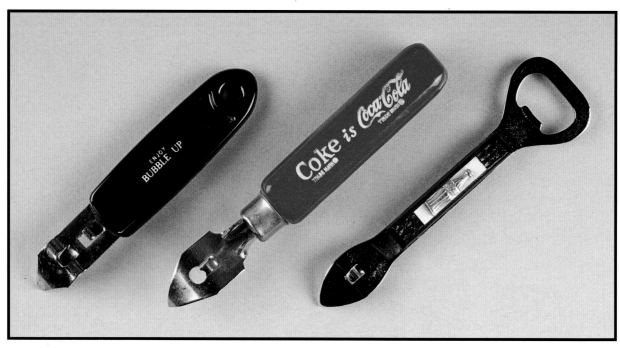

Top: M-29 Cap lifter and can piercer with plastic handle. Flat end. Developed by Mr. Lipic of St. Louis, Missouri, in the early 50s. 5 5/8".
Middle: M-30 Cap lifter and can piercer with plastic handle. Pointed end. 5 3/4".
Bottom: M-83 Cap lifter and can piercer. Plastic handle. Handle and end molded as one piece. 6 1/8".

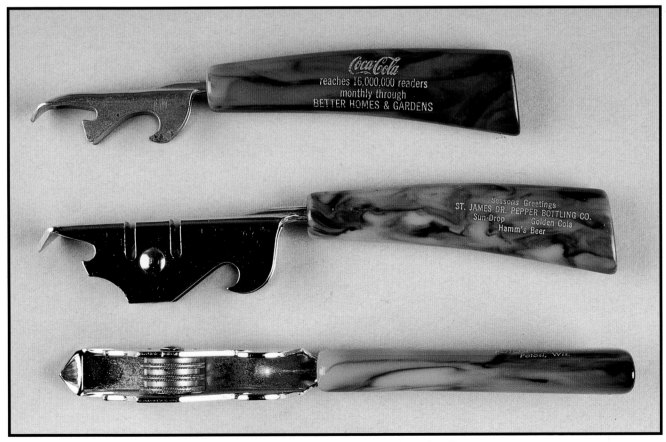

Top: M-40 Cap lifter and can piercer with plastic handle.
Made by Langer Mfg. Co. of New York, New York. 5 3/4".
Bottom two: M-69 Cap lifter, can piercer, and knife sharpener (shown in bottom view). Plastic handle. 7 1/2".

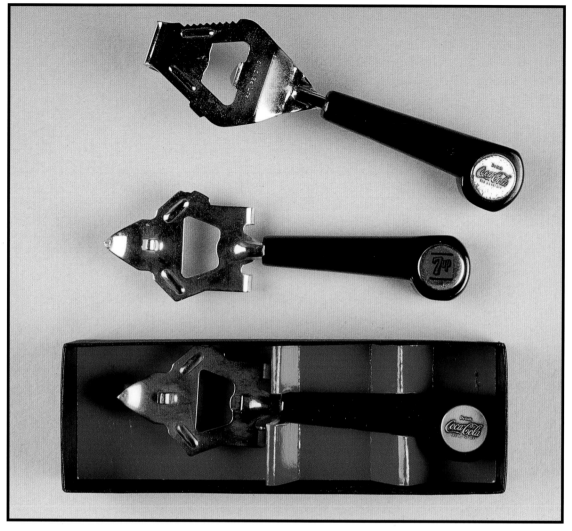

Above:
Top: M-501 Cap lifter and can piercer. Plastic handle with medallion insert. 7 5/8".
Bottom two: M-85 Cap lifter and can piercer. Plastic handle with medallion insert. Part of a set—see P-512. 7 3/8".

Right:
M-503 Cap lifter. Bottle Shape. Marked MADE IN ITALY. 7 7/8".

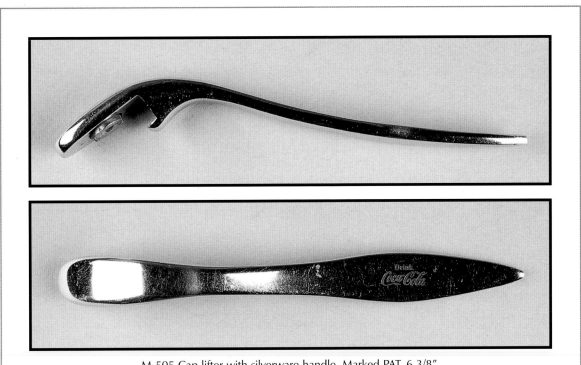

M-505 Cap lifter with silverware handle. Marked PAT. 6 3/8".

Left: M-502 Cap lifter and can piercer with wood handle. Marked
STAINLESS STEEL JAPAN. 6 3/4".
Right: M-506 Cap lifter and can piercer with wood handle. Hand in shape
of "okay figure." Marked BARLOW STAINLESS STEEL JAPAN. 7 7/8".

M-504 Cap lifter and can piercer with silverware handle. Comes in a set of four: bottle logo, cup logo, glass logo, and label logo. Marked CAPRI ITALY STAINLESS. 7 1/4".

Top two: M-39 "Tap Boy." Cap lifter, can piercer, and corkscrew. Made by Vaughan Company, Chicago. American design patent 170,999 for a "Bar Tool" issued to Michael J. LaForte, December 1, 1953. The tool was manufactured by Vaughan Company of Chicago under the name "Tap Boy." Usually marked VAUGHAN'S TAP BOY, PAT. NO. 170,999, CHICAGO 24, U. S. A. 4 3/4".
Bottom two: M-23 Combination cap lifter, can piercer, and corkscrew. Made by EKCO, Chicago. Plastic handle. 5 1/4".

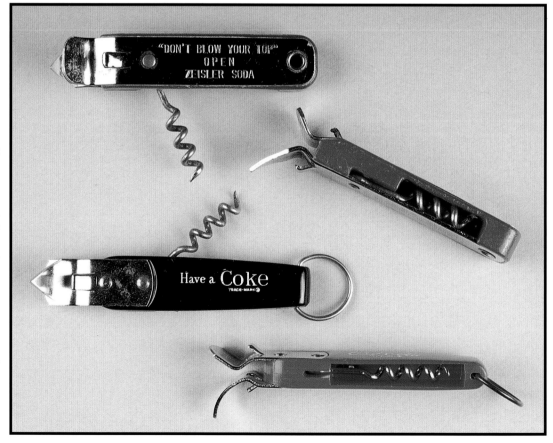

NOVELTY OPENERS

A wide variety of openers fall under this category, which, generally, includes those openers that have accessories to serve other purposes. There are knives, cigar cutters, shoe horns, pencils, jar openers, jiggers, button hooks, and bottle sealers and resealers.

Top: N-22 Cap lifter with pencil. Marked AMERICAN PENCIL CO. NEW YORK PAT. PEND. U. S. A. KAPOFF OPENUP. 7″ (length will be less if pencil sharpened!).
Middle five: N-29 Cap lifter. Bullet end contains a pencil that reverses and is inserted into the handle for use. Marked G. FELSENTHAL & SONS, CHICAGO. 4 5/8″.
Bottom: N-67 Mechanical pencil with cap lifter. 5 1/2″.

Right:

Top: N-7 Cap lifter with sliding cigar cutter, nail puller, and Prest-O-Lite key. Marked PAT. 10.12.09. American patent 936,678 issued to John L. Sommer, October 12, 1909. 3".

Bottom two: N-8 Cap lifter with sliding cigar cutter, cigar box opener, nail puller, and Prest-O-Lite key. Marked PAT. 10.12.09. American patent 936,678 issued to John L. Sommer, October 12, 1909. Obverse and reverse shown. 3".

Below:

Top three: N-10 Cap lifter with bottle stopper. Marked PAT'D U. S. A. DEC. 9, 19, NOS. 1,324,256. American patent 1,324,256 issued to William B. Langan, December 9, 1919. Patent assigned to the Koscherak Siphon Bottle Works, Hoboken, New Jersey. 3 1/8".

Bottom: N-79 Cap lifter with bottle stopper. Marked IT'S-A-CORKER PAT. PEND. 3 5/8".

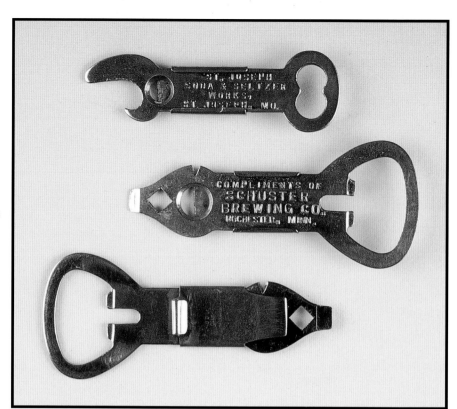

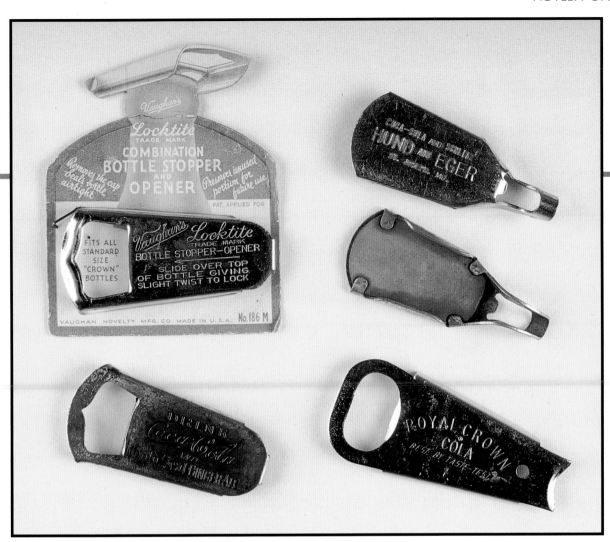

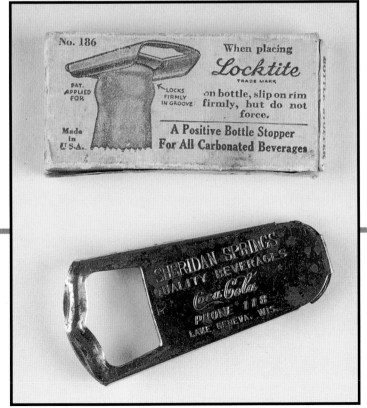

Left two: N-9 Cap lifter and bottle resealer. Appears in a 1937 Vaughan Novelty Manufacturing catalog as "Locktite (Trade Mark) Bottle Stopper and Opener Combination." It is described as "Removes the crown caps. The rubber gasket seals bottle air tight, preserving the unused portion for future use. Will last for years. Large space for advertisement." 3 1/8".

Top right two: N-62 Cap lifter with bottle resealer. Marked PAT. PEND., B & B, ST. PAUL (Brown & Bigelow Company). American design patent 98,486 issued to M. E. Trollen, February 4, 1936. 3 1/4".

Bottom right: N-512 Cap lifter with graduated jar opener. 3 1/2".

Top: N-503 Folding cap lifter. 3 1/4" opened and 2 1/4" folded.
Bottom two: N-11 Cap lifter on shoe horn. Marked PAT APL.
FOR. Shown in a 1961 Handy Walden catalog. A slightly
different design is shown in a 1971 Vaughan catalog. 3 3/8".

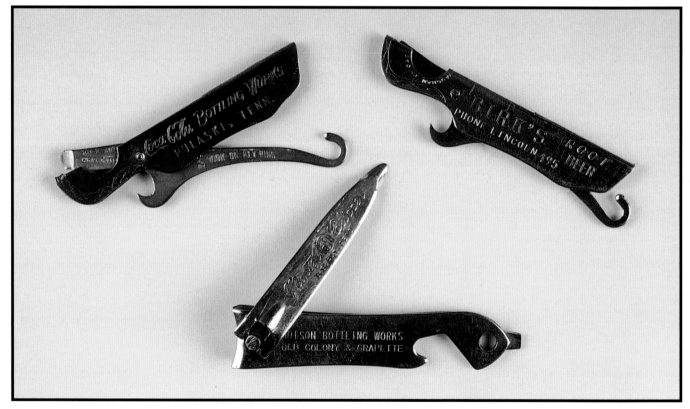

Top two: N-20 "Jim Dandy." A 4 in 1 pocket tool by Vaughan
Company with bottle opener, button hook, cigar cutter, and
screwdriver. Shown in a 1922 Vaughan catalog. 3".
Bottom: N-38 Nail clipper/file with cap lifter and screwdriver
on handle. Marked MASTER GSI (IN CIRCLE) CLIPPER, U. S.
PAT. PEND. 3 1/8".

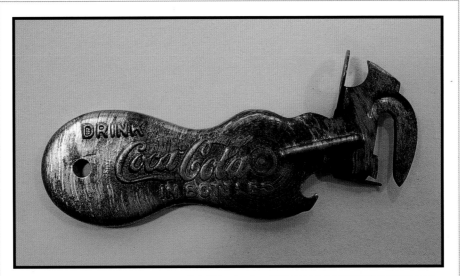

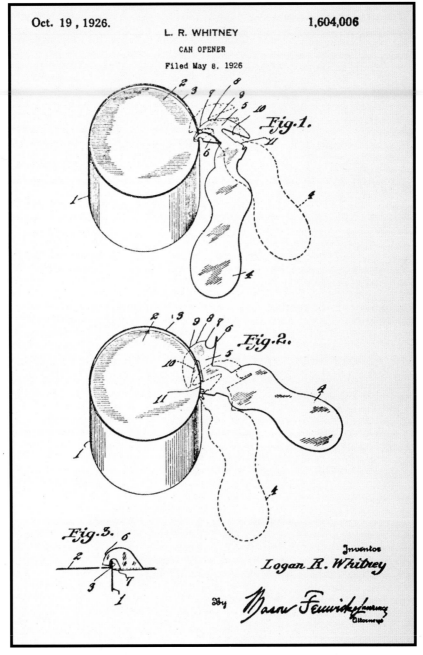

N-511 Cap lifter and can opener. American patent 1,604,006 issued to Logan R. Whitney of Louisville, Kentucky, October 19, 1926. 5 7/16".

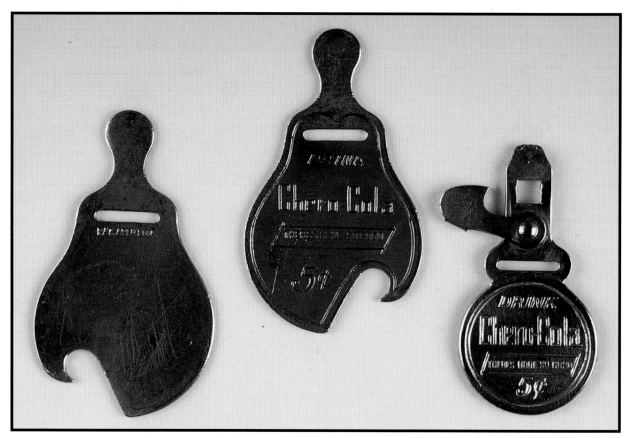

Left two: N-501 Cap lifter and watch fob. Marked PAT. APLD FOR. 2 5/8".
Right: N-502 Cap lifter, screwdriver, Prest-O-Lite key, and watch fob.
Marked PAT OCT. 8, 1912. Patented by Arthur Merrill. 2 3/8".

N-510 Cap lifter and door lock.
Cap lifter 3 3/8"; door lock 3 5/8".

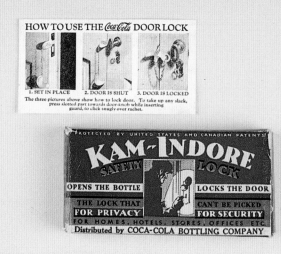

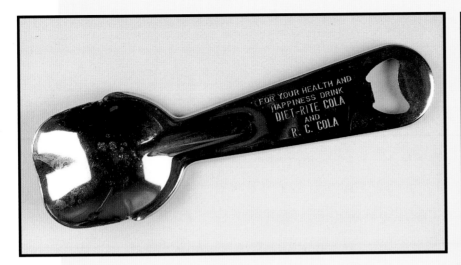

Above: N-513 Cap lifter and ice cream spoon. 8 1/8″.

Right: N-505 Cap lifter with bottle cap handle. 4 1/8″.

Below: N-506 Cap lifter with bottle handle for the 50th anniversary of the Nashville Coca-Cola Bottling Co. 3 3/4″.

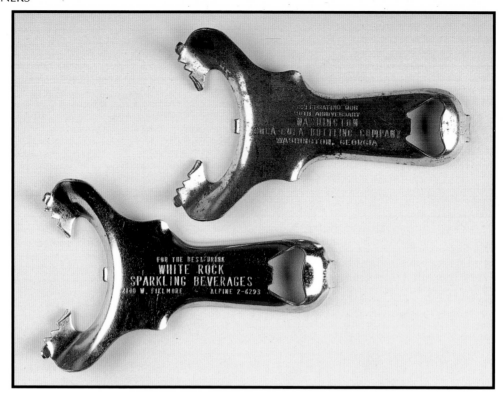

N-26 Cap lifter, lid prier, and jar top opener. Marked B&B ST. PAUL, MINN. U. S. A. REMEMBRANCE PATENT 2,493,438 2,501,204, 2,501,205. American design patent 176,518 issued to James L. Hvale, January 3, 1956. 5 1/2".

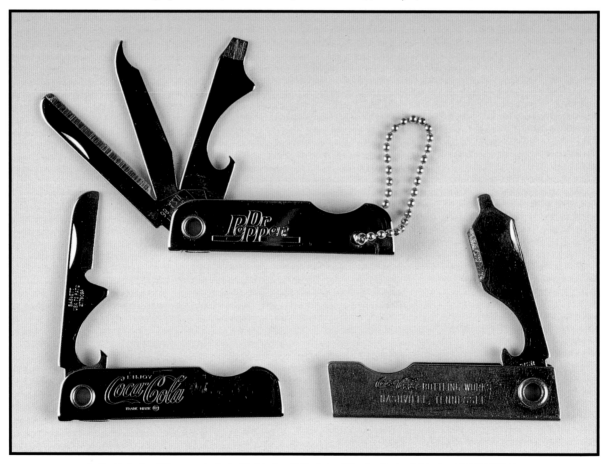

Left: N-3 Cap lifter on single knife blade. Called the "Derby Duke." Marked BASSETT U. S. A. PATD, 2,779,098. American patent 2,779,098 issued to Edward J. Pocoski and William G. Hennessy, January 1, 1957. 2 1/4".
Middle: N-56 Knife with three blades including cap lifter. 2 3/8".
Right: N-84 Single blade knife, cap lifter, and screwdriver blade. Marked U. S. A. 2 3/8".

Above: N-4 Cap lifter built into handle of single blade knife. Marked ETCHED P. CO., L. I. C., N. Y." (L. I. C. is Long Island City) or G. SCHRADE BPORT, CT. (Bridgeport, Connecticut). 3".

Left: N-5 Cap lifter on bolster of two blade knife. Boot shape with ivory handles. May be marked HENRY SEARS & SON 1865 MADE IN GERMANY. 3 1/4".
N-85 (Not shown, see chapter on Fantasy Openers). Cap lifter on handle of single blade knife. Boot shape with metal handles. Marked REMINGTON UMC. 3 1/4".

Left: N-24 Cap lifter formed in handle of single blade knife. Marked
STAINLESS, SHEFFIELD, ENGLAND. 3".
Right: N-43 Single blade knife with cap lifter formed in handle. 3 1/4".

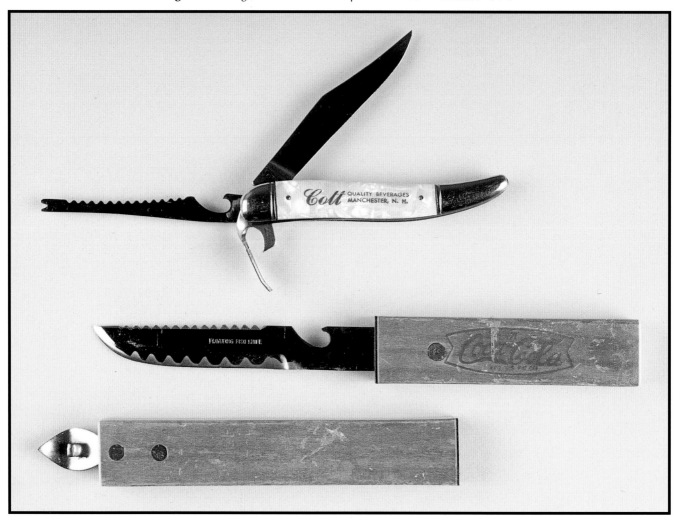

Top: N-42 Fishing knife with cap lifter. Master blade marked P2170537 & 2281712, IMPERIAL
PROV. U. S. A. Fish scaler blade marked BEVERAGE CAN OPENER 2361-889. 4 1/2".
Bottom: N-521 Cap lifter on concealed blade of floating fish knife. Marked WARCO,
STAINLESS STEEL, JAPAN. 10".

Left:
Top two: N-44 Knife with master blade and cap lifter blade. 3 1/2″.
Bottom: N-504 Knife with master blade and cap lifter blade. Celluloid handles. 3 3/8″.

Below:
Top: N-514 Four blade Scout knife. Bone handles. 3 3/4″.
Bottom three: N-515 Four blade Scout knife. Lengths and shapes of cap lifter blades vary. Composition handles. 3 3/4″.

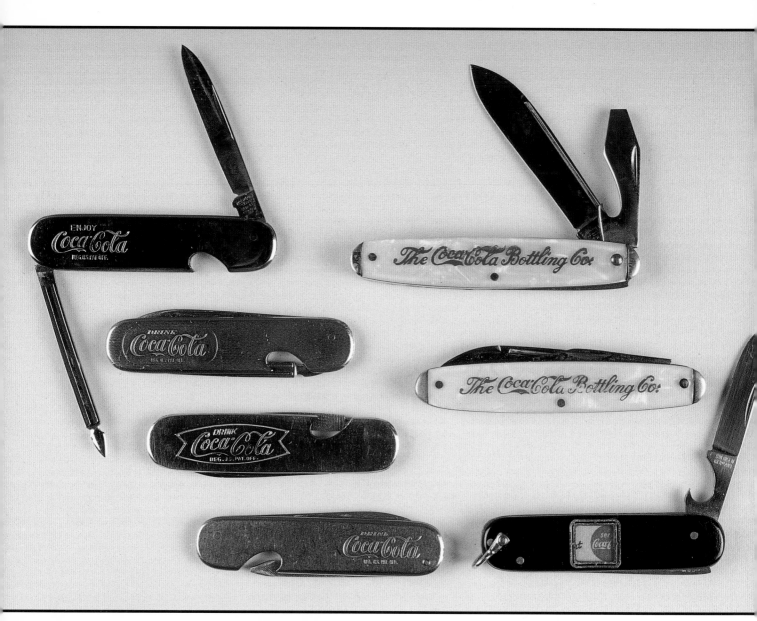

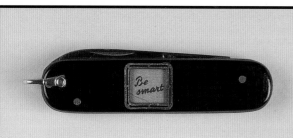

Left four: N-508 Knife with master blade, file blade and cap lifter in handle. Metal handles. Marked AUG. MULLER SOHNE, SOLINGEN, GERMANY. 3".

Top right two: N-509 Knife with master blade and cap lifter blade. Plastic handles. Marked CAMILLUS, NEW YORK, U. S. A. or CAMCO U. S. A. 3 3/8".

Bottom right: N-507 Knife with cap lifter in knife blade. Black celluloid handles. Marked PAT. PEND. 2 3/4".

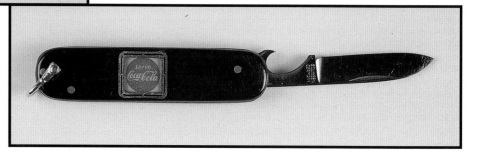

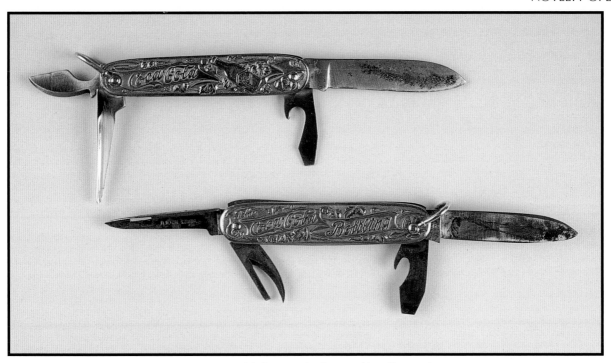

Top: N-516 Four blade Scout knife. Metal handles. 3 5/8".
Bottom: N-517 Four blade Scout knife. Metal handles. One blade is marked D.R.G.M. 429321 (German 1910). 3 1/2".

Top: N-518 Two blade knife. Composition handles. 3 1/16".
Middle: N-519 Single locking blade knife with cap lifter in handle. 3".
Bottom: N-520 Single blade knife with cap lifter in handle. Marked ROSTFREI. 3 3/8".

WALL MOUNT STATIONARY OPENERS

At one time the wall mounted bottle cap remover was a standard fixture in roadside motels. The owners screwed them to the wall in hopes that they would still be there at check out time—much less of a risk than leaving an opener on the dresser that could conveniently be pocketed on the way out. It was also insurance against the whims of the thirsty traveler who might otherwise resort to ripping a cap off using the underside of the bathroom counter or a hinge on a door. Although many wall mounts were produced with beer advertising, the traveler was more likely to find a plain example or one advertising Coca-Cola on his bathroom wall.

Cap lifters were also mounted in handy spots behind the tavern bar to save the bartender the constant frustration of locating an opener. In the soda advertising arena it is the soda pop machine that saw a large use of wall mount openers. Whether they were stand alone, on the side of a machine, or used in conjunction with a bottle cap catcher, this is where the wide variety of soda advertising wall mounted openers gained their fame.

The Orange-Crush matchbook had a special offer inside: "Get This De Luxe Wall-Type Home Bottle Opener Today. Only 10¢. Worth Much More!"

Left two: O-2 Enameled wall mounted cap lifter with four screws. Made by Erickson Company, Des Moines, Iowa. 2 1/8" wide, 3 5/16" high.
Right two: O-6 Enameled wall mounted cap lifter mounts with three screws. Probably made by Erickson Company, Des Moines, Iowa. 2 5/8" wide, 4" high.

Five outside: O-4 Vaughan's "Never Chip" models #1 and #2 wall mounted cap lifter. Mounts with two screws. American patent 1,029,645 issued to Harry L. Vaughan, June 18, 1912. The opener appears in Vaughan's 1922 and 1970 catalogs. Single packed in box claiming "It's the only *Stationary* Bottle Opener made which will remove 'the cap' without chipping the bottle, it's flexible." 2 1/2" wide, 1 13/16" high.
Middle: O-504 Vaughan's "Never Chip" wall mounted cap lifter. Mounts with two screws. Marked PAT. DEC. 21,09. Earlier variation of Vaughan's "Never Chip" wall mounted opener. 2 1/2" wide, 1 9/16" high.

Left: O-5 "Starr" wall mounted cap lifter with two screws. Manufactured by Brown Manufacturing Co., Inc., Newport News, Virginia. Trademarked as STARR X. American patent 2,033,088 issued to Raymond M. Brown, November 2, 1943. In a 1946 advertisement, we learn that the Starr is "The World's Best Opener. Eliminate loss of bottles and contents. Prevent danger to the public. Have long life." 2 3/4" wide, 3 5/16" high.
Right: O-502 "Starr" "side-mount" wall mounted cap lifter with two screws. Manufactured by Brown Manufacturing Co., Inc., Newport News, Virginia. 2 11/16" wide, 2 3/4" high.

O-506 Wall mounted cap lifter with two screws. Similar to type O-5 but bigger face for advertising. 2 3/8" wide, 2 1/2" high.

Left: O-503 Coca-Cola "Hood" wall mounted cap lifter with two screws. 2" wide, 3 1/4" high.
Right: O-523 All steel Coca-Cola "Hood" wall mounted cap lifter with two screws. Marked Reg. U.S. Pat. Off. 1 13/16" wide, 4 1/4" high.

O-511 Coca-Cola "Hoof" wall mounted cap
lifter with two screws. 1 7/8" wide, 2 1/8" high.

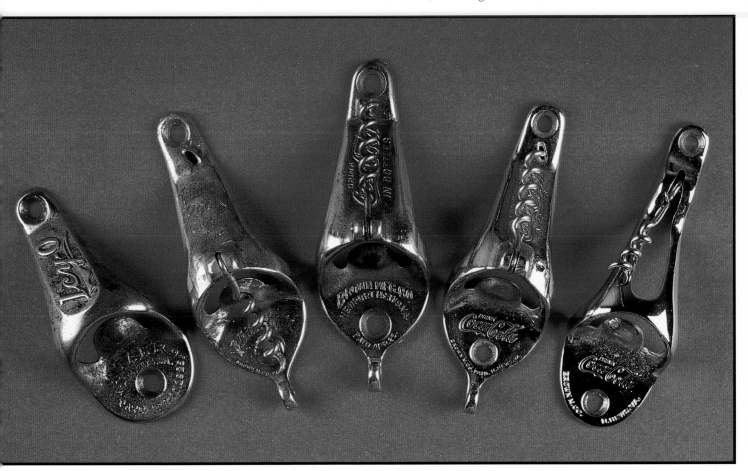

Left: O-505 "Long Neck Starr" wall mounted cap lifter with two screws. Marked STARR N'PT NEWS,
VA. PATD. APR.21, 1925 BROWN MFG CO. MADE IN U.S.A 1 7/8" wide, 4 1/8" high.
Middle three: O-516 "Long Neck Starr" corkscrew and cap catcher hook wall mounted cap lifter
with two screws. Marked BROWN MFG CO. NEWPORT NEWS, VA. PAT. 4,25. 1 3/4" wide, 5" high.
Right: O-515 "Long Neck Starr" corkscrew wall mounted cap lifter with two screws. Manufactured by
Brown Manufacturing Co., Inc., Newport News, Virginia. 1 11/16" wide, 4 7/8" high.

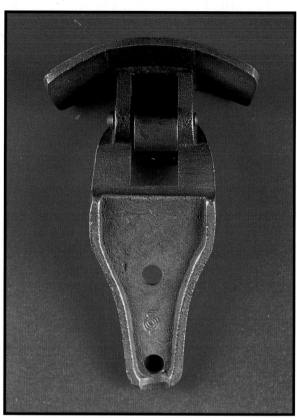

O-501 Coca-Cola "Swivel Hook" wall mounted cap lifter with two screws. Rotating hook acts as cap lifter. Marked PAT. APPL. FOR. Probably manufactured by Brown Manufacturing Co., Inc., Newport News, Virginia. 2 5/8" wide, 4 1/4" high.

O-507
Pepsi=Cola "Tear
Drop" wall
mounted cap lifter
with two screws.
Marked PAT.
PEND'G
VAUGHAN
CHICAGO. 2 1/4"
wide, 4 7/8" high.

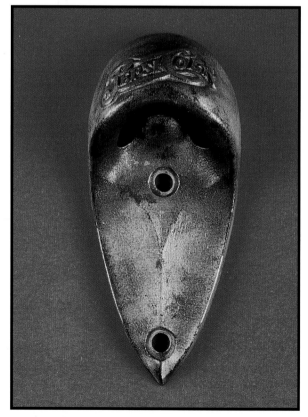

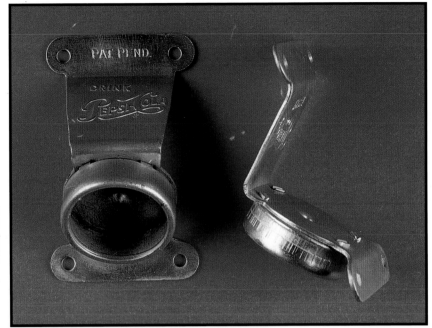

O-508 All steel Pepsi=Cola wall mounted round cap lifter with four screws. Marked PAT. PEND. 2 1/16" wide, 3 3/8" high.

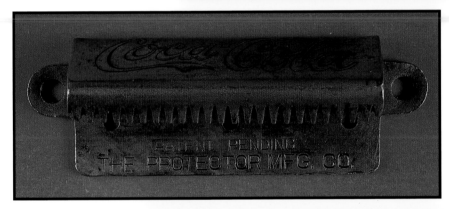

O-18 Toothed cap lifter mounts with two or three screws. May be marked PATENT PENDING THE PROTECTOR MFG. CO. 4" wide, 1 3/8" high.

O-517 Coca-Cola "Acton Crown Puller" wall mounted cap lifter with two screws. Manufactured by Hemp and Company Division of The American Thermos Products Company Macomb, Illinois. 1 5/8" wide, 2 3/8" high.

Left: O-509 "Deluxe De-Capper" wall mounted cap lifter with two screws. Marked DELUXE EZE-DECAPPER S&S PRODUCTS CO. LIMA, O. PATD. OR PAT 9-34. 2 3/8 wide, 2 3/4" high.
Right: O-518 "Ledge Mount" wall mounted cap lifter with one screw. Manufactured by S&S Products Co. of Lima, Ohio. 1 1/2" wide, 1 3/4" high.

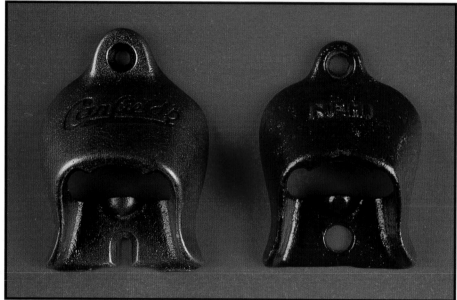

Left: O-512 Cast iron "Hood Type" wall mounted cap lifter with two screws. 2 1/8" wide, 3" high.
Right: O-522. Cast iron "Hood Type" wall mounted cap lifter with two screws. 2 1/8" wide, 2 3/4" high.

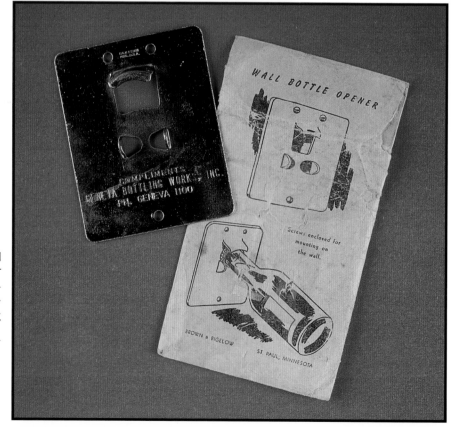

O-524. All steel wall mounted cap lifter with three screws. Marked B & B ST. PAUL MINN., U. S. A. 2 5/8" wide, 3 1/4" high.

O-513 Formed steel wall mounted cap lifter with two screws. Made by Dacro which claimed *"The handy way to remove—Dacro milk caps, beverage caps, pry-off type caps."* The box says "Attach to wall, door frame or any rigid structure." 1 1/2" wide, 3 1/2" high.

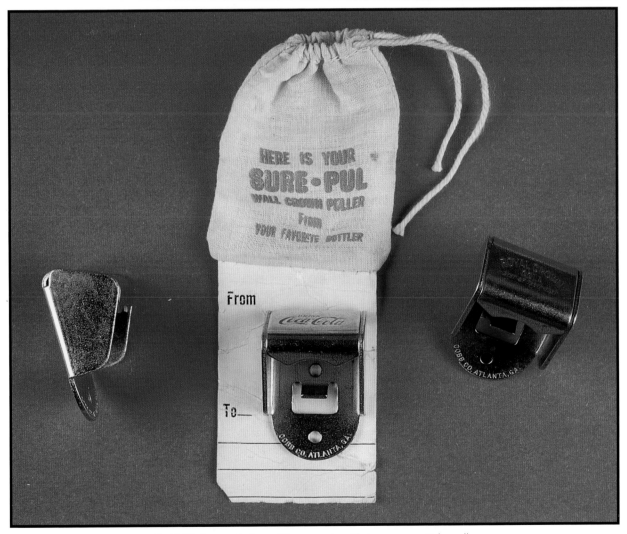

O-16 Wall mounted cap lifter mounts with two screws. Side walls. Marked COBB CO. ATLANTA, GA. 1 3/8" wide, 2 1/16" high.

O-8 Wall mounted cap lifter with four screws. American patent 1,711,678 issued to Thomas
Harding of Newark, New Jersey, May 7, 1929. Produced by J. L. Sommer Manufacturing Company.
Also covered by Canadian patent 289,495. Bottom center example not formed. 2" wide, 3" high.

O-19 Wall mounted cap lifter mounts with three screws. 2" wide, 3 3/8" high.

Left two: O-10 Squared top wall mounted cap lifter mounts with three screws. 2" wide, 3 1/4" high.
Right two: O-510 Pointed top wall mounted cap lifter mounts with three screws. 2" wide, 3 3/16" high.

Left: O-14 Plastic wall mounted cap lifter with bottle cap (to show what it's for!). Mounts with one screw. 1 11/16" wide, 3 7/16" high.
Right: O-514 Steel wall mounted cap lifter with bottle cap. Mounts with two screws. 1 13/16" wide, 2 1/2" high.

O-520 Steel wall mounted C-19 type cap lifter with reinforcing ribs for opener that is bent out 45 degrees. Mounts with two screws. Marked SCOVILL WATERBURY. 1 5/8" wide, 3 3/4" high.

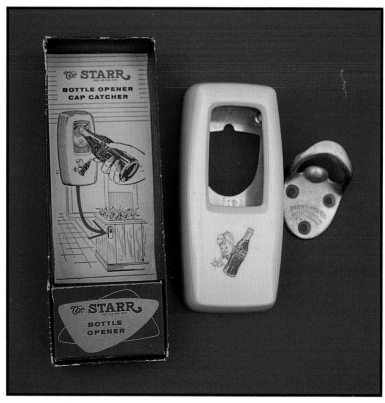

Above: O-17 Bottle opener and cap catcher. 2 5/8" wide, 6" high.

Right: O-521 Plastic wall mounted cap lifter with steel opener. Mounts with two screws. Marked MADE IN CANADA A.S.I. 7930. 2 7/8" wide, 3 1/4" high.

O-519 Bottle opener and cap catcher. Contains an Acton crown puller. Box reads "Akbilt bottle opener and cap catcher. Manufactured by Hemp and Company Division, The American Thermos Products Co., Macomb, Illinois." 2 5/8" wide, 6" high.

O-525 Wall mount cap remover. Manufactured by Brown Mfg. Co., Newport News, Virginia. Shown with type O-505 for size relationship. 1 5/8" wide, 3 1/4" high.

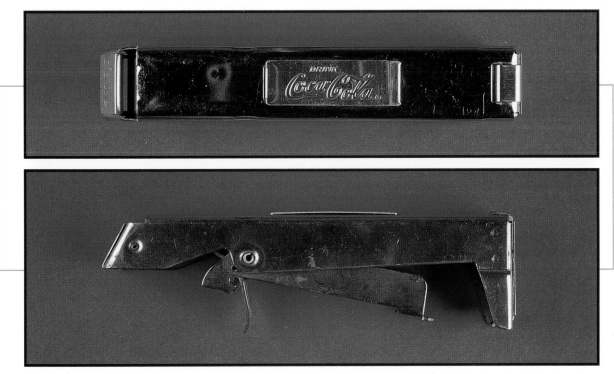

O-526 Wall mount can piercer. Marked TOPMASTER U. S. PAT. NO. 2687569 U. S. A. 1 5/16" wide, 2" high, 7 1/4" long.

CORKSCREWS

Corkscrews played an important role in soda advertising and as a necessary tool in the 1800s and into the early 1900s. Prior to the invention of the crimped bottle cap, breweries used corks that were secured by wire or string to the bottle. The corks protected the precious soda inside. For many years the corkscrew was *the* opener for soda as well as beer, medicines, inks, photographic liquids, perfumes, whiskey, and wine. The bottle cap did not become commercially available until the late 1890s and many skeptical bottlers continued to favor the cork until the early twentieth century.

When searching for soda advertising corkscrews, the advertising collector will often butt heads with the corkscrew addict. These addicts are usually relentless in their pursuit of corkscrew types that will fill the holes in their collections. To them it doesn't matter whether there is soda advertising or not. Meanwhile the soda advertising corkscrew collector may desperately want to add another brand name to a type he already owns. The struggle begins when they both need the same corkscrew. What they will ultimately find is that some corkscrews will bring a higher price amongst corkscrew collectors for the type, while advertising collectors may be willing to pay a higher price for the brand name on any example. This dilemma is reflected in the wide range of values shown on types in this category.

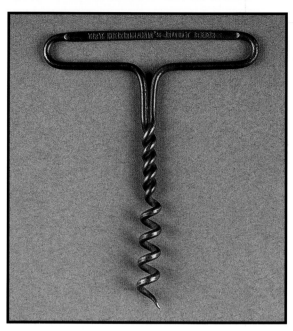

P-88 Steel wire formed corkscrew with twisted shank and single helix. American patent 172,868 issued to William R. Clough, February 1, 1876.

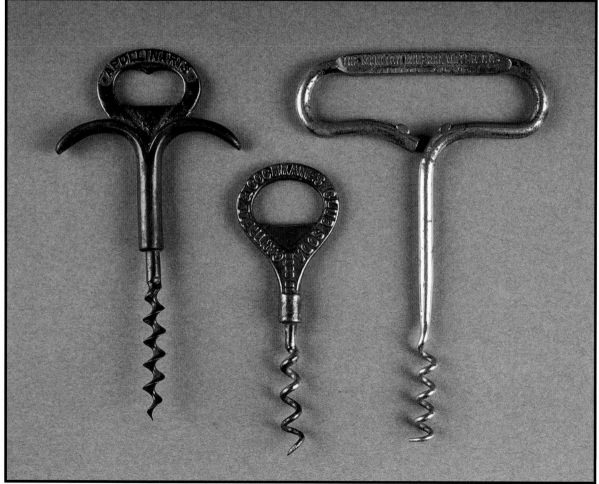

Left: P-505 Cast iron corkscrew and cap lifter T-handle. **Middle:** P-513 Cast iron corkscrew and cap lifter. **Right:** P-508 Steel loop handle corkscrew.

Left: P-8 Wood handle corkscrew with cast bell. American patent 501,975 issued to Edwin Walker, July 25, 1893.

Right: P-10 Wood handle corkscrew. Wire breaker and cap lifter are part of cast bell. American patent 647,775 issued to Edwin Walker, April 17, 1900.

Left: P-22 Wood handle direct pull corkscrew. Made by Williamson. Some found with "speed worm."

Right: P-51 Wood handle corkscrew with cast iron wire breaker and cap lifter above cast bell. American design patent 29,798 issued to William A. Williamson, December 13, 1898.

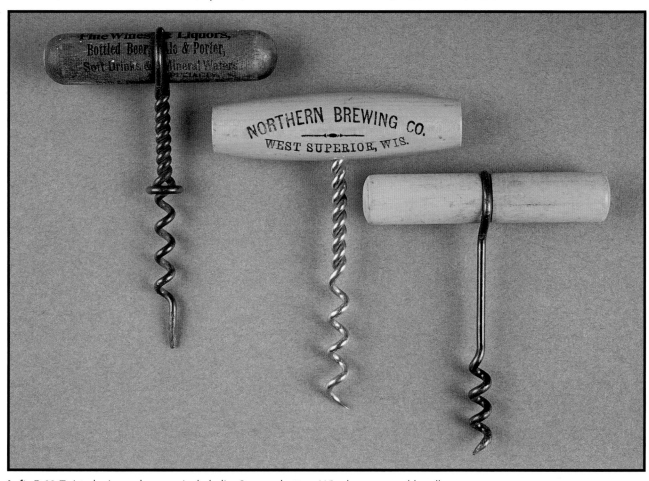

Left: P-60 Twisted wire corkscrew, single helix. Stopper button. Wire loops around handle.
Middle: P-90 Wood handle twisted wire corkscrew with single helix.
Right: P-95 Wood handle corkscrew with worm wire wrapped around handle.

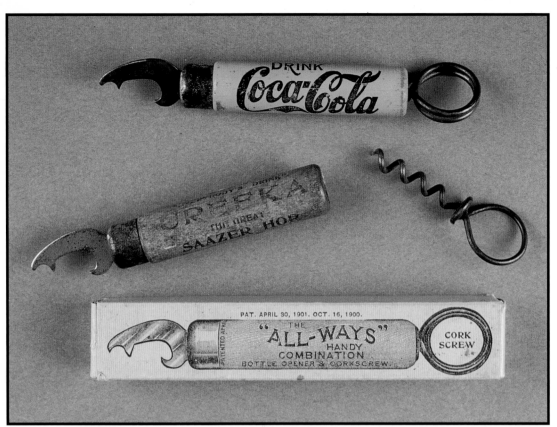

P-7 The "All-Ways" handy combination bottle opener and corkscrew. Advertised as "No two ways about this being useful, it's useful in four ways—Pulling a Cork, Taking out Aluminum Stopper, Removing a Seal, Lifting a Crown Cap." 1900 patent date on these is a reference to Clough's machine for bending wire into a corkscrew. A 1901 patent date on these is John Baseler's patent for a "Stopper Extractor." The patent was for the cap lifter with the point at the front end of the crescent designed to punch a hole in the cap so it could not be re-used. A 1916 *Western Brewer* magazine advertisement from A. W. Stephens Company of Waltham, Massachusetts, proclaims "One of these openers hung up in the kitchen beats a hundred of the other kind scattered on the cellar floor." Supplier names are usually included in small print and often with the incorrect patent dates March 30, 1901, and April 30, 1910.

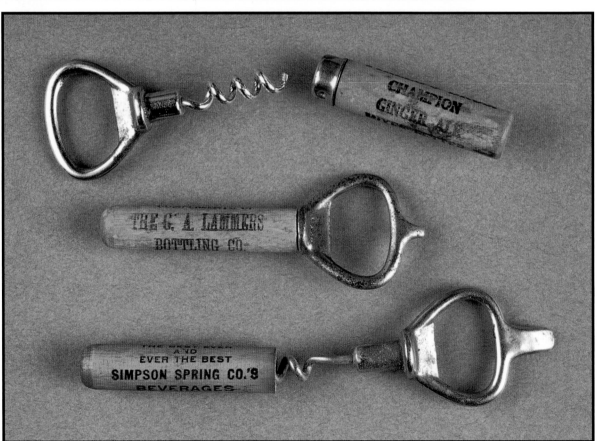

Top: P-6 Cap lifter and corkscrew. Wooden sheath protects worm.
Middle: P-31 Cap lifter with wire breaker and corkscrew. Wooden sheath protects worm.
Bottom: P-85 Cap lifter with screwdriver tip and corkscrew. Worm protected by wooden sheath.

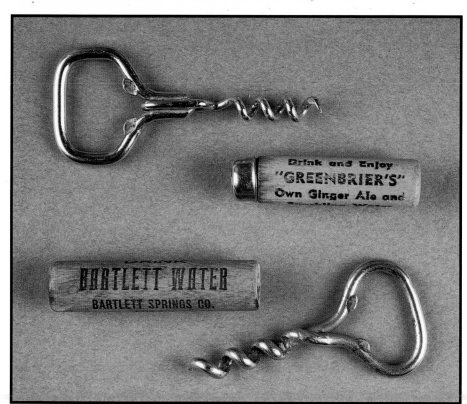

Left: **Top:** P-53 Corkscrew with two fret wire formed cap lifter. Wood sheath protects worm.
Bottom: P-74 Two fret cap lifter and corkscrew. Worm protected by wooden sheath.

Below: **Top three:** P-19 Single/double ring wire handle corkscrew with wooden sheath (made by the gazillions).
Fourth: P-54 Single/double ring wire handle corkscrew with "Decapitator."
Bottom: P-501 Cap lifter (two nibs) and corkscrew with wooden sheath.

Top: P-502 Cap lifter with wire breaker and corkscrew. Wooden sheath to protect worm also reverses for handle of ice pick.
Bottom: P-138 Cap lifter with wire breaker and corkscrew. Wooden sheath to protect worm is also handle of ice pick.

P-58 Key shape cap lifter with concealed corkscrew. Shown with hanger and with the advertising on the bottom of the key.

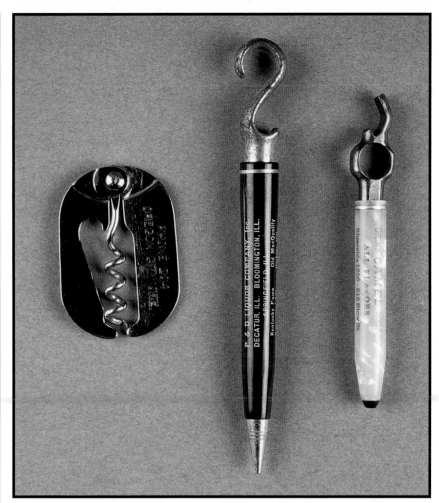

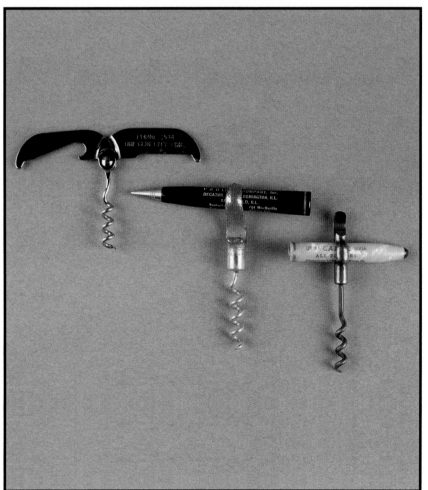

Left: P-11 The "Tip Top" by Williamson of Newark, New Jersey. A packaging card for the Tip Top proclaims "Lies flat in your vest pocket."
Middle: P-506 Corkscrew, cap lifter and pencil. American design patent 109,879 issued to Walter Ruby, May 31, 1938.
Right: P-509 Picnic corkscrew with celluloid sheath.

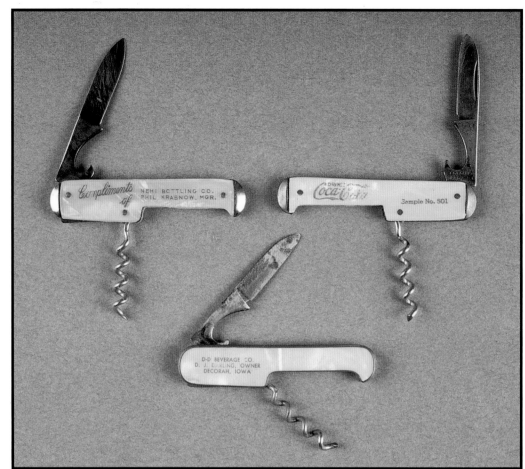

Top two: P-14 Corkscrew knife with master blade having a cap lifter at the base. Marked CAMCO, U. S. A. or KENT, N. Y. C. or COLONIAL, PROV., R. I.
Bottom: P-36 Single blade knife with cap lifter at base of blade. Corkscrew on opposite side of blade.

Top: P-515 Single blade corkscrew knife with cap lifter formed in pearlized handle.
Middle: P-15 Single blade corkscrew knife with cap lifter (handle does not cover cap lifter) formed in plastic handle.
Bottom: P-504 Single blade corkscrew knife with cap lifter (handle does cover cap lifter) formed in plastic handle.

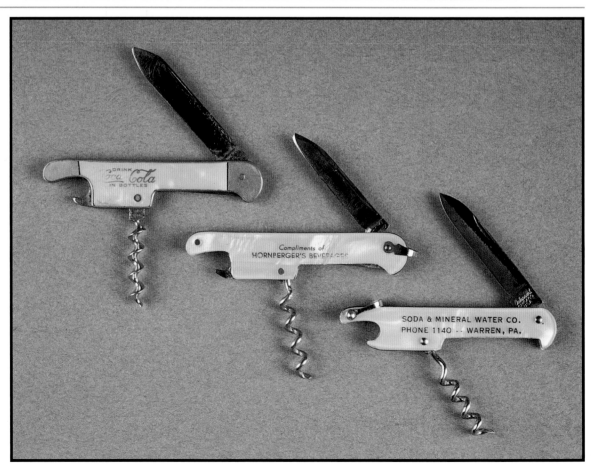

Top: P-507 Single blade knife with cap lifter and corkscrew. Ornate handles.
Bottom: P-514 Double blade knife with cap lifter and corkscrew. Ornate handles.

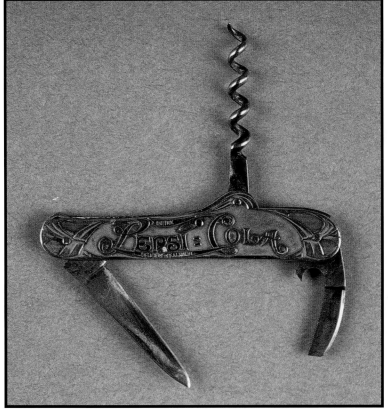

P-69 Double blade knife with corkscrew.
Ornate handles. Back and front views.

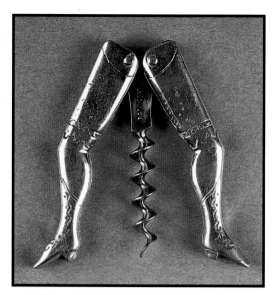

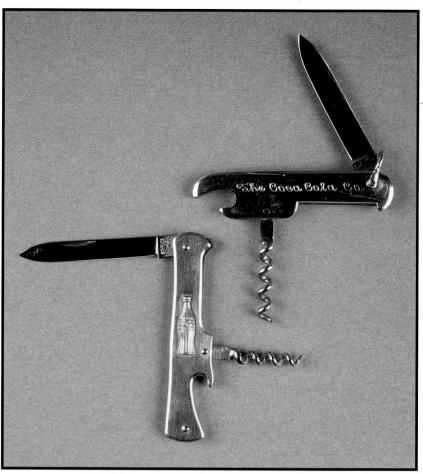

Above:
P-79 Folding gay nineties legs. Nickel plated brass. Made in Germany.

Right:
Top: P-510 Single blade knife with cap lifter in handle and corkscrew. Key ring hook.
Bottom: P-511 Schrade-Walden knife with cap lifter in handle and corkscrew. Metal handles.

Left: P-104 Swiss Army knife with corkscrew. Marked VICTORINOX SWITZERLAND STAINLESS ROSTFREI, OFFICIER SUISSE. Plastic handles.
Right: P-512 Five blade knife with cap lifter blade and corkscrew. Plastic handles.

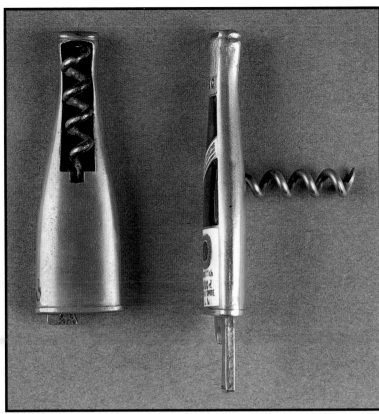

P-503 Clicquot Club Eskimo bottle corkscrew and cap lifter. Corkscrew folds out of the back of the bottle and the cap lifter drops out of the bottle.

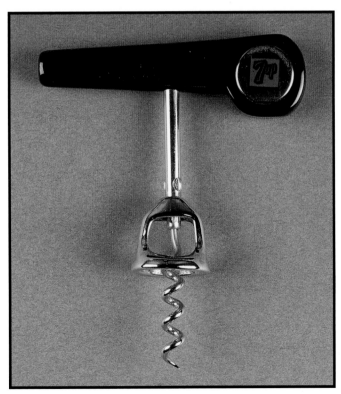

P-131 Plastic handle corkscrew with cast bell. Medallion in handle. Part of a set-see M-85. Made by Williamson.

FIGURALS (3-D)

The figural or 3-D category is only represented by two examples in soda, a figural fist and a figural ladies' leg. Beer advertisers have offered a wide range of openers in this category but it is one area where soda openers lag behind.

R-501 Figural fist. Cap lifter is between thumb and fingers. 2".

R-502 Figural ladies' leg. Marked PAT. 3".

══ AMERICAN PATENTS ══

The story of the evolution of the advertising openers can easily be viewed by a look at the patents issued:

1876, February 1. P-88. "Duplex Power Cork Screw." Patent 172,868 by William R. Clough.

1893, July 25. P-8 Wood handle corkscrew. Patent 501,975 by Edwin Walker.

1894, February 6. D-6 & M-45. "Capped bottle opener." Patent 514,200 by William Painter.

1894, January 1. P-79 Folding gay nineties legs. German patent 21,718 by Steinfeld & Reimer.

1897, June 1. L-2 Mini bottle roundlet corkscrew. Patent 583,561 by William A. Williamson.

1898, December 13. P-51 Wood handle corkscrew. Design patent 29,798 by William A. Williamson.

1900, April 17. P-10 Wood handle corkscrew. Patent 647,775 by Edwin Walker.

1900, September 4. L-2 bottle roundlet corkscrew. Patent 657,421 by Ralph W. Jorres.

1901, February 19. B-18, B-19 and B-21 openers. Design patent 34,096 by Augustus W. Stephens.

1905, November 28. B-7 Handy Pocket Companion. Patent 805,486 by Julius T. Rosenheimer.

1909, July 13. G-5 Cap lifter with flat handle. Patent 928,156 by Adolph Rydquist.

1909, October 12. N-7 and N-8 Cap lifter. Patent 936,678 by John L. Sommer.

1911, September 11. M-1 and M-2 Lithographed cap lifter. Design patent 41,807 by Harry L. Beach.

1911, November 7. A-42 Fish. Design patent 41,894 by John L. Sommer.

1911, November 7. A-13 Automobile. Design patent 41,895 by John L. Sommer.

1912, March 12. A-28 and A-29 Bottle. Design patent 42,305 by John L. Sommer.

1912, March 12. A-7 and A-35. Fancy lady's boot. Design patent 42,306 by John L. Sommer.

1912, June 18. O-4 "Never Chip." Patent 1,029,645 by Harry L. Vaughan.

1912, October 8. N-502 Cap lifter, screwdriver, cigar cutter, Prest-O-Lite key, and watch fob. Patent by Arthur Merrill.

1912, November 26. F-6 "Four in 1 Handy Tool." Design patent 43,278 by Thomas Harding.

1913, June 17. A-4 and A-5 Girl clothed (calendar) and nude (Early Morn). Design patent 44,226 by Harry L. Vaughan.

1913, November 25. A-30 and A-53 Dancer legs. Design patent 44,945 by Harry L. Vaughan.

1914, April 28. A-34 Powder Horn. Design patent 45,678 by John L. Sommer.

1914, August 18. A-9 Baseball player in pitching position. Design patent 46,298 by John L. Sommer.

1914, August 25. F-18 Cap lifter with ice pick. Design patent 46,311 by Thomas Harding.

1914, November 24. F-13 Cap lifter and cake server. Design patent 46,702 by John L. Sommer and Thomas Harding.

1914, December 8. Type A-1 Bathing girl, mermaid or surf-girl. Design patent 46,762 by Harry L. Vaughan.

1915, August 17. E-8 Single wire loop. Patent 1,150,083 by Edwin Walker.

1916, December 5. B-13 Nifty. Patent 1,207,100 by Harry L. Vaughan.

1919, December 9. N-10 Cap lifter with bottle stopper. Patent 1,324,256 by William B. Langan.

1924, April 15. H-1, H-2, and H-3. Over-the-top cap lifter. Design patent 1,490,149 by Harry L. Vaughan.

1926, October 19. N-511 Can and bottle opener. Patent 1,604,006 by Logan R. Whitney.

1928, August 14. B-35 Pocket opener and corkscrew. Patent 1,680,291 by Thomas Harding.

1928, December 13, and February 12, 1929. H-4 Over-the-top cap lifter with folding corkscrew. Patents 1,695,098 and 1,701,950 by William Hiering.

1929, May 7. O-8 Wall mounted cap lifter. Patent 1,711,678 by Thomas Harding.

1931, September 22. F-2 Spoon with cap lifter. Design patent 85,178 by Thomas Harding.

1933, November 7. G-9 Cap lifter with wood handle. Patent 1,934,594 by Harry G. Edlund.

1935, April 2. I-7 The original cap lifter/can piercer. Patent 1,996,550 by Dewitt F. Sampson and John M. Hothersall.

1935, October 22. B-24 Vaughan's "Never Slip" bottle opener. Patent 2,018,083 issue by James A. Murdock.

1936, February 4. N-62 Cap lifter with bottle resealer. Design patent 98,486 by M. E. Trollen.

1938, May 31. P-506 Corkscrew, cap lifter and pencil. Design patent 109,879 by Walter Ruby.

1943, November 2. O-5 "Starr." Patent 2,033,088 by Raymond M. Brown.

1945, December 25. I-4 Cap lifter/can piercer. Design patent 143,327 by Michael J. LaForte.

1948, February 3. M-19 Cap lifter and muddler. Design patent 148,535 by Frank E. Hamilton.

1949, September 20. J-9 Can piercer with tubular handle. Design patent 155,314 by Joseph G. Pessina.

1950, August 1, and September 4, 1951. I-23 "Easi-Ope" Cap lifter/can piercer. Design patent 164,448 and Mechanical patent 2,517,443 by Harland R. Ransom.

1950, October 17. O-16 Wall mounted cap lifter. Design patent 160,453 by Davis J. Ajouelo.

1950, October 31. F-3 Spoon with cap lifter and can piercer. Design patent 160,1950 issue by Le Emmette V. De Fee.

1950, December 16. A-39 Turtle with three screwdrivers. Design patent 161,321 by Le Emmette V. De Fee.

1952, October 28. I-20 Cap lifter/can piercer. Design patent 168,053 by Michael J. LaForte.

1953, December 1. M-39 "Tap Boy." Design patent 170,999 by Michael J. LaForte.

1956, January 3. N-26 Cap lifter, lid prier, and jar top opener. Design patent 176,518 by James L. Hvale.

1957, January 1. N-3 "Derby Duke." Patent 2,779,098 by Edward J. Pocoski and William G. Hennessy.

OPENER MANUFACTURERS

The best way for an opener manufacturing company to advertise was for them to use their own products featuring their company name. The manufacturers would often assign catalog numbers to their openers as well as catchy slogans. Besides opener manufacturing companies, advertising sales specialty firms also used this method.

Above:
Top row: Enameled opener by Electro-Chemical Engraving Co.; G. P. Coates & Co.; Cigar Box Opener by L. F. Grammes.
Second row: B-31 "Crown Opener" made by Williamson Mfg Co. (No. 110); "Crown Opener" by Williamson (No. 108).
Third Row: Improved Crown & Seal Co; "The Presto Bottle Opener and Gas Tank Key"; Enameled opener by J. K. Aldrich.
Fourth Row: Vaughan Novelty Mfg Co's "Item #3."; Enameled opener by J. K. Aldrich with ad for "Advertising Metal Material."
Bottom: Enameled opener by J. K. Aldrich with ad for "Bottle Openers."

Right:
Top left: Two Dow pin openers by Louis F. Dow Co. Marked ST PAUL 4 MN NO. X 2500 and ST. PAUL 14 MN NO. 29-076.
Middle: Enameled bottle by America Etching Co.
Right: Clothed lady advertising "Crown Throat & Opener Company Makers Chicago"; Fish from John L. Sommer's Chicago office. Sommer was headquartered in Newark, New Jersey; Dancer legs opener could be purchased through the "American Novelty Co. Niagara Falls, N. Y. 10 Cents Each."
Bottom Left: Lady "U-Neek" Bottle Opener & Auto Gas Tank Key.

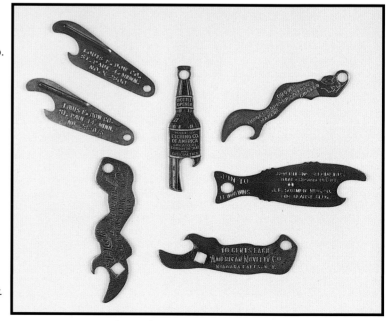

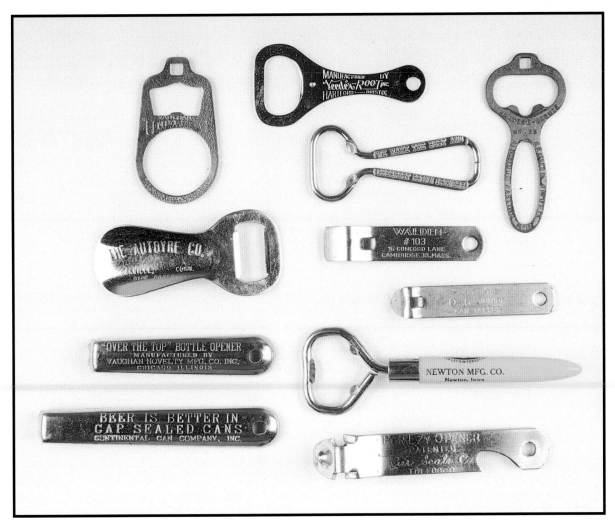

Left top to bottom: Vaughan's "Universal" opener with gas key made by Crown Throat & Opener Co; Shoehorn opener by Autoyre (pronounced "Auto Wire"); "Over The Top" bottle opener by Vaughan; "Over The Top" advertising "Continental Can Company" for "Cap Sealed Cans."
Second column top to bottom: Spinner opener by Veeder-Root Inc. of Hartford-Bristol (Connecticut); Wire opener made by Autoyre; Cap lifter by Walden of Cambridge, Massachusetts; "Vaughan's O-G Junior Can Tapper"; By Newton Mfg. Co.; Heavy steel can piercer called "Por-Ezy Opener" by Air Scale Co. of Toledo, Ohio.
Top Right: "Quick & Easy" made by Erie Specialty Co. of Erie, Pennsylvania, with gas key. Back side marked FOUNDERS OF MANGANESE-BRONZE BRASS GERMAN SILVER AND ALUMINUM CASTING.

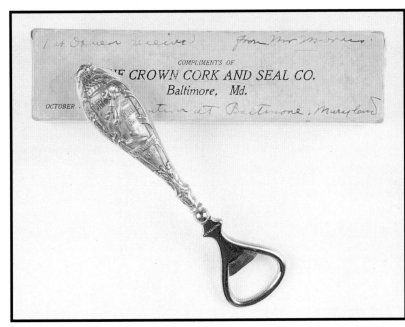

Beautifully engraved opener produced by the Crown Cork and Seal Co. of Baltimore, Maryland. Produced as a convention souvenir from 1908.

When one drinks soda pop, the soda fountain and soda jerk come to mind. The wooden wall mount opener is not shown as a type because a non-advertising opener is attached. It is still a highly sought after Coca-Cola collectible worth $125-150. Major brands have many origins and dates of beginning. Two of the most important were Coca-Cola, which was invented in 1886 by John Pemberton of Atlanta, GA, and Pepsi-Cola, which was invented in 1898 by Caleb Bradham of New Bern, NC.

Above: A purchase order from The Atlanta Coca-Cola Bottling Company for bottle openers.

Right: A Pepsi-Cola Company purchase order for bottle openers.

Below: A colorful Squirt letterhead.

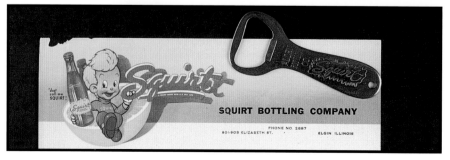

SLOGANS

Bottle and Can Openers were an ideal place for producers, bottlers, and distributors to emblazon their slogans. Here are a few found in this book.

A delicious food drink—Malted Grape Nuts
A drink of good taste—High-N-Dry Ginger Ale
A drink of merit—Rader's Root Beer
A drink without a kick—Mint Cola
A flavor you can't forget—Nu-Grape
A knockout for thirst—Phillip Bros. Champion Ginger Ale
A nickel drink worth a dime—Pepsi Cola
A pal for your palate—Eskimo Pop
A pure beverage—De Luxe, Chicago Beverage Co.
A pure drink of natural flavors—Coca-Cola
A pure liquid food, the peer of all soft drinks—Reif's Special
Absolutely pure—Double Eagle Ginger Beer
Adventure in good taste—Cola Moca
All ways blends best—quenches thirst all ages—7 Up
America's biggest nickel's worth—Pepsi=Cola
America's greatest beverage—Dy-Yo
An extra glass in every bottle—Phillips Bros. Champion Ginger Ale
An investment on good taste—Maydale Beverages, Maynard, Mass.
An invigorating beverage—Gipp's Barlo
Anyway you get Kist it's delicious—Kist Beverages
Assorted flavors you can't forget—Nu Icy
Atlantic City's own finest in drinks—Kramer's beverages
Best by taste test—Royal Crown Cola
Best by test—Spar-Ko
Best by test, made by new process—Zee-Mo
Best in the state—Des Moines Steam Bottling Works
Best mixing sodas—Kiel
Better beverages—Graham's
Better beverages—Husting's
Better in bottles—Coca-Cola
Better taste calls for R C—Royal Crown Cola
Bigger'n better—Big-Giant Cola 16 oz.
Biggest thirst value under the sun—Pop Kola
Bottled at the springs—Crystal Rock
Call for it by name—Tenn-Cola
Champagne of Ginger Ales—Canada Dry
Contains no habit forming drugs—"3-C Nectar"
Cures headache, constipation, Etc.—Heptol Splits
Delicious and zestful—D&Z Bottling Co
Delicious beverages—Eberle's, Jackson, Mich.
Delicious refreshing—Coca-Cola
Deliciously different—Vernor's Ginger Ale
Deliciously different, everybody's choice—La Vida Beverages
Delightfully invigorating—Cola-Cocktail
Distinctively different—Dr. Pepper
Distinguish the best from the rest—Grand-Pop Bottling Co.
Don't blow your top—Zeisler Soda, St Charles, Mo.
Drink a bite to eat at 10, 2 & 4 O'Clock—Dr. Pepper
Easy to say easier to drink—Neerit
Eat, drink and be merry Phone—Sterilized Bottling Works, Scranton, PA

Every bottle sterilized—Coca-Cola
Every drop pure—Hydrox Beverages
Everybody's drink, nourishes the body quenches the thirst on sale everywhere—Ureeka, Boston, Mass.
Everybody's drinken it—Lemon-Kola
Famous Ginger Ale—Dean's, Connellsville, Pa.
Fine flavor—Mr. Cola
Fine natural flavors—Kern's Beverages
Fine temperance beverages—Simpson Spring
First for taste—Buck, National Beverage Company, Chicago
First for thirst—Buck, National Beverage Company, Chicago
First for thirst—Old Scotch Ginger Ale
Flavors you can't forget—Nugrape Nuicy
For a good understanding—Ne-Hi
For health's sake—So Good Ciardi & Co. Dover, N. J.
For particular people—Mohawk Beverages
For particular people—Queen City Beverages
For the 7 hangovers/for the stomach sake—7 Up
For the best drink—White Rock
For the stomach—Sulpho-Saline
For your health and happiness—Diet-Rite Cola and R.C. Cola
Fresh up—7 Up
Good and good for you—A.B.C.B. Washington, D.C.
Good for life—Dr Pepper
Good for what ales you—Broad Rock Ginger Ale
Good to the last drop sold everywhere—Kurth Company's Beverages
Grapefruit-lemon refresher—Quiky
Hang me up in the kitchen—Hill's High Grade Beverages
Have one more—Avon
Healthful invigorating—Pepsi-Cola
Healthful-refreshing—Black Bear Beverages
High grade beverages—Kamp Fire Bottling Co.
Hires to you! so refreshing—Hires
Imitation grape a flavor you can't forget—Nugrape
In bottles—Coca-Cola
In sterilized bottles—Coca-Cola
It gingers you up—Gin-Cera
It hasta be Shasta—Shasta
It's a bear of a drink—Black Bear Beverages
It's always pure—Hires
It's better—Gay-Ola
It's Cott to be good—Cott
It's delicious—Glee Cola
Its elegant—Sand Springs Ginger Ale
It's good and wholesome—Barq's
It's great pop—Towne Club Beverages
It's made for you all flavors—Big Lu, St Louis, Mo.
It's real orange juice, say it by it's full name to avoid substitutions—Orange Crush
It's refreshing—Par Fay, Illinois Parfay Co. Champaign, Ill.
It's the best fruit beverages—Frank's

It's the real thing enjoy—Coca Cola
It's the water—Mt. Shasta Bottling Works
J-C for all occasions—J-C Bottling Co.
Just to stir up a little business—Hund & Eger Coca-Cola
Keep a case in the home—Coca-Cola
Keep me busy—Batchelor's
King of beverages—Dr. Pepper
King of beverages vim, vigor, vitality—Dr. Pepper
King of table waters—Saratoga Vichy
Leaves a Good Taste with You—Eagle Bottling Works & Fixture Co. Inc. Seattle
Lithiated lemon for health or the 7 hangovers—7 up
Made famous by the public—Sunny Kid Pale Dry Ginger Ale
Made from pure fruit flavors—Hydrox Beverages
Made from real oranges—Nesbitt's of California
Made ginger pure and wholesome—Conner Bottling Wks. Newfields, N. H.
Made of herbs only—Giant Tonic
Made of pure cane sugar—Tip Top Soda Water
Made where the ginger grows—Hawaiian Dry
Made with Waukesha spring water—Fox Head Beverages
Makes a perfect lemonade—Jackson's Napa Soda
Makes good drinks taste better—Country Club Beverages
Makes you glad you're thirsty—Bludwine
Makes you glad you're thirsty—Hyklas Dry Ginger Ale
Merely a matter of good taste—Manhattan Pepsin Ginger Ale
More bounce to the ounce—Pepsi-Cola
More flavor for your money—Sun Crest
More than wet—Roxa Kola
More zip in every sip!—B-1 Lemon-Lime
Most delicious very healthful—Pepsi Cola
Mountain high in quality—Mount Kineo Ginger Ale
Natural gas carbonation makes it better naturally—Original Manitou
Naturally better—Shasta Water
Naturally good—Mission Orange
Naturally good—Grapico, J. Grossman's Sons, New Orleans, La.
Never an after-thirst—Squirt
None better—Superior Ginger Ale
Nourishing as beer—Becco, Becker Products Co. Ogden, Utah
Often imitated never equaled—Whistle
One and only one—Dr. Brown's Ginger Tonic
One bottle means another—Tuck's Ginger Ale
One of America's best—Berkeley Club Ginger Ale
Pure as sunlight—Coca-Cola
Purest of all waters—Chippewa, Chippewa Springs Co. Chippewa Falls, Wis.
Purity is sealed in a bottle—Coca Cola
Quality beverages—Big Ben
Quality beverages—Fladung's
Quality beverages since 1856—Fleck's
Quenches thirst for all ages—7 Up
Real orange goodness—Sun Spot
Refreshing invigorating—Coca-Cola
Refreshing and invigorating—Busch's Special Root Beer, John B. Busch Brg. Co.
Satisfies thirst—Gay-Ola
Serving the public 25 Years—Goldy Rock Beverages
Sheboygan Mineral Water and Ginger Ale chief of them all— Sheboygan Mineral Water and Ginger Ale
Sheboygan's best mixers—Lakeside Beverages
Since 1858 better beverages—Bartle's
Smile!—Cheerwine

Soft drinks the best-our motto—Zipf Bros., Niles, O.
Stimulating—Celery Cola
Strongest alkaline water known—Kalak Water Co. Brooklyn, N. Y.
Superior to laxatives—Adlerika
Taste that beats the others cold—Pepsi Cola
Tastes best ice cold—Coca Cola
That's the beer—Old English Ginger Beer, Hoster, Columbus, Ohio
The best ever and ever the best—Simpson Spring
The best in the west—Crawford's, Sedalia, Mo.
The best of the grade—Pierce Juice
The best since 1873—Grafs Beverages
The best what gives—Grafs
The delightful cola drink—Ceco
The drink of drinks—Limetta
The drink of the Gods—"3-C Nectar"
The drink with tone and tickle—Mo-Ro
The finest—Bay City Beverage Co.
The finest orange soft drink ever made—Nesbitt's
The friendly "Pepper-Upper"—Dr Pepper
The high grade beverages—Emaus Bottling Works, Emaus, Pa.
The improved—Ocola
The great teetotaler's beverage—Te-To, Willow Springs Beverage Co. Omaha, Nebraska
The greatest beverage, Sy-Ro, Methuen, Mass.
The most delicious cereal beverage—Gozo, Goetz Co., St. Joseph, Mo.
The national drink—Welch's Westfield, N. Y.
The old reliable—Havelock Ginger Ale
The perfect neutralizer—Calso Water
The prince of ales—Tacoma Dry Ginger Ale
The prince of drys—Sand Springs, Williamstown, Mass.
The royal drink—King-Cola
The satisfying soft drink, a pure wholesome and refreshing beverage—Moer-Lo
The strongest alkaline water of commerce—Kalak
The taste tells—Nehi
The world's greatest tonic—Lipsey's Products Co., Chicago
There's none so good—Chero-Cola
They're naturally better—Lavida
Thirsty or not! Enjoy—Grapette
Thirsty? just Whistle—Whistle
Three times as good—Trio Beverage Co., Wheeling, W.Va.
To your health—Dy-Yo
Tops in taste—Royal Crown Cola
Unequaled non intoxicating cereal beverage—Barma Blatz-Mil.
Very refreshing—Polar Ginger Ale
Viteminized—B-1
Water of health—Mt Zircon Spring Water Co., Rumford, Maine
When in doubt try Old Fashioned—Harbor Grape Juice Co., Long Beach Calif.
Wholesome beverages—Barq's
Wholesome refreshing—Moxie
Wholesome refreshment—Bubble Up
You can't lose if you drink Cola-Moca the all year-round drink—Cola-Moca
You like 7 Up it likes you—7 Up
You lose if you do not use our mixers—Lyons Bottling Co.
You remember the taste—Deerfield Ginger Ale
You won't kick if you drink Wineberg's Beverages—Wineberg
You'll like it—Pisco Punch
You'll love it!—Frostie Root Beer

From the beginning many openers were distributed in packages attached to sales cards. Manufacturers were always trying to come up with ingenious ways to "double" advertise their products. Early packages were mainly envelopes and later followed by cardboard displays. Boxes in the early years were reserved for corkscrews and later on wall mounts.

I'm a Good Mixer

CANADIAN GRENADIER
Place 2 large tablespoons of vanilla ice cream in a tall glass, then fill the glass with "Canada Dry." Garnish with red cherries cut in circlets.

HAWAIIAN NECTAR
Combine 1 cup of fresh pineapple juice with the juice of ½ lemon and 1 lime. Stir in 1 large teaspoon powdered sugar. Pour in tall glass and fill with "Canada Dry." Add tiny balls of pineapple or other fresh fruit garnishing. (Portion for 1 person).

CONTINENTAL PUNCH
Combine a quart of grape juice and a pint of orange juice with a half cup of sugar, a third cup of lemon juice, eight sprigs of crushed mint, and four bottles of "Canada Dry." Add two quarts of crushed ice; mix and serve garnished with mint. (Courtesy of Ida Bailey Allen).

"CANADA DRY" NIGHT CAP
Try this refreshing drink just before retiring. Squeeze the juice of ½ lime into a tall glass. Pour in "Canada Dry" thoroughly chilled.

Betty Beldon

"CANADA DRY"
Reg. U. S. Pat. Off.

The Champagne of Ginger Ales

THE HOSTESS PACKAGE

Include this compact carton in your next order. The Delicious Dozen, so snugly reposing within, will complete your hours of hospitality.

Reserve a little corner in the pantry for this emergency kit — it will answer the call of any refreshment hour.

Invite me to your party

Above & left: Canada Dry inserted their B-6 type opener into this four page cardboard foldout. In addition to touting the "emergency call for an opener," drink recipes were also included.

Below: Even though a brewing company envelope is shown, one can imagine soda openers also being distributed in the same style paper package. Claims were well founded for this "3 tools in 1" bottle opener, ice pick, and milk bottle opener.

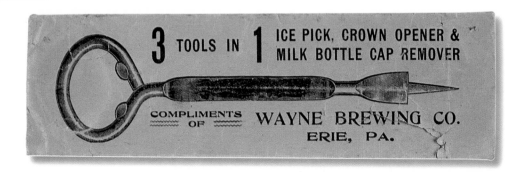

3 TOOLS IN 1 — ICE PICK, CROWN OPENER & MILK BOTTLE CAP REMOVER

COMPLIMENTS OF WAYNE BREWING CO. ERIE, PA.

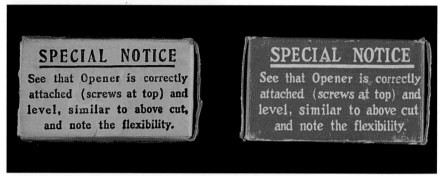

Vaughan of Chicago crammed a lot advertising on these little boxes for wall mount opener type O-4 called their "Never-Chip." The off-white box on the left is the earlier version. It was certainly a favorite opener of soda makers as almost all major brands at one time or another advertised on this type.

The Seven-Up Bottling Co. of Tulsa, Oklahoma, came up with a nice presentation box containing a combination bottle opener/can piercer, corkscrew, and a drink strainer. The velvet-lined cardboard box adds a nice touch to an advertising giveaway with each piece marked with the company name, address, and phone number.

MODERN SODA OPENERS

Like their beer counterparts, soda openers have seen a tremendous number of recent productions. Despite the invention of pull-tabs and screw-off bottle caps, several soda companies have produced many new types. As with older styles, Coca-Cola is the leader in the collectibles of the future. All of the examples shown in this chapter can be found for under $10.

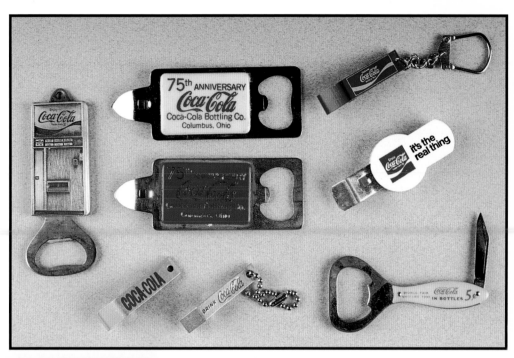

Coca-Cola as with pre-1970 openers leads the way in the production of new openers. One of the latest style openers is the one at the left made of pewter. The two 75th anniversary openers in the middle are examples of using a plastic insert instead of stamping a steel opener. Using plastic saves money in the opener production process. Please note the opener at the lower right advertising World's Fair Chicago 1933 is a recent fantasy opener. This opener has also been produced with Pepsi and Chicago 1933 along with examples of Coca-Cola and Pepsi 5 cents. These examples are valued at $2-3.

More Coca-Cola openers of recent vintage. The diet Coke opener in the upper right is the most popular style bottle opener in today's market especially for beer openers. The tag-master at the lower left is a combination twist-off opener and "tab popper" for pull-tab cans.

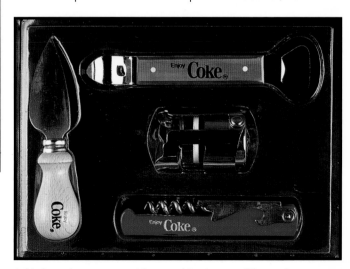

A kitchen giveaway set with a combination cap lifter and can piercer at the top, a cheese cutter at the left, a bottle cap sealer in the middle, and a "waiter's friend" at the bottom with a corkscrew and cap lifter/neckstand.

Opener in original package shaped like a Coca-Cola bottle. Nice heavy opener that has a good feel to it when being used to open a bottle. These typically sell in the $8-10 range.

Other brands have joined the new opener market. At the top is a 7 Up opener made by Alexander Husky. The middle two openers at left and center are fairly common new styles while the opener at the right center is a cheap tab-popper. A very unusual style is shown at the bottom. With a tab-popper, twist-off opener, and a cap lifter, one really has to wonder how well the cap lifter holds up to daily use.

Recent nail clippers production with a plastic covered handle. Once again the manufacturer saves costs by using plastic instead of stamping steel. A sister opener to the "World's Fair" opener in the first picture in this chapter. Both recent 1970s-80s production. Widely available and the example shown in this picture was probably authorized by Pepsi-Cola. Value is like the World's Fair example, $2-3.

A recent multi-tool.

FOREIGN SODA OPENERS

Unlike their American counterparts, foreign soda openers rarely appear as figurals and are mainly found in formed and over-the-top type openers.

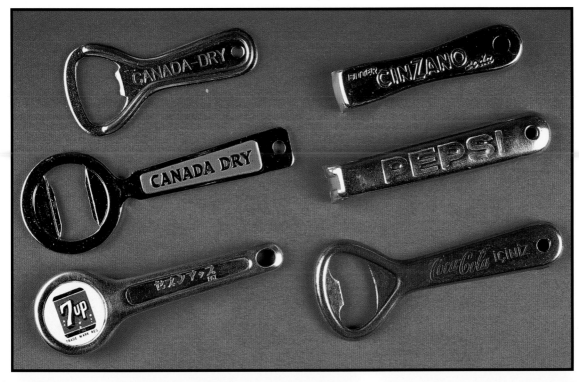

Various "C" and "G" style foreign openers. Identifying countries is usually guess work but these openers can add color and style to a collection.

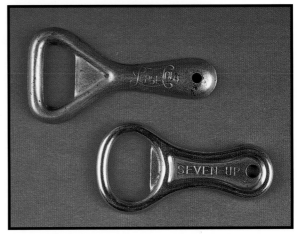

Above: Two "G" types. The one on the top is German. It is frequently seen and comes with Coca-Cola advertisement also. The bottom opener is a Canadian soda opener made by Lunn of Montreal.

Left: Three "C" types with an interesting folding cap lifter opener at the right. The Coca-Cola bottle shape opener is from Germany.

FANTASY OPENERS

Like most areas of collectibles, fantasy openers have made their presence felt in the soda opener market. Buyers beware: most fakes are made in brass. Carry a magnet when looking for openers. If the magnet does not stick, you probably are looking at a fake. Exceptions are styles B-1, B-2, and B-27. Fantasy openers are fine to buy as long as you know they are fake and the prices are low.

The wall mount O-5 style shown has been gold-plated. Though technically not a fantasy opener, it is a recent production and should be bought as such. Starr X openers have been produced since the late 1920s with the latest versions being cast with Germany. This example even comes with a "COA" (certificate of authenticity). $10-12.

Three recent figurals reproduced with Coca-Cola advertising. All made in brass. The A-9 baseball player on the left is stamped "Canton City Ohio" instead of Canton Ohio. The You Pay spinner at top right has "spin to see who wins" stamped on the front instead of on the back like the originals. The A-12 sword style at the bottom right seems to always turn up with a much darker tone than the other brass fakes. Careful comparisons with originals show all three examples as slightly larger than the real earlier versions. $5-10.

Fake Coca-Cola knives are also fairly common. Usually they are very easy to spot because the blade tang is stamped Japan instead of Kastor Bros Germany. The corkscrew worm is also new looking while the handles themselves lack the detail of the originals. $10-20.

Right: Crudely made cast iron Coca-Cola opener. Has a somewhat old look but is definitely a recent fantasy item. Detail is very rough. $3-5

Far right: 1970s reproduction of the 1930s Remington Nehi knife. This is frequently sold as the real thing. Fakes are always in mint condition. The original knife has a sharply detailed grid pattern on the Nehi bottle while fakes have a faint grid pattern. As with other fake knives, in general the overall handle detail is not as sharp as the original, but if you don't have an original to compare with you might be out of luck.

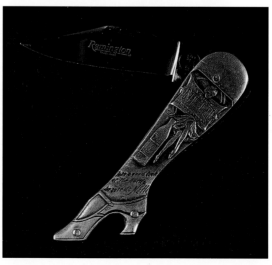

USING THE RIGHT OPENER

Openers can be basically used with two methods, straight lift and over-the-top. Regular lift openers are more natural to use, but over-the-top openers are favored by collectors of bottle caps as they usually leave only a slight dent in the cap.

A type H-9 over-the-top opener in action.

A type F-501 combination spoon, corkscrew, regular lift-up opener.

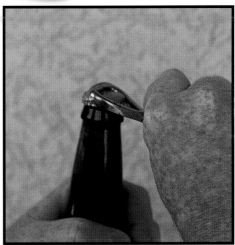

A firm grip on a type G-1 opener.

A type I-17 Coca Cola can piercer opening a beer can.

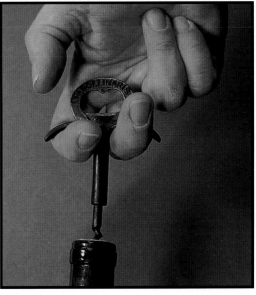

A two-finger pull corkscrew extracting a cork.

119

GRADING OPENERS

Grading any collectible can be a tough job and openers certainly fall in the tough category. Most have at least two sides and many times one side can be very nice while the other side can be bad. Many collectors grade the two sides of an opener separately when buying, selling, or trading. The five pictures represent the ten grades of openers using a 10 point scale.

Top: Grade 1; poor, pitted, a filler item only.
Bottom: Grade 2; fair, mostly readable but also has some pitting.

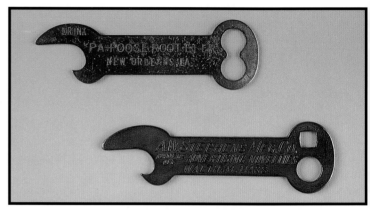

Top: Grade 3; almost good, readable but very worn.
Bottom: Grade 4; good, clean opener with definite wear.

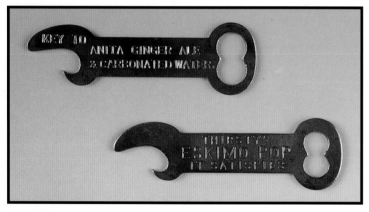

Top: Grade 5; good-to-very good, clean opener, some wear or staining.
Bottom: Grade 6; very good, nice even wear, may have stain or some rust if a lot of chrome remains.

Top: Grade 7; very good+ or excellent-, nice even wear with no stain or rust marks.
Bottom: Grade 8; excellent, 90 percent original plating remains with minimal wear, could also be a sharp strike opener with no plating remaining and no rust marks at all.

Top: Grade 9; excellent+, 95 percent of plating with only a small mark to distract from the appearance.
Bottom: Grade 10; mint or near mint, as issued by the manufacturer, may have the slightest wear to plating.

BROWN MANUFACTURING COMPANY

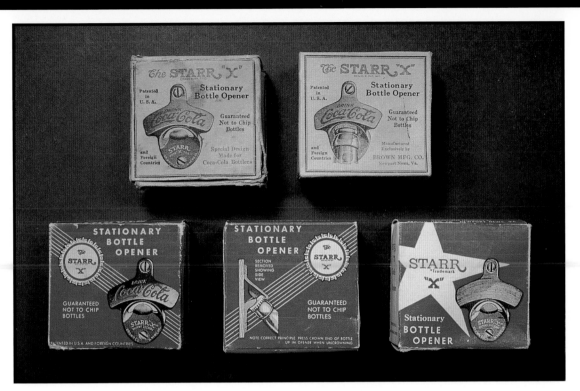

Raymond M. Brown of Newport New, Virginia, owned the local Coca-Cola Bottling Plant and also was the father of the type "O-5" bottle opener along with the type O-505 "Long Neck" or "Oblong," which was his first patented opener on April 21, 1925. Brown Mfg. called it their "Standard" and they were also known as the "Starr X Sanitary Bottle Opener." The "O-5" was patented on November 2, 1943, but had been produced at least as early as 1928 as shown in some Coca-Cola advertisements. His patent would lead to the production of tens of thousands of Starr X openers. The "Long Neck" O-505 also shows this patent date and was pro-duced in fairly large numbers with Coca-Cola leading the way as it did on the O-5s.

Today every other flea market table has a Coca-Cola O-5 for sale. Some O-5s are marked PAT PEND. and we can assume they were produced before the patent was approved in 1943. Business was brisk from the 1930s through the 1960s. Even when Brown moved produc-tion to Germany in 1971, Coca-Cola openers were pro-duced in great numbers along with many other brands. The business held on until recently when the Brown family sold the bottling plant, Starr X patents and the warehouse where the openers were made.

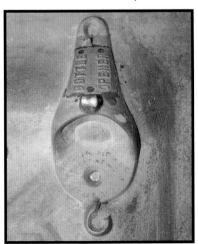

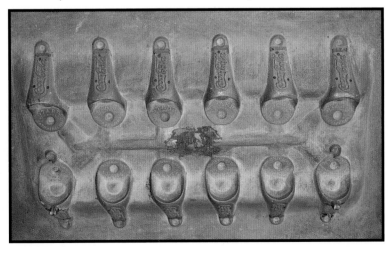

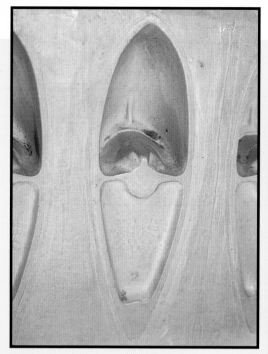

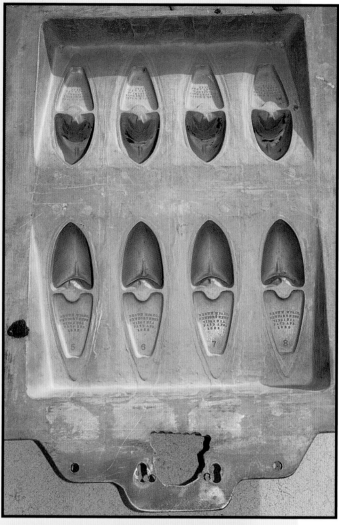

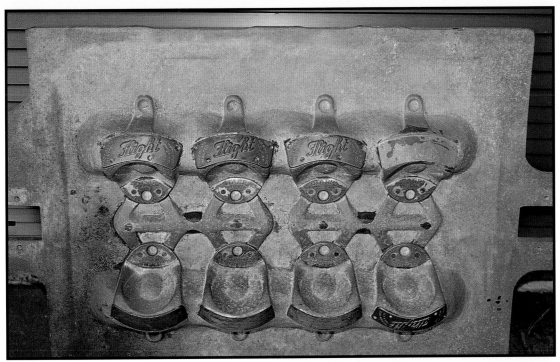

Just For Openers member Clayton Denny is a friend of the Brown family. In 1995, the Brown family bought the warehouse back with all of its contents. The family was planning to discard the contents and told Clayton he could take what he wanted. He had to do the moving himself with no help and had a little over a day to gather everything he could. Three tractor trailer loads (hopefully they were all Coca-Cola) still went to the dump except for what the truck drivers kept. Clayton managed to gather a very impressive collection of the original molds, cases of original openers and a lot of documentation.

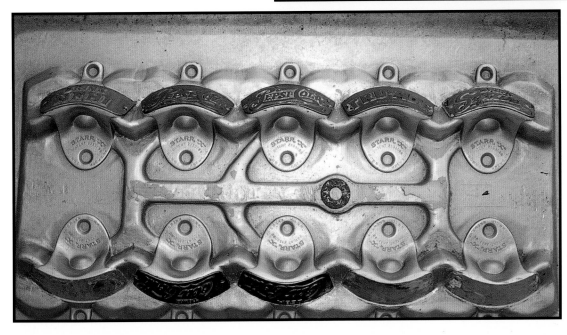

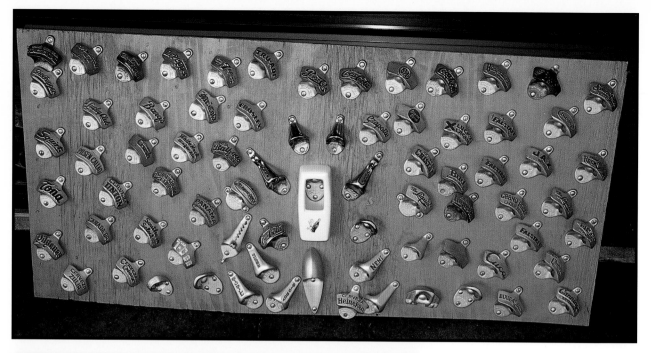

Stanley arranged a meeting where Clayton brought a large selection of openers and a lot of molds for photographs. The opinion held by many novice collectors and dealers is that the numbers on the backside of O-5s may have been the years they were made and are considered variations. Clayton pointed out that they were simply mold numbers. Molds could either make 10 or 12 openers. It was a sand cast process and they were numbered 1 through 10, 11 through 20, and so on, or 1 through 12, 13 through 24, and so on. The names were made by adding a brass name tag to the mold and each brass tag was numbered to match the individual opener mold. Clayton was able to obtain most of the brass plate names for each brand made by Brown. Once made, the painting department staffed by women, would paint the opener using a rubber roller to apply the color. After 1971 the imported German openers were still painted in Newport News. German-made openers are usually zinc plated to prevent rusting, which also gives the opener a very rough appearance.

Brown Manufacturing Co. is presently located in Alpharetta, Georgia, near Atlanta. They have started to produce Starr X openers for college sports teams. Information can be obtained on the Internet at http://www.bottleopener.com/.

HOW'S THIS FOR OPENERS?

Do you remember the old service station just outside of your town where people would hang around the soda machine sipping a cold one? And the soda machine in the bus station? How about all of those service stations with their soda machines lining Route 66? In the heat of the day, you could stop just about anywhere, put a nickel or a dime in the machine and get instant relief from a cold drink. Today you may spot a rusting hulk of a machine outside of an old, closed building but most are being snatched up as collectors' items.

Restorers turn healthy profits using their dent removers and fresh paint.

The old machines have been replaced with shiny new machines picturing race car drivers, fancy slogans, and the like. The old machines had a built-in or attached bottle opener to pop the cap. The new machines filled with pop-top cans and twist-off bottle caps no longer need that accessory.

Upright and chest type machines abound with Coca-Cola and Pepsi-Cola logos emblazoned on them. The picnic coolers can be found with the big names as well as the occasional regional brand name. Today these have

been replaced with plastic or foil insulated coolers ideal for taking a six pack to a day at the races.

Although the brand names on coolers and machines may be household words, certainly most of the names of the manufacturers are not. The 1940s and 1950s were the hottest years for production of soda machines which had openers—some merely attached by a chain or string! Manufacturers such as Vendo, Cavalier, Narco, Jacobs, and Kelvinator produced machines that would

hold from a couple of dozen to a gross of cold ones. One "household" name found on Coke machines is Westinghouse.

Advertising for the machines was targeted to the soda distributor while cooler advertising was mainly aimed at the consumer market. Low cost, easy to maintain, simplicity, and trouble-free performance were some of the machine selling features.

There was a lot of great advertising for portable coolers in the 1940s and 1950s. One Coca Cola cooler advertisement says "This portable cooler puts more fun in your vacations and outdoor outings." It goes on to tell of the many uses: picnics, vacation, travel, hunting and fishing, sporting events, farmers and outdoor workers, and auxilliary home storage. Progress Refrigerator Company of Louisville, Kentucky, offered their "Special Events Cooler" advertising Royal Crown Cola. The cooler was furnished complete with detachable legs, which stored in the cooler, and could be carried by "one man" to be filled at an event with Royal Crown and ice. They were produced with three, five, and nine case capacities. Their advertising proclaimed that their cooler was ideal for "Picnics, Social Events, Barbecues, Fish Fries, and Ball Games." Meanwhile Thermos advertised its cooler with "Need only 1/3 the ice…hold more Coke."

So if you are indeed really serious about collecting soda advertising openers, shouldn't you add a machine or two to your collection? And why not throw in a few chest coolers for the smaller spaces in your home?

CLEANING OPENERS

Many collectors consider cleaning openers a sin and do not even attempt to clean their openers. For those who wish to clean their openers, here are several methods.

In the first issue of *Just For Openers* (April, 1979), Ed Kaye wrote: "Each opener (if not mint) I get from whatever source, is first wire brushed, then dipped in Naval Jelly, then rinsed in cold water, transferred to extremely hot water, hand dried, and finally buffed."

In July, 1984, Jack Lennon reported that he cleaned openers with fine steel wool and car polish compound. He would then clear spray them.

In July, 1986, Jim Hollinger's letter contained this explanation on how he cleaned openers: "I use various methods for cleaning my openers depending on the original condition. The various steps used in cleaning include:

1. Naval Jelly: For very poor condition openers. Openers such as this usually are not worth the effort due to excess pitting.

2. Fine Wire Brush: Fine wire brush is used in a drill press for removing spotty rust areas. A fine wire brush does not scratch the opener finish.

3. Polishing Compound: Automobile paint scratch and blemish remover is used with a soft cloth to buff all openers. This removes dirt and discoloration.

4. Paste Car Wax: All my openers receive a coat of car wax as the final step. This returns the original sheen of the plating as well as it leaves a protective coating against further corrosion."

IN JULY, 1990, JOHN STANLEY PRESENTED THIS PROCESS:

1. Prepare a solution of oxalic acid (can collectors use this) using about 3 tablespoons of crystals for 2 pints of water. I also use a narrow lidded glass container so the opener will not lay flat in the bottom of the jar. The oxalic acid can be purchased at your local drug store (they may have to special order) and the cost is about $6 for 16 ounces.

2. Depending upon the condition I will soak an opener in the solution from 30 minutes to 4 hours (for one with a lot of rust). I cleaned an A-13 Car for Gary Deachman at the convention soaking it for about 4 hours. It came out so nice he didn't want to trade the opener to me.

3. At the end of the soaking time, remove the opener from the solution using an old ice pick or awl (unless opener has no key ring hole then you need to pour acid into another container and remove opener). Thoroughly rinse skin if acid contacts.

4. I then scrub the opener with a soapy "SOS" pad. I dry the opener thoroughly with paper towels. If the opener has a moving part I will add some machine oil.

NOTES:

1. Do not try to clean any openers with enameling using the acid solution.

2. If an opener is pitted, I use a Dremel (small electric drill). The Dremel is used by jewelers and anyone needing a small drill but it can leave brush marks. The wire brush attachment is very handy for cleaning pitted openers. You cannot remove the pit marks but the discoloration can be cleaned off.

3. An alternative to the Dremel is using a regular drill with a "copper" wire brush.

4. Cleaning openers with "celluloid" parts is very tough. Use warm soapy water to clean the celluloid part. A soapy SOS or just a piece of fine steel wool is used to clean the metal opener. Celluloid is very tough because if the lettering is worn, you are just plain out of luck.

5. Enameled Openers present a real challenge because any rubbing of the enamel will take it right off.

OTHER SUGGESTIONS COME FROM:

Harold Queen: "When using Oxalic Acid, it is safe to use with your bare hands, since the acid is diluted with water. I use 2 heaping teaspoons to about 6 ounces of water. I then use a soapy SOS pad and finally use a fine wire brush to complete the process."

Joe Knapp: "I use Dow Bathroom Cleaner with Scrubbing Bubbles and a fine brass wire brush. I complete the process with chrome polish."

Ollie Hibbeler: "I use white distilled vinegar, soaking the opener for about 12-15 hours."

Part 3

CATALOG OF OPENERS

OPENER LISTINGS AND VALUES

In this section, openers are listed by type and alphabetic key advertising word. Each opener has been assigned a number within the type and a value range. To determine value, the collector should first determine the opener type by using Part 1 of this book and then look up the advertising in this section.

A-1
1) Drink A-1 (10-12)
2) Avon More "Have One More" (10-12)
3) Drink B-1 (10-12)
4) Bay View Bottling Works 305 Logan Avenue (10-12)
5) Drink Burk's Soda Water (10-12)
6) Drink Caton Ginger Ale Catonsville, Md. (15-20)
7) Chero-Cola Bot. Co. Gainesville, Ga. (40-50)
8) Coca-Cola (Script) Bottling Co. Baltimore, Md. (175-200)
9) Compliments of Coca-Cola (Script) Bottling Co. Grand Island, Nebr. (175-200)
10) Oriente Coca-Cola (Script) Bottling Co. (175-200)
11) Sayre Coca-Cola (Block) Bottling Co. Sayre, Okla. (175-200)
12) Compliments of Cocheco Bottling Works, Inc. Rochester, N. H. (10-12)
13) Cream of Cola St. Albans Bottling Wks. (20-25)
14) Drink Dresch Soda Water (10-12)
15) Drink Fladung's quality Beverages (10-12)
16) Grafs drink Lemon-Life (10-12)
17) Grafs drink Lemon Lime (10-12)
18) Grafs drink Orange Life (10-12)
19) Grafs drink "The Best What Gives" (10-12)
20) Grafs Seal (10-12)
21) Drink Hello! Kid (20-25)
22) Hub City Soda Works Marysville, Cal. (20-25)
23) Jamaica Pale Dry Ginger Ale (10-12)
24) Keen Drinks (10-12)
25) King-Cola the royal Drink (20-25)
26) Las Vegas Bottling W'ks. Las Vegas, Nevada (20-25)
27) The Lithia Bottling Company Pueblo, Colo. (20-25)
28) Compliments of the Manhattan Bottling Works Milwaukee (10-12)
29) Compliments of the Manhattan Bottling Works Milwaukee, Wis. (10-12)
30) Manhattan Bottling Works Milwaukee (10-12)
31) Manhattan Bottling Works Milwaukee, Wis. drink Pale Dry ale (10-12)
32) Market Beverage & Supply Co. 1403 Market St. San Diego (10-12)
33) Mt. Shasta Bottling Works it's the water (20-25)
34) Nugrape Nuicy flavors you can't forget (20-25)
35) Drink Orange Crush Real Oranges (60-75)
36) Drink Par Fay (20-25)
37) The Original Pisco Punch you'll like it. (10-12)
38) Drink Quako 5c (10-12)
39) Range Bottling Works Hibbing Minn. (10-12)
40) Compliments Roxboro Bottling Co. Roxborough, Phila. (10-12)
41) Spokane Bottle Supply Co. 408 Sprague Spokane Phone Main 3580 (10-12)
42) Spokane Bottle Supply Co. 408 W. Sprague Main 3580 (10-12)
43) Compliments Wineber Bottling Works Vancouver, Wash. (15-20)
44) Yankee Dry Ginger Ale (20-25)
45) Yuncker Bottling Works Indianapolis (10-12)
46) Zeisler's Bottling Works St. Charles, Mo. (20-25)

A-3
1) Dixon Bottling Co Phone 375 Dixon Ill (20-25)

A-4
1) Appleton Bottling Wks. Appleton, Minn. Red Rose Sweet 17 (20-25)
2) Drink Brainol 5c (20-25)
3) "J.H. Bryant Bottling Works" (10-12)
4) Drink Buck National Beverage Co. Chicago (10-12)
5) Drink Chero-Cola 5c 5c (35-40)
6) Coca-Cola (Script) Bottling Works Indianapolis (Brass Plated) (175-200)
7) Compliments of Coca-Cola (Script) Bottling Works Cairo, Ill. (175-200)
8) Drink Bottled Coca-Cola (Script) Wichita, Kans. (175-200)
9) Drink Coca-Cola (Script) in Bottles (175-200)
10) Cola-Nip Nips the Thirst (30-35)
11) Cold Spring Brewing and Mineral Water Co. (25-30)
12) Curo Soda Water Ginger Ale Omaha (10-12)
13) J.J. Flynn & Co. Carbonated Waters Quincy, Ill. (10-12)
14) John Graf the best what gives (10-12)
15) A.W. Happy Soda & Mineral Waters (Jefferson City, Mo.) (10-12)
16) Buy Hek Crystal Bottling Co. (20-25)
17) Hillsdale Bottling Works Hillsdale, Mich. (10-12)
18) Hub City Soda Works Marysville, Cal. (20-25)
19) Compliments of Kershaw Bott. Wks. Kershaw, S. C. (20-25)
20) Merchant Bot. Wks. Winston-Salem, N. C. (20-25)
21) The-Meyersdale Bottling Works C. E. Deal Prop Meyersdale, Pa. (10-12)
22) Get Neerit easy to say easier to drink (10-12)
23) Par Fay (10-12)
24) Raleigh Pepsi=Cola (Script) Bottling Co. Raleigh, N. C. (175-200)
25) The Wadesboro Pepsi-Cola (Block) Bottling Co. (175-200)
26) Drink Purity Soda Moberly, Mo. (10-12)
27) "Richard's Soda" (10-12)

28) Sequoia Soda Works L. A. Deveggio Prop. (20-25)
29) Taka-Cola Fredericksburg Bot. Works You Will Take No Other (40-50)
30) Tip Top Bottling Works Blytheville, Ark (10-12)
31) Ask for Utica Club Pilsener—Ginger Ale (15-20)
32) Compliments Walla Walla Bottling Works (20-25)
33) Waukon Bottling Works Waukon, Iowa (10-12)
34) Drink Wineberg's Grape Punch Vancouver, Wash (20-25)

A-5

1) "Ace-Hy" The Electro-Pure Water Company 81-83 Seventeenth Street Toledo, Ohio Adams 7251 (10-12)
2) Aliquippa Sanitary Bottling Works (10-12)
3) Atlantic Beverage & Products Company, drink XXX Atlantic City, N. J. (40-50)
4) Atlas Bottling Co. 12170 Conant TO 7-1414 (10-12)
5) Blue Anchor Pale Dry (10-12)
6) Drink Buck National Beverage Co. Chicago (10-12)
7) Charles City Bottling Works Charles City, Iowa (10-12)
8) Cherry Blossoms Sanford Pepsi-Cola (Block) Bot. Co. (100-125)
9) Coca-Cola (Script) Bottling Works Distilled Water Ice (175-200)
10) Curo Soda Water Ginger Ale Omaha (10-12)
11) Deluxe Beverages Chicago Beverage Co. 3423-31 W. 13th Pl. Chicago (10-12)
12) Compliments Endicott Bottling Co. 16 Odell Ave. Endicott N. Y. Phone 819R (15-20)
13) Ask for Epicure Club Ginger Ale Boston, Mass. (15-20)
14) Ask for Flecks quality Beverages since 1856 (15-20)
15) Drink Grafs "The Best What Gives" (10-12)
16) Jamaica Pale Dry Ginger Ale (10-12)
17) Drink Keystone Soft Drinks (10-12)
18) Drink Lime Cola (35-40)
19) Rumford Bottling Co. Rumford, Maine (15-20)
20) Sagalowsky Bottle Co. Bottler's Supplies 605 S. Capitol Ave. Drexel 2104 (10-12)
21) Sagalowsky Bottle Co. 806 So. Capitol Ave. Indianapolis Riley 7104 (10-12)
22) Sebewaing Beverage Co. Sebewaing, Michigan (20-25)
23) Compliments Springer Bros., Inc. quality Soft Drinks Louisville, K. Y. (10-12)
24) Ask for Utica Club Pilsener Ginger Ale (10-12)
25) Thirsty? just Whistle (25-30)
26) Drink Whitman's Beverages Philadelphia Pa. (15-20)
27) Drink Woolner's Beverages Toledo (20-25)

A-7

1) H.A. Bortner, Bottler Phone 623 Hanover, Pa. (12-15)
2) Butte Bottlers Supply Co. 115 S. Main St. Phone 549-J Malt Syrup Hops Bottles (15-20)
3) Butte Bottlers Supply Co. 115 So. Main St. Butte, Mont. Phone 549-J (15-20)
4) Crystal Ice Cream & Bottling Co. (15-20)
5) John Harvilla Soft Drinks (10-12)
6) Manhattan Bottling Works Pale Dry Ale & White Soda Milwaukee, Wis. (15-20)
7) Drink Nehi in all Flavors (30-35)
8) Phone 1080, drink Nehi, all Flavors (30-35)
9) Compliments of Orange Crush Dry (25-30)
10) The Whistle Bottling Works San Luis Obispo, Cal. Whistle & Cherry Blossom "Often Imitated Never Equaled" (25-30)

A-9

1) Atlas Bottling Co. 12170 Conant St. Arlington Phone 4654 (35-40)
2) Butte Bottlers Supply 112 So. Main St. Phone 2522 (75-100)
3) Drink Coca-Cola (Block) Canton City Bottling Works, Canton, Ohio. (250-300)
4) Drink Coca-Cola (Script) in Bottles (350-400)
5) Drink Fan Taz (50-60)
6) Drink Fan Taz <835>(50-60)
7) Drink Glee Cola it's delicious (35-40)

8) Hires Root Beer Twin Size Beverages (75-100)
9) Drink Lawrence Beverages made of Spring Water Tel. 3-1510 (35-40)
10) Drink Pe-Ne-To (35-40)
11) Drink Pe-Ne-To J B Lambert, Woonsocket, Ri. (35-40)
12) Richter's Bottling Works Fresno, Calif. Phone 30 (60-75)
13) "Drink Schusters Root Beer" (50-60)
14) Top Notch Products Co. 421 Hamilton St. Allentown, Pa. (50-60)
15) Top Notch Products Co. 421 Hamilton St. Allentown, Pa. Phone 23293 (50-60)
16) Union Beverage Co., New Orleans Bingo a hit every time (50-60)
17) Try a Ginger Ale. made by Warwick Bottling Wks. Arctic, R.I. (35-40)
18) Wards Orange-Lemon & Lime Crush in Krinkley Bottles (100-125)
19) Drink Whistle bottled only by John Friedrich Phila. (50-60)

A-12

1) Drink Bottled Coca-Cola (Script)/London Dry (Ginger Ale) (1 Line) (150-175)
2) Drink Bottled Coca-Cola (Script)/London Dry (Ginger Ale) (2 Lines) (150-175)
3) Drink Bottled Coca-Cola (Script)/"Purity is Sealed in a Bottle" (150-175)
4) John Graf Co. (15-20)
5) John Graf Co./Jamaica Pale Dry Ginger Ale (15-20)
6) Drink Jamaica Dry (15-20)
7) London Dry Ginger Ale (2 Var (A) Straight Text (B) Curved Text) (10-12)
8) Meyer's Beverage Co./Drink Meyer's quality Beverages (10-12)
9) Always drink Palermo Beverages Garfield 8161 (10-12)
10) Drink St. Francis Dry Ginger Ale/Meyer's Specialty Beverage Co. (15-20)
11) Drink St. Francis Orange Dry Ginger Ale/Meyer's Beverage Co. San Francisco (15-20)
12) Drink St. Francis Orange Dry Ginger Ale/Meyer's Specialty Beverage Co. (15-20)
13) Shasta Water from Shasta Springs "Naturally Better"/Shrine Victory Convention July 1946 San Francisco (15-20)

A-13

1) Cobb's Bottling Co. Taunton, Mass. (25-30)
2) David City Bottling Works, David City, Nebr. (25-30)
3) "Drink to Your Health" Dy-Yo America's greatest Beverage, Dy-Yo Beverage Co. Phone S. Boston 1317 (25-30)
4) Comps the Empire Bottling Works Reading, Pa. (25-30)
5) Compliments of Fairmount Soft Drink Mfrs. 2139-41 Mt. Vernon St. Phila. (25-30)
6) Drink Giant Tonic made of herbs only (25-30)
7) Jones Bros. Bottling Works, Jeannette, Pa. (25-30)
8) Rob't McCarter East End Ginger Ale 1508-10-12 Ritner St. Phila., Pa. (25-30)
9) Polar Ginger Ale (35-40)
10) George J. Rittmann Bottler 444 So Broad St. Trenton, N. J. (20-25)

A-15

1) Anton Bottling Works Hannibal, Mo. (20-25)
2) Drink Berkshire Spring Soda (15-20)
3) "J. Burk & Co. Soda Waters Keokuk Ia." (15-20)
4) Calumet Bottling Works 12056 Emerald Ave. Phone Pullman 0253 West Pullman, Ill. (15-20)
5) Drink Chero-Cola 5c (50-60)
6) Coca-Cola (Script) Bottling Works, A. L. Anderson, Prop'r Rochester, N. Y. (100-125)
7) Drink Coca-Cola (Script)/Saginaw Bottling Co. (100-125)
8) Drink Coca-Cola (Script) in Bottles (100-125)
9) Drink Coca-Cola (Script) in Bottles/Drink Goldelle Ginger Ale (100-125)
10) Diamond a Ginger Beer Syracuse N. Y. (15-20)
11) Best Drink Eagle Soda Water 5c Large Bottle (20-25)

12) Drink Golf Ginger Ale/H. C. Schrank Co. fine flavors, Milwaukee, Wis. (20-25)
13) M. Jacob & Sons bottles 2903 Beaubien Detroit (15-20)
14) "Limetta" the drink of drinks (15-20)
15) Drink Nee-Ska-Ra Milwaukee Ginger Ale (20-25)
16) Drink Roxa Kola "More Than Wet" (20-25)
17) "Its Elegant" Sand Springs Ginger Ale Williamstown, Mass. (20-25)
18) Standard Bottling Works Wm. Krieger Phone 6703 (15-20)
19) Drink Tenn-Cola call for it by name (40-50)
20) Drink Tenn-Cola 5c made in Knoxville, Tenn. (40-50)
21) Vitaqua Sparkling Water (15-20)
22) Drink Zee-Mo Ginger Ale best by test, made by new process. (20-25)

A-16
1) Key to Aldworth's Soft Drinks Phila. (15-20)
2) Argenta Bottling Works Argenta (Ill) (15-20)
3) Blakeslee Brothers Beverages (30-35)
4) H. C. Breimeyer Bottling Co. Hummer Brand Soda Water Central 2712 1940-42 No. Ninth St. St. Louis, Mo. (35-40)
5) Charles City Bottling Works Charles City, Iowa (15-20)
6) Drink Coca-Cola (Script) in Bottles (250-300)
7) Key to Herb-Ola (20-25)
8) Kirsch's Beverages (15-20)
9) Drink Mohawk Beverages French & French South Boston, Mass. (15-20)
10) Drink Mount Kineo Ginger Ale "Mountain High in Quality."/ Same (15-20)
11) Return these Keys to Spokane Bottle Supply Co. 408 W. Sprague Spokane, Wa. (15-20)
12) Drink Tenn-Cola 5c made in Knoxville, Tenn. (40-50)

A-17
1) Drink Big Bill (20-25)
2) Drink "Cascade Ginger Ale (20-25)
3) Coca-Cola (Block) Bottling Co. Baltimore, Md. (125-150)
4) Drink Coca-Cola (Script) in Bottles (100-125)
5) Drink Coca-Cola (Script) in Bottles/Drink Goldelle Ginger Ale (100-125)
6) Drink Dr. Pepper (Script) King of Beverages Vim, Vigor, Vitality/Austin Bot. Co. Distributors (250-300)
7) Drink Gay-Ola "It's Better" (30-35)
8) Drink Gesco Pale Dry/General Seltzer Co. Quincy, Mass. (20-25)
9) Leco Pure Beverage Co. Inc. Marietta, Pa. (15-20)
10) Lenz Bros. Soda Waters Phone 6511 (15-20)
11) Logsdon Mfg. And Bottling Co. Dallas, Texas (20-25)
12) Odiorine's White Label Ginger Ale (15-20)
13) Drink Par Fay 5c it's refreshing/Illinois Parfay Co. Champaign, Ill. (20-25)
14) "Penn Brand" Chester Beverage Co. Chester, Pa. (20-25)
15) Drink Schooner Brew in Bottles (Glass of Beer) (30-35)
16) Drink Tenn-Cola call for it by name (40-50)

A-20
1) Drink Coca-Cola (Script) in Bottles (100-125)
2) Drink Coca-Cola (Script) in Bottles/Ford F. T. Branch, Ind. (100-125)
3) Drink Coca-Cola (Script) in Sterilized Bottles (100-125)
4) Drink Coca-Cola (Script) in Sterilized Bottles/Bellingham Bottling Works, Inc. Bellingham, Wash. (100-125)
5) Fox sparkling Beverages (10-12)
6) Kamp Fire Bottling Co. high grade Beverages 5415-17 Haverford Ave. Phone All. 7173/Beer Distributors day & night service free delivery 1 dozen & up (10-12)
7) Spin for Orange Crush the Winner/Belton Bottling Co. Phone 2 (25-30)
8) Buy Royal Crown Cola in Cartons it's more economical Nehi Bottling Co. Coatesville, Pa. (25-30)
9) Spin for Tom's Orange Pale Dry Ginger Ale/Tom's Golden Ginger Ale (15-20)

A-21
1) Bartle's since 1858 better Beverages (5-8)
2) Canada Dry Gettelman Schlitz Kessler Yellowstone Distributing Miles City (25-30)
3) Spin around and pick up some Cheer Up at Rovner's P-X Phone 5536
4) Smile! drink Cheerwine (25-30)
5) Compliments Coca-Cola (Block) Bottling Co. Tell City Ind. (100-125)
6) Drink Coca-Cola (Script) (1997-1998 Manufacture) (5-10)
7) Drink Coca-Cola (Script) in Bottles (100-125)
8) Give Coca-Cola (Block) a whirl (100-125)
9) You can't lose if you drink Cola-Moca the all year-round drink (10-12)
10) Drink Hearty Crystal Rock Reading, Pa. Dial 9-1611 (5-8)
11) You Pay Dad's Root Beer Falstaff Stag Harold L. Paul Distributor (15-20)
12) Spin for a De-Lux Cola De-Lux Cola Co. Atlanta, Ga. (25-30)
13) Hund & Eger (15-20)
14) J-C Bottling Company drink "J-C" for all Occasions (5-8)
15) Lyons Bottling Co. Phone 105 you lose if you do not use our Mixers (5-8)
16) Have you tried "Old Sol" you will like it Newport, N. H. (5-8)
17) Drink 7 Up Lithiated Lemon for health or the 7 hangovers Birrell Bottling Co. Salt Lake City (15-20)
18) Sterilized Bottling Works Scranton, Pa. Eat, Drink and be Merry Phone 3-2811 (5-8)
19) Trio Beverage Co. "Three Times as Good" Wheeling, W.Va. (5-8)

A-23
1) Brown Bottling Co. Hunters of Ky. Prestonsburg, Ky. (10-12)
2) Drink Coca-Cola (Script) in Bottles (35-40)

A-24
1) Nu-Grape a flavor you can't forget (15-20)

A-28
1) Acme Bottling Works Palmyra, Pa. Phone 131 (8-10)
2) Batchelor's Ginger Ale Woonsocket, R.I. (8-10)
3) Beaver Dam Bottling Co. Beaver Dam, Wis. (8-10)
4) Blue Label Bottling Works Geneva, N. Y. (8-10)
5) Drink Coca-Cola (Block) (75-100)
6) Cola-Nip (Script)/Drink Cola Nip (30-35)
7) Curo/-Extra Dry- Ginger Ale Curo Mineral Springs, So. Omaha, Neb. (15-20)
8) Deans famous Ginger Ale Connellsville, Pa. (8-10)
9) John G. Epping established 1863 Epp's Cola & all High Grade Soda. (8-10)
10) Gra-Rock Ginger Ale & Mineral Water, Canton, Conn. (8-10)
11) N. G. Gurnsey & Co., Soda Mfrs., Keene, N. H. (8-10)
12) Havelock Ginger Ale, the Old Reliable. (8-10)
13) Hekelnkaemper Bros., Soda Water Atchison, Kansas. (8-10)
14) Drink Horlacher's Soft Drinks Horlacher Bottling Co. Slatington, Pa. (15-20)
15) Horlacher Bott. Co. Slatington, Pa. Horlacher's 9 month old "Perfection" and Soft Drinks (15-20)
16) Drink King-Cola (12-15)
17) Drink Lime Cola a Cola with Lime/Drink Lime Cola (12-15)
18) Drink Lithia high grade Soda Waters, Pueblo, Colo. (8-10)
19) Drink Mo-Ro 5c "The Drink with Tone and Tickle" (12-15)
20) Quakertown Bottling Works Otto Martin, Prop. Quakertown, Pa. (12-15)
21) Rec-Ola/Recker Syrup & Bottling Works. Vincennes, Ind. (8-10)
22) St. Joseph Soda & Seltzer Company Phone 6-0331 (8-10)
23) Drink Schooner Brew in Bottles (20-25)
24) "Drink Schuster's Root Beer" (12-15)
25) Drink Schuster's Root Beer and Ginger Ale Cleveland, Ohio (12-15)
26) Drink Star Cola The Clarksburg Bottling Works Phone 592 (15-20)
27) Superior Mineral Water Co. 175 Enfield St., Thompsonville, Conn. (8-10)

28) Tutti Frutti Bev. Co. Inc. 292 Knickerbocker Ave. Bushwick 0860 Bklyn./Ma-Mi (15-20)
29) Wakefield Bottling Co. G. D' Agata, Prop. 96 Water St. Wakefield, Mass. Tel. Crystal 51476 (8-10)
30) White Ribbon Mineral Water, Harrison Valley, Pa. (8-10)
31) Drink Woluco Brand Soda/Independent Bottling Co. Tacoma. (15-20)
32) Drink Zest Beverages (12-15)

A-29
1) Drink Blue Wing Brand Soft Drinks Mpls. Bottling Co./Drink Bobby Burns Pale Dry Ginger Ale (8-10)
2) For your Health drink Breunig's natural Mineral Water Leeds, N. Y. (8-10)
3) Drink Bromo Kola 5c/Same (2 Var (A) (Girls Skirt Outline instead of Bottle) (B) No Skirt Outline) (20-25)
4) Butte Bottlers' Supply Co. Inc. 112 S. Main St. Phone 2522/ Malt Syrups Bottles Cordials Glassware (15-20)
5) Butte Bottlers' Supply Co. Inc. 112 S. Main St. Phone 3236/ Malt Syrup Cordials Mission Orange Dry (15-20)
6) Butte Bottlers' Supply Co. Inc. 112 & 114 S. Main St. Phone 3236/Malt Syrup Cordials Mission Orange Dry (15-20)
7) "Chemung Spring Water Co." Phones Elmira 3152 Waverly 12F12 Corning 731 Owego 164 (8-10)
8) Drink Chero-Cola there's none so good (25-30)
9) Drink Cherry Flip West Tusc. Bottling Co. Garf. 4465 Canton, O. (12-15)
10) Drink Chin-Ekee Soda Water Lyman, Wyoming Montpelier, Ida. (8-10)
11) Anheuser-Busch & Coca-Cola (Block) Products L.C. Frick Service Co. Distributors (50-60)
12) Cola-Cocktail Cola Cocktail Corp. of Amer/Cola-Cocktail delightfully invigorating (12-15)
13) Crystal Rock Soft Drinks Bottled at the Springs (8-10)
14) Bottled by C. Damhorst Soda Water Co. Estd. 50 years Phone Garfield 6920 & 6921/Laurel Brand (8-10)
15) Delaware Punch patented min. con. 6 fl. oz. (12-15)
16) Deutscher Club Pale Dry Ginger Ale/Independent Mil. Br'y Deutscher Club Pale Dry Ginger Ale (15-20)
17) The Double Eagle (Pic of Eagle) Bottling Co. Cleveland Ginger Beer/Double Eagle Bottling Co. 6517 St. Clair Ave. Phone Rand. 4629 (12-15)
18) Dr Pepper good for life 6 1/2 ozs./Drink a bite to eat (with 10-2-4 Clock) (50-60)
19) Dr Pepper good for life 6 1/2 ozs./Drink a bite to eat (with 10-2-4 Clock) ("You Pay" Spinner) (75-100)
20) Drink Eberle's delicious Beverages Jackson, Mich. (12-15)
21) Emerson's Ginger Mint Julep Ginger Mint Julep serve ice cold/Drink Ginger-Mint Julep (8-10)
22) The Flora Co. Inc. Manufacturers High Grade Soft Drinks Beacon 2289 Seattle, U. S. A. (8-10)
23) Drink Forest Spring Water/Drink Hub Extra Dry (8-10)
24) Harbor Grape Juice Co. 937 E. Anaheim St. Long Beach Calif./When in doubt try Old Fashioned (15-20)
25) Horlachers Bott. Co. Slatington, Pa. Horlachers 9 months old Perfection and Soft Drinks (15-20)
26) Laurel Brand/Bottled by C. Damhorst Soda Water Co. Estd. 50 Years Phone Chestnut 3940 3941 (St Louis, Mo) (8-10)
27) Drink Long Distance Soda Martinsburg, W. Va. (20-25)
28) Mavis Chocolate Drink serve ice cold or hot shake well (8-10)
29) Maydale Ginger Ale Maynard, Mass. (8-10)
30) Drink Mello-Mix it satisfies (8-10)
31) Mt Zircon Spring Water Co. Rumford, Maine/Mt Zircon Ginger Champagne Pale Dry Grape "Water of Health" (8-10)
32) Mumms Extra Dry Ginger Ale Rapken & Co. Ltd/Mumms imported Extra Dry Ginger Ale Raphen & Co Ltd sole distributors (12-15)
33) Mumms Belfast Ginger Ale imported Rapken & Co. Ltd/ Mumms imported Extra Dry Ginger Ale S. Feibusch Company 64 West Randolph St. Chicago, Ill. (12-15)
34) Mumms Extra Dry Ginger Ale Rapken & Co. Ltd/Geo B. Winfrey Co. Southern California Brokers Mumms Extra Dry

Ginger Ale Los Angeles, Calif. (12-15)
35) Mumms imported Extra Dry Ginger Ale Parrot & Company Distributors for Southern California (12-15)
36) Napa Rock Mineral Water Bohemian Ginger Ale (15-20)
37) Drink genuine Ne-Hi for a good "Understanding" (Ladies Legs)/Barberton Chero-Cola Bottling Co. Barberton 230 Barberton, Ohio. (25-30)
38) Drink genuine Ne-Hi for a good "Understanding" (Ladies Legs)/Chero-Cola & Ne-Hi Bottling Co. Youngstown, Ohio. Phones 3-3333, 3-3334 (25-30)
39) Drink genuine Ne-Hi for a good "Understanding" (Ladies Legs)/Chero-Cola & Ne-Hi Bottling Co. Belleville, Ill. Phone 2302 (25-30)
40) Drink genuine Ne-Hi for a good "Understanding" (Ladies Legs)/Elgin Bottling Co. 350 Brook St. Phone 5415 (25-30)
41) Drink Ne-Hi St. Joseph Soda & Seltzer Company (15-20)
42) "First For Thirst" Old Scotch Ginger Ale (8-10)
43) O'Donnell Bros. Bottlers of Soda Summit Hill, Pa. (initials G. B.) (8-10)
44) Orange Crush Bottling Co. (20-25)
45) Orange Crush Dry (15-20)
46) Pacific Coast Glass Company Bottles Factory San Francisco Seattle Portland Los Angeles (12-15)
47) Big Pepsi=Cola (Script) 5c/Same (35-40)
48) Polar Ginger Ale Pale Dry/Same (8-10)
49) Enjoy Red Rock Cola (8-10)
50) Drink Saegertown Beverages/Saegertown old style Saegertown Lime Rickey Aristocrat Extra Dry (8-10)
51) Drink Saegertown Ginger Ale/The Aristocrat Saegertown the Aristocrat of old style Ginger Ale (8-10)
52) You like 7 Up it likes you (12-15)
53) Drink Silver Spring Beverages Manufactured by Silver Springs Company Madison, Wisconsin (8-10)
54) Drink Smile a darn good Drink (8-10)
55) For refined Taste St. Francis-Dry-Pale Ginger Ale Meyer's Specialty Beverage Co. (12-15)
56) Suburban Club Ginger Ale/Suburban Club Extra fine (8-10)
57) Suburban Club Ginger Ale/Suburban Club fine Drinks (8-10)
58) Sunset Sunset Dry Ginger Ale/Sunset Club Beverages 8862 Sunset Blvd Oxford 5696 (8-10)
59) Drink 3 Centa Gastonia 3 Centa Bottling Co. (20-25)
60) Visalia Soda Works Beverages (12-15)
61) The Western Bottle Co. Home Bottling Supplies 818 Wade St. West 4436 West 0229 Cin'ti. Ohio (8-10)
62) Wheeling Bottle & Cork Co 2142 Main St Wheeling W.Va. all Wheeling 1955 Bottle Supplies and Malt/Barrels & Crocks Wholesale Prices our Specialty Wheeling 1955 (12-15)
63) Whistle (20-25)
64) Whistle/Thirsty just Whistle Phone Jefferson 0590 (15-20)
65) Wyandotte Mineral Springs General Offices 1 South Fourth Street Columbus, Ohio/Ginger Ale Plain and Carbonated Mineral Waters Bottled at the Springs (8-10)

A-30
1) Acme Bottling Co. 976 So. Preston St. City 9548 (15-20)
2) Anderson Bottling Works Carlinville, Illinois (15-20)
3) Big Frosty Bottling Co. Greensboro, N. C. Phone 724 (20-25)
4) Drink "Cascade" Ginger Ale (20-25)
5) Compliments of Coca-Cola (Script) Bottling Co. Sapulpa-Bristow (150-175)
6) Nehi (40-50)
7) Nehi Bottling Co. Wichita, Kansas (40-50)
8) Nehi Wichita, Kas. (40-50)
9) Compliments Rosebud Bottling Co. Forsyth, Mont. (25-30)

A-33
1) Distributed by Raleigh Coca Cola Bottling Works Falls City Beer Wins by Test (175-200)

A-34
1) Olivo Albertini Manufacturer of High Grade Soft Drinks 38-40 No. Maple St. Mt. Carmel, Pa. (40-50)

2) Ocean Park Beverage Co. 2719 Main St. Ocean Park, Calif. (60-75)
3) Rivo Products Co. Rivo Cola, Hires Welchade and Ginger Ale Louisville. (100-125)

A-35
1) Afri-Kola Co. Atlanta. (12-15)
2) H.A. Bortner Bottler Phone 623 Hanover, Pa. (8-10)
3) Drink Chero-Cola 5c (35-40)
4) Compliments of Crown Bottling Works Up-To-Date Soft Drinks, Brownsville, Pa. both phones. (10-12)
5) Drink Federal Bottling Works Orange Julep (10-12)
6) Drink Gay-Ola it's better/Same (10-12)
7) Drink Gay-Ola it's better/Drink Gay-Ola satisfies Thirst (Brass) (10-12)
8) Drink Gay-Ola it's better 5c/Drink Gay-Ola satisfies Thirst 5c (10-12)
9) Drink Gay-Ola it's better the improved Cola 5c/A Champagne delightfulness as a Soft Drink it satisfies Thirst (10-12)
10) Drink Gay-Ola it's better the improved Cola 5c/A Champagne delightfulness as a Soft Drink or a Highball (10-12)
11) Drink Jellico-La (10-12)
12) Soft Drinks R.G. Keller No Kick Pottstown Beer Porter Smith's Ale (30-35)
13) Liberty Beverage Co. the best Soft Drinks Connellsville, Pa. (10-12)
14) The Manitou Springs Mineral Water Co. Manitou, Colo./ Drink original "Manitou" Table Water & Ginger Champagne. (12-15)
15) Drink Power & have Pep. (12-15)
16) Drink Quench-O Mfd by Sher-A-Coca Bottling Co. Lexington, Ky. (20-25)
17) Compliments of Richwood Bottling Works Richwood, W.Va. (20-25)
18) Vartray Ginger Ale (10-12)
19) You won't kick if you drink Wineberg's Beverages. (8-10)
20) Zipf Bros. Mfrs-Soft Drinks The Best-Our Motto Niles, O. (12-15)

A-39
1) Drink Coca-Cola (Script) in Bottles (10-12)
2) Enjoy Coca-Cola (Script) (10-12)
3) 7up Bottling Co. St. Cloud, Minnesota (20-25)

A-42
1) Compliments of Anaconda Bottlers' Supply Co. Anaconda, Mont. Phone 665 207 Cherry St. (25-30)
2) Don't be a Fish drink Ingleside Ginger Ale, Ingallis Bros. Portland, Me. (15-20)
3) George J. Rittmann Bottler 444 South Broad St. Trenton, N. J. (15-20)

A-43
1) Coca-Cola Bottling Co Waterloo, Iowa (175-200)
2) Orange Kist (40-50)
3) "Penn Brand" Chester Beverage Co. Chester, Pa. (35-40)
4) Drink Penn-Cola (40-50)

A-44
1) "Ace" Beverage Co., Inc. 584 Perry Street Phone 3-0024 (15-20)
2) Acme Bev. Co. 1524 Olive Way CA 1112 (15-20)
3) Drink Allouez Beverages Green Bay, Wis. (15-20)

A-46
1) Elk-Club Ginger Ale made with Lithia Water (15-20)
2) Standard Bottling Works (15-20)

A-53
1) Drink "Cascade Ginger Ale (20-25)
2) Drink Coca-Cola (Script) in Bottles (150-175)
3) Drink Coca-Cola (Script) in Bottles 5c (150-175)

4) "Compliments Emporia Bottling Works Emporia, Kans." (20-25)
5) Compliments of Higginsville Bottling Works Higginsville, Mo. (20-25)
6) Drink Nifty Cola (35-40)

A-57
1) American Bottling Co. (25-30)
2) Compliments of Roesner & Hoyt Thornton Mineral Springs Product Thornton, Ill. (20-25)

A-59
1) Chero-Cola in Bottles 5c Chero-Cola (40-50)

A-501
1) Open a Bottle of Arrowhead Pale Dry Ginger Ale (100-125)

A-502
1) Drink Try-Me Try Me (20-25)

A-503
1) Coca-Cola (Script) Bottle Coolers Glascock Bros. Mfg. Co. Muncie, Ind. (150-175)

A-504
1) Crush Dry/Compliments Orange-Crush Dry (8-10)
2) Orange Crush/Compliments of Orange Crush Bottling Co. (8-10)

A-505
1) Clicquot Club Ginger Ale/(Eskimo) Clicquot Club Pale Dry Ginger Ale (50-60)

A-506
1) White Rock Water & Ginger Ale (3-5)

A-507
1) White Rock Water & Ginger Ale (5-8)

A-508
1) Drink Concord Grape Soda (20-25)

A-509
1) Nehi Quality Drinks (25-30)

B-1
1) Bacon's Pure Non-Alcoholic Beverages Harrisburg, Pa. (35-40)
2) Jackson's Napa Soda California's Sparkling Table Water makes a Perfect Lemonade (60-75)

B-2
1) Drink Coca-Cola (Script) in Bottles (2 Var (A) (Brass/Red on Black) (60-75) (B) (Steel/Red) (100-125))
2) Eastside Bottling Works Cheyenne, Wyo. Soda Water Hello 264 Beer (50-60)

B-5
1) G. A. Straub, Bottler Quakertown, Pa. (30-35)

B-6
1) Drink "Canada Dry" Pale Ginger Ale (5-8)
2) Coca Cola (Block) (75-100)
3) Drink Dr. Brown's "One and Only One"/Ginger Tonic (25-30)
4) Pluto Water America's Physic/Same (5-8)
5) Drink Profile & Brobe Beverages (8-10)
6) Drink Welchs Grape Juice (12-15)

B-7
1) Coca-Cola (Script) Bottling Co. Memphis (100-125)
2) Coca-Cola (Script) Bottling Wks. Paducah (100-125)
3) Coca-Cola (Script) Bottling Wks. 2nd Louisville, Ky. (100-125)
4) C.W. Elliott Co. Bottlers. (10-12)
5) Lomax's Original Pepsin Ginger Ale Phone Harrison 1869 (15-20)
6) Drink Rainbow Ginger Ale (15-20)

B-8
1) Drink Brandimist (20-25)
2) Drink Gin Su you'll like it 5c (20-25)
3) Standard Soda Water Co. Columbus, Ohio. (20-25)
4) Drink Woolner's Toledo's Best Beverages (30-35)

B-9
1) The Lithia Water Bottling Co. Soda Fountain & Bar Supplies Pueblo, Colo. (15-20)

B-13
1) Beaufont Extra Dry Pale Ginger Ale The Beaufont Co. Inc. Richmond, Va. (8-10)
2) Butte Bottlers' Supply Co. Inc. Butte 112 S. Main St. (15-20)
3) Church's Grape Juice it is Healthful/Church Grape Juice Company Kennewick, Washington (5-8)
4) L.D. Claus Carbonated Beverages (5-8)
5) Coca-Cola (Script)/Coca-Cola (Script) Bottling Works (60-75)
6) Coca-Cola (Script) Bottling Co. Terre Haute, Indiana (60-75)
7) Diamond Ginger Ale (8-10)
8) "Dubois Special Pale Dry Ginger Ale" (8-10)
9) Eagle Bottling Works & Fixture Co. Inc. Seattle/"Leaves a Good Taste with You" (5-8)
10) J.G. Fox & Co. Seattle, Wash. (8-10)
11) Golden State Beverage Co./New Crow (8-10)
12) Hawaiian Dry "Made Where the Ginger Grows" (8-10)
13) Jamaica Pale Dry Ginger Ale/John Graf Co. "The Best What Gives" (5-8)
14) McCulloch's Ginger Ale (8-10)
15) Mendota Bottling Co. Mendota, Ill./High Grade Sodas and Ginger Ale Agents for Bohemian Bottle Beer (20-25)
16) Montana Dry Ginger Ale/Carlstrom's Hamilton, Mont. (15-20)
17) Montana Dry Ginger Ale/Compliments of Nevin-Frank Co. (15-20)
18) Compliments Nevin-Frank Co. (15-20)
19) New Century Beverage 820 Pacific St., S. F./Drink Pale Dry Niagara (8-10)
20) Drink Nite Club Ginger Ale/Drink Bohemian Club (8-10)
21) Drink O-T sold everywhere (8-10)
22) Old English Ginger Ale (8-10)
23) Olympic Dry Ginger Ale Co. (8-10)
24) Pepsi-Cola—- Modesto Jacob Richter (30-35)
25) Quencho Pure Syrup Beverages/Baxter Bottling Co. Paterson, N. J. Tel. Lambert 1281 (8-10)
26) Prima Company Beverages Chicago (8-10)
27) Drink Red Rock Cola (20-25)
28) Red Rock (12-15)
29) Wm. Roesch Bottling Works Pendleton, Oregon (15-20)
30) Drink Saserac Ginger Ale (8-10)
31) Drink Schuster's Root Beer Made in Cleveland, Ohio (15-20)
32) Fresh up with 7 Up (12-15)
33) Sprau's Ice Cream & Beverages (5-8)
34) Star Bottling Co. Marshfield (5-8)
35) Drink Sunny Kid Pale Dry Ginger Ale made famous by the Public (8-10)
36) Tech Dry Ginger Ale/Iron City Lager (5-8)
37) Tom Moore Ginger Ale (8-10)
38) Drink Western Club Special (5-8)
39) Ben Herr sells White Rock Water (8-10)
40) Whistle Bottling Co. Allentown, Pa. (12-15)
41) Yankee Dry Ginger Ale (8-10)

B-14
1) Apollo Bottling Co. 30th Anniversary 1949 Apollo, Pa. (5-8)
2) Barq's (5-8)
3) Drink Berghoff/Dry Ginger Ale (5-8)
4) Beaufont Dry Ginger Ale/Same (5-8)
5) Beaufont Dry Ginger Ale/Beaufont Lime Dry (5-8)
6) The Beaufont Co. Inc. Richmond, Va. Pale Dry/Extra Dry Beaufont Pale Ginger Ale (8-10)
7) Drink Becco nourishing as Beer/Becker Products Co. Ogden, Utah (15-20)

8) Berkeley Club Ginger Ale one of America's Best (5-8)
9) Berkeley Club Ginger Ale one of America's Best/Same (5-8)
10) Drink Bludwine makes you glad you're thirsty (5-8)
11) Bobby Burns Pale Dry Ginger Ale/Minneapolis Bottling Company Minneapolis, Minn. (5-8)
12) Drink Broad Rock Ginger Ale "Good for What Ales You" (5-8)
13) Calmar Bottling Works Calmar, Iowa Phone 11 (5-8)
14) Cerva made in St. Louis/Cerva a Soft Drink (15-20)
15) Coca-Cola (15-20)
16) Coca-Cola (Script)/Crown Bottling Works 702-706 S. Wolfe St. Phone Wolfe 1565 (20-25)
17) Coca-Cola (Script) Bottling Co. Ft. Smith, Ark. (25-30)
18) Coca-Cola (Script) Bottling Co. Greenwood (25-30)
19) Coca-Cola (Script) Bottling Co. Okmulgee, Okla. (25-30)
20) Coca-Cola (Script) Bottling Co. Springfield, Mo. (25-30)
21) Coca-Cola (Script) Bottling Works, Inc. Danville, Ky. (25-30)
22) Coca-Cola (Script) Bottling Works New Albany, Miss. (25-30)
23) Coca-Cola (Script) drink Crown Ginger Ale (20-25)
24) Coca-Cola (Script) The Springfield Bott. Co. Springfield, O. (25-30)
25) Coca-Cola (Script) 3-1392/Same (20-25)
26) Compliments Coca-Cola (Block) Bottling Co. Bloomington-Indiana (2 Var (A) Block Coca-Cola (B) Script Coca-Cola (25-30)
27) Compliments Coca-Cola (Script) Bottling Co. Newberry, S. C. (25-30)
28) Compliments Gastonia Coca-Cola (Block) Bottling Company (25-30)
29) Compliments Tell City Coca-Cola (Block) Bottling Co. Tell City, Ind. (25-30)
30) Drink Coca-Cola (Script) (15-20)
31) Drink Coca-Cola (Script)/Bottled in Greenville, S. C. (2 Var (A) Small Letters (B) Large Letters) (25-30)
32) Drink Coca-Cola (Script) Coca-Cola (Script) (10-12) (2 Var (A) Drink Block Letters (B) Drink Cursive Letters)
33) Drink Coca-Cola (Script) Coca-Cola (Script)/Coca-Cola (Block) Bottling Works, Inc. Bethlehem, Pa. (25-30)
34) Drink Coca-Cola (Script) in Bottles (15-20)
35) Drink Coca-Cola (Script) in Bottles (Vaughan) (15-20)
36) Drink Coca-Cola (Script) Shelby, N. C. (25-30)
37) Drink Double Cola (10-12)
38) Dr. Pepper (Script) (40-50)
39) Dr. Pepper (Script)/Dr. Pepper (Block) Bottling Co. Ft. Smith, Ark. (50-60)
40) Compliments of Dubois Products & Cold Storage Co. Dubois, Pa. (10-12)
41) Eskimo Pop a pal for your palate/Same (8-10)
42) Eskimo Pop a pal for your palate/Eskimo Syrup Co. Pittsburgh, Pa. one dollar reward for return of these Keys 1904 (Numbered at least 1 to 2000) (8-10)
43) Drink Eureka Puraqua Products & Ice Co. Smithton, Pa. (5-8)
44) Felix Dry Ginger Ale/Felix Orange Dry Felix Club Soda (5-8)
45) Felix Dry Ginger Ale Felix Orange Dry/Felix Grapefruit Dry Felix Club Soda (5-8)
46) Drink Fitger's Beverages (15-20)
47) Drink Fitger's Non-Alco (15-20)
48) Freeburg Bottling Co. (5-8)
49) Fresno Beverage Co. Sierra Brew pasteurized Sodas/Fresno Beverage Co. Hi-B Ginger Ale pasteurized Sodas (20-25)
50) Drink Gipps Barlo an invigorating Beverage (15-20)
51) Gluek Indian Maid Ginger Ale/Gluek Pilsener Pale (5-8)
52) Gluek's Indian Maid Ginger Ale/Gluek's Pilsener Pale (5-8)
53) Goudy's Beverages 119 State St. Oil City, Pa. (5-8)
54) John Graf Co./Jamaica Pale-Dry Ginger Ale (5-8)
55) Griesedieck Bev. Co. St. Louis buy Hek (15-20)
56) Drink Hamm's Beverages St. Paul, Minn./Windsor Club the real Beer Taste (10-12)
57) Hauensteins New Ulm, Minn. quality Beverages (10-12)
58) Hauensteins New Ulm, Minn. quality Beverages/Ed Korrman Clements, Minn. 1938 (10-12)
59) Hekelnkaemper Bros. Soda Water Atchison, Kansas (5-8)
60) Hoster-Columbus Company Inc. Columbus, Ohio/Hoster is Bruin Non-Intoxicating a Cereal Beverage (15-20)

61) Hoster drink Bruin a Cereal Beverage/Hoster's famous Old English Ginger Beer Columbus, Ohio (15-20)
62) Hoster Drink Bruin a Cereal Beverage/Hosters' Columbus, Ohio "That's The Beer" Old English Ginger Beer (15-20)
63) Hub Brand Hub Bottling Works Mason City, Iowa (5-8)
64) Just ask for Joe's Ginger Ale Johamkneckt's (5-8)
65) Kiel "Best Mixing Sodas" (5-8)
66) Lakeside Beverages/"Sheboygan's Best Mixers" (5-8)
67) Drink Min Rize/Mix with Min Rize (5-8)
68) Drink Mohawk Brand Soda (5-8)
69) Compliments of F. W. Muller Sons Arlington Heights, Ill. Pale Dry (5-8)
70) Nehi (20-25)
71) Oxford Club Pale Dry Ginger Ale/Drink Hamm's Master Brew St. Paul, Minn. (10-12)
72) Oxford Club Pale Dry Ginger Ale/Hamm's Master Brew St. Paul, Minn. (10-12)
73) Oxford Club Pale Dry Ginger Ale/Drink Hamm's Special Brew (10-12)
74) Pepsi=Cola Bros./Humbolt Bott. Wks. Genoa (25-30)
75) "Drink Quench" (5-8)
76) Sand Springs Extra Dry "The Prince of Drys" Williamstown, Mass. (5-8)
77) Serenader's Club Pale Dry Ginger Ale (5-8)
78) Sheboygan Mineral Water and Ginger Ale chief of them all (5-8)
79) Drink Spur Canada Dry 5c (10-12)
80) Tally Non-Intoxicating Non-Alcoholic/Same (5-8)
81) Three Star Ginger Ale O. Altpeter Baraboo, Wis. (5-8)
82) Triangle Beverage Snohomish, Wn. (5-8)
83) Joe Vaccaro Soda Water Mfg. Co. Kansas City, Mo. 922 E. 5th St. (10-12)
84) White Label Bottling Co., Inc. Hartford, Conn. Beverages (10-12)
85) Widmer's Grape Products Industry/Use Widmer Products Widmer Wine Cellars Naples, N. Y. U. S. A. (3-5)
86) Widmer's Grape Products Industry use Widmer Products Widmer's Wine Cellars Naples, N. Y. U.S.A.(3-5)

B-15
1) Drink Big Boy (15-20)
2) Drink Coca-Cola (50-60)
3) Dublin Dry Ginger Ale/Always demand Schreiers by Name (15-20)
4) Otto Eberlin Sodas (Hermann, Mo) (15-20)
5) Haberle Congo Syracuse/Same (20-25)
6) Huesing's Lemon Soda (15-20)
7) Mt. Zircon Spring Water Co. Rumford, Me./Mt. Zircon Ginger Champagne (10-12)
8) Pur-Ox Beverages (10-12)
9) Reading Bottling Works 313 Chestnut St. (10-12)
10) Drink Zang's Beverages Denver/Same (15-20)

B-16
1) Haberle Congo Syracuse/Same (20-25)
2) Drink Lime Cola (15-20)

B-17
1) Compliments of Macon Bottling Wks. Macon, Mo./Same (15-20)
2) Zizz the drink with fizz (15-20)

B-18
1) Key to Anita Ginger Ale & Carbonated Water. (5-8)
2) Arcadian Club Ginger Ale Waukesha (5-8)
3) Arcadian Ginger Ale Waukesha (5-8)
4) The Arlington Bottling Co. Wash, D.C. (10-12)
5) Arrowhead Ginger Ale and Kwas. (5-8)
6) Ballardvale Lithia Water absolutely pure (5-8)
7) Try Ballardvale Spring Water the Perfect Blender (5-8)
8) Bangor Bottling Co. Bangor, Pa. (5-8)
9) Banquet Beverages (5-8)

10) Drink Beacon Rock Camden Bottling Co. Camden, N. J. (5-8)
11) Beaufont Ginger Ale Richmond, Va. (10-12)
12) Bethlehem Beverage & Cold Storage Co. (5-8)
13) Drink Big Bill Beverages (10-12)
14) Drink Big Frosty Pale Dry Greensboro, N. C. (10-12)
15) Birdsboro Bottling Works, T.R. Lacey, Prop. (5-8)
16) Drink E.A. Boemler House Springs, Mo. (5-8)
17) Bowman Ice & Soda Works Chico, Calif. (12-15)
18) Compliments of Geo. E. Bryan Bottling Works. (5-8)
19) Buffalo Rock Ginger Ale (10-12)
20) Drink Buffalo Ginger Ale (10-12)
21) Compliments of Carrington Bottling Works (5-8)
22) Cascade Ginger Ale (5-8)
23) Castle Rock natural Mineral Water (5-8)
24) Key to Chesterman's-Famous-Ginger Ale (10-12)
25) Coca Cola (Block) Bottling Works Inc. Lynchburg, Va./Bottlers Coca Cola (Block) Ginger Ale and Soda Water. (40-50)
26) Coca-Cola (Script) Bottling Co. Buffalo, N. Y. (40-50)
27) Compliments Coca-Cola (Script) Bottling Co. Columbia, S. C. (40-50)
28) Compliments Coca-Cola (Script) Bottling Co. Oklahoma City (40-50)
29) Compliments Coca-Cola (Script) Bottling Co. Peoria, Ill. (40-50)
30) Compliments Coca-Cola (Script) Bottling Co. Union, S. C. (40-50)
31) Compliments of Coca-Cola (Script) Company Memphis, Tenn. (40-50)
32) Compliments of The Coca-Cola (Script) Bottling Works Richmond, Va. (40-50)
33) Compliments of The Coca-Cola (Script) Bottling Works Washington D.C. (40-50)
34) Key to Coca-Cola (Script) drink a Bottle (40-50)
35) Key to Coca-Cola (Script) drink a Bottle/Sold everywhere 5cts. (50-60)
36) Lawrence Bottling & Mfg. Co. Coca-Cola (Block) & Soft Drinks New Castle, Pa. (40-50)
37) The Coca-Cola Bottling Works Cumberland, Md. (40-50)
38) Key to Colby Pop (5-8)
39) Key to Colby Pop/J. A. Westermeier Maker, Colby, Kansas (10-12)
40) Columbia Bottling Co. (5-8)
41) Corona Lithia Water/California's Best (12-15)
42) Crown Steam Bottling Works Callahan Bros. Prop's Clearfield, Pa. (5-8)
43) Key to C. Damhorst Soda Water Co's Sodas (5-8)
44) This Key unlocks Delaney & Young's Bottles (Eureka, Ca Soda Manufacturer) (15-20)
45) Des Moines Steam Bottling Works Best in the State (5-8)
46) Drink Eagle Brand Ginger Ale/Eagle Bottling Works Davenport, Iowa (5-8)
47) Drink Eagle Brand fine Beverages (5-8)
48) Eagle Soft Drink Co Phone 27W South Milwaukee, Wis./Drink Old Manhattan (5-8)
49) Edelweiss Products/Green River (5-8)
50) Thirsty? Eskimo Pop it satisfies/Same (5-8)
51) Key to Excelsior Bottling Co's. Bottled Goods 37 & 39 Maple St., Reading, Pa./T.J. Fessler proprietor (12-15)
52) Key to Excelsior Soda Works Los Angeles, Calif./C. B. Strohm (5-8)
53) Drink Fan Taz/Drink Fan Taz Drink of the "Fans" (in Ball Bat) "League" (in Ball) (60-75)
54) Forest Park best ever Beverages (5-8)
55) Key to Geo. L. Franck's Soda, Ginger Ale Etc. 4 E. Broad St. Richmond, Va. (10-12)
56) Drink Fuhs Bottled Beverages/Same (5-8)
57) Compliments of Gettysburg Bottlery Gettysburg, Pa. (10-12)
58) Compliments of Geyser Spring Co. Saratoga Spring, N. Y. (5-8)
59) Goetz Co. St. Joseph, Mo. Gozo/The most delicious Cereal Beverage (15-20)
60) Goetz Co. St. Joseph, Mo. Gozo Non-Intoxicating (15-20)
61) Key to Golden West Soda Water Somps & Paillet 1619 O'Farrell St. S. F. (15-20)

62) Key to Gravel Springs Water Highest Award St. Louis World's Fair (15-20)
63) Harsch's Coyote Water Albuquerque./Same (5-8)
64) Key to Heptol Splits "The Bestway"/Cures Headache, Constipation, Etc. (5-8)
65) Drink Hilleman's Beverages (5-8)
66) "Joy" Cereal Beverage (5-8)
67) Keystone Bottling Works Lebanon, Pa./Compliments of I. E. Rabold (5-8)
68) Kutztown Bottling Works. (5-8)
69) Drink Lime Cola (12-15)
70) Drink Liquid Force The A. R. Champney Co. Elyria, O. (5-8)
71) Compliments Los Angeles Soda Works (10-12)
72) Majestic Ginger Ale Goetze, Spiro & Goetze San Francisco, Cal./Distributors Boyes Springs Mineral Water (20-25)
73) Majestic Ginger Alee (Ale is misspelled) made from Distilled Water/Goetze, Spiro & Goetze, S. F. (20-25)
74) Drink Mizz/Delicious new Beverage made in Chicago. (8-10)
75) Drink Molto Blairs Root Beer Blair Beverage Co. (10-12)
76) Compliments of New London Bottling Works (5-8)
77) Oxford Club Pale Dry Ginger Ale/Drink Hamm's Master Brew St. Paul, Minn. (12-15)
78) Ozarka Water and Ginger Ale/Eureka Springs Water Co. Eureka Springs, Ark. (5-8)
79) Pacific Bottling Works drink "Beerine" (20-25)
80) Drink Pa-Poose Root Beer New Orleans, La. (20-25)
81) Drink Peacock Beverages/Weisbrod & Hess Phila. (15-20)
82) Drink Pepsi Cola (Block) and Van Doren's Ginger Ale (35-40)
83) Drink Pepsi Cola (Block) Charlotte Pepsi-Cola Bottling Co. (40-50)
84) Remember H.A. Petersen Beer & Soda Water (5-8)
85) Drink Pin-Ap-Ola trade mark 5c (5-8)
86) Pioneer Soda Water Co. San Francisco, Cal. (12-15)
87) Drink Ple Zee the best Soft Drink on Earth. (5-8)
88) Pureoxia Ginger Ale made from Distilled Water (5-8)
89) Drink Quex the Beverage Peninsula Products Co. Wilmington-Delaware. (12-15)
90) W.H. Raubenhold Bottler, Hamburg, Pa. (5-8)
91) Key to Red Rock Ginger Ale America's Finest Hagan & Dodd Co. Atlanta, Ga. (5-8)
92) Key to Red Rock Hagan & Dodd Co. Atlanta, Ga. (5-8)
93) Key to Red Rock The Red Rock Co. (5-8)
94) Rock Spring Water Ginger Ale (5-8)
95) Drink W.F. Roesen's Soda & Mineral Waters (5-8)
96) Compliments San Luis Obispo Soda-Works/L. Albert Prop. Phone Main 42 (20-25)
97) Schlitz Pale Dry Ginger Ale/Schlitz in Brown Bottles (12-15)
98) Schmidt Bottling Works Hanover, Pa. (5-8)
99) Drink Shasta Ginger Ale. (5-8)
100) Simpson Spring fine Temperance Beverages (5-8)
101) Drink Star Cola Diehl & Lord Nashville, Tenn. (20-25)
102) Compliments of The Star Bottling Works. (5-8)
103) Drink Statue Brand Hygienic Aerated Waters (5-8)
104) Key to Stoeckle's Beer & Crown Ginger Ale bottled by Foord (20-25)
105) Telluride Bottling Works George W. Tallman (20-25)
106) Drink "3-C Nectar" the drink of the gods (5-8)
107) "Tuck's" Ginger Ale/"One Bottle Means Another" (5-8)
108) "Drink Viva" The Viva Food Co. Atlanta, Ga. (8-10)
109) Venetian Ginger Ale/A Tait Bros. Product. (5-8)
110) Exclusive bottlers of Whistle & Hires/Bangor Bottling Co. Mc Aloon & Geagan, Props. (20-25)

B-19

1) Drink Famous Arrowhead Brands. (5-8)
2) Drink Beaufont Ginger Ale (12-15)
3) Drink Beaufont Ginger Ale made in Richmond, Va. (12-15)
4) Drink Bevetone/Des Moines Beverage Co. Des Moines, Iowa (5-8)
5) Drink Celery-Cola Reg. U.S. Pat. Off./Bottled by Sanitary Bottling Co. (8-10)
6) Key to Clicquot Club Ginger Ale (8-10)

7) Coca-Cola (Script) in Bottles/When Thirsty Try a Bottle (30-35)
8) Drink Deep Rock Ginger Ale the World's Best (5-8)
9) Dixie Brewing Company -Dixo- Beverage (20-25)
10) Gerst's Sodas are Best/Try our Cola Phone M. 2578 (25-30)
11) Kola Chalaca Angel Derossi & Co. (5-8)
12) Drink Lemon Kola (8-10)
13) J. Melmod mfr. of Soft Drinks Atlantic City, N. J./Distributor of Phila. Brewing Co. and Aco (20-25)
14) Drink Moer-Lo the satisfying Soft Drink/A pure wholesome and refreshing Beverage
15) Mt Laurel Spring Water Co. (5-8)
16) My-Coca Company, Birmingham, Ala./Made from the Original Coca-Cola (Block) Formula (75-100)
17) Oakland Pioneer Soda Water Co. (15-20)
18) Drink Pepsi-Cola (Block) Charlotte—Rockhill Columbia (35-40)
19) Drink Pepsi——-Cola (Block) Charlotte—Rockhill Columbia (35-40)
20) Drink Pepsi-Cola (Block) 5 Cts. Rock Hill, S. C. (35-40)
21) Drink Pepsi-Cola (Block) very refreshing, Charlotte, Rockhill, Columbia (35-40)
22) The Key to Peter's Soda/Washington Bottling Works, Washington, Mo. (15-20)
23) Drink "Quality" Ginger Ale Compliments of Federal Bottling Co. W. Lynn, Mass. (5-8)
24) Drink Quex the Beverage Peninsula Products Co. Wilmington, Delaware. (12-15)
25) Drink Red Seal Ginger Ale/Fairmount Beverages 2139-41 Mt. Vernon St. (5-8)
26) Key to Red Rock Hagan & Dodd Co. Atlanta, Ga. (5-8)
27) Reif's Special "A Pure Liquid Food" "The Peer of All Soft Drinks" (20-25)
28) Jacob Richter Fresno, Cal. (12-15)
29) A.W. Schrader Co. 726 Adams Ave. Scranton, Pa./Schlitz Beer and Mineral Waters (15-20)
30) Taka-Cola Out of Bottles Clean Fresh & Stimulating/Winchester, Harrisonburg, Virginia (15-20)
31) Willow Springs Beverage Co. Omaha (15-20)
32) Willow Springs Beverage Co. Omaha, Nebraska/Drink Te-To the Great Teetotaler's Beverage (15-20)

B-21

1) Drink Ala-Cola (5-8)
2) Drink Alhambra Spring Water & Sodas (5-8)
3) American Table Water Co. Inc., Ephrata, Pa. (5-8)
4) Andy's Beverages Emaus Bottling Works Emaus, Pa. (5-8)
5) Frank Banko Soft Drinks of quality Bethlehem, Pa. (5-8)
6) Bay City Beverage Co./The Finest (12-15)
7) Drink Beaufont Ginger Ale (5-8)
8) The Bon Ton Bottling Works/Bottlers of "Schlitz" Beer and All Sodas (15-20)
9) Drink California Grapine 5c at All Soft Drink Places (15-20)
10) Drink Celery Cola Stimulating. (5-8)
11) Cereal Beverages Sunbury Bottling Works (5-8)
12) Chippewa Purest of All Waters (5-8)
13) Chippewa Springs Co. Chippewa Falls, Wis./Chippewa Purest of All Waters (5-8)
14) Chippewa Springs Company Chippewa Falls, Wis./Chippewa Purest of All Waters (5-8)
15) Clarinda Bottling Works, Clarinda, Iowa (5-8)
16) Drink Clauss Birch Beer (10-12)
17) Drink Clinton Lithia Water (8-10)
18) Compliments of Coca-Cola (Script) Co. Memphis, Tenn. (40-50)
19) Drink Coca-Cola (Script) in Bottles/Every Bottle Sterilized. (40-50)
20) Drink Concord Drips/Emaus Bottling Works Andrew Jagnesak Prop. Emaus, Pa. (5-8)
21) Crawford's Famous Bottled Soda Water. The Best in the West. (Sedalia, Mo) (12-15)
22) Crystal Bottling Works Crocker, Mo. (12-15)
23) Call for Deerfield Ginger Ale you remember the taste (5-8)
24) This Key unlocks Delaney & Young's Bottles (Eureka, Ca Soda Manufacturer) (15-20)

25) Key to Emaus Bottling Works Emaus, Pa. the High Grade Beverages (5-8)
26) Excelsior Bottling Co. T.J. Fessler Prop Reading, Pa. (5-8)
27) The Ferro-Phos Co. Soft Drinks Pottstown, Pa. (5-8)
28) J.G. Fox & Co. Seattle/Drink Fox Beverages (10-12)
29) Gosman's Ginger Ale (5-8)
30) Gra-Rock Ginger Ale (5-8)
31) Hays Bottling Works/Manufacturers of Soft Drinks (15-20)
32) Key to J.B. Hronecz Bottling Works Shenandoah, Pa. (5-8)
33) Jackson Lithia Spring Water Co. Kansas City, Mo. Tels. M2190 (5-8)
34) Buy Koenig High Grade Soda Brand Owensville, Mo. (10-12)
35) Kreutzer Bottling Works for thirst try us first Peru, Ind. (5-8)
36) Lombard's Ginger Ale, Jackson, Mich. (10-12)
37) Manhattan Food Specialty Co. Malt-Brew 2403 First Ave. N. Y. (12-15)
38) Drink Ocean Breeze in Bottles (10-12)
39) Drink Orange Fizzade Phone Bryant 826 New York (5-8)
40) Compliments of The Owens Spring Water Co. Glenwood, Minn. (5-8)
41) Drink Petersburg Pop/Same (10-12)
42) Polar Ginger Ale/Same (5-8)
43) Wm. H. Raubenhold bottler Hamburg Pa. (5-8)
44) Red Goose Root Beer (10-12)
45) The Reiners Co. Bottlers Huntingdon-Pa. (5-8)
46) Riverside Beverage Co. G. & H./Ginger Ale you can taste the Ginger (5-8)
47) Drink Rye-Ola/Quitman Ice & Bottling Works Quitman, Ga. (15-20)
48) Key to Sand Springs Ginger Ale Williamstown, Mass. (5-8)
49) Key to Saratoga Vichy king of table waters/Keep young while growing old (5-8)
50) Schmidt Bottling Co. Hanover, Pa. (5-8)
51) Drink Silver King brewed Ginger Ale/Silver King sparkling Mineral Water (5-8)
52) Demand Soterian Ginger Ale/Drink Sulpho-Saline for the Stomach (10-12)
53) Southern Fountain Co. Little Rock Ark. (5-8)
54) Drink Sulpho-Saline for the Stomach (5-8)
55) -Tuscaloza- Bottling Works (5-8)
56) Key to Vogel's Famous Bottled Sodas & Cola Henderson, Ky. (15-20)
57) Waukesha Arcadian Ginger Ale (5-8)
58) Just Whistle/Spitzer & Co. Scranton, Pa. (15-20)

B-22
1) American Cereal Beverage (5-8)
2) Compliments of The Coca-Cola (Script) Bottling Works Phila Pa. (40-50)
3) Dickson Coca-Cola (Script) Bottling Co. Dickson, Tenn. (40-50)
4) Key to "Gluek Root Beer" "Glix" Beverage Gluek Brg. Co. Minneapolis (10-12)
5) Key to Granite State Spring Water Ginger Ale & Tonic (5-8)
6) Buy Hek Griesedieck Bev. Co. St. Louis (15-20)
7) The Lorain Bottling Co. (5-8)
8) Drink J. J. McCraw & Bro Ginger Ale (5-8)
9) My-Coca Company Birmingham, Ala./Made from the Original Coca-Cola (Block) Formula (75-100)
10) Murphysboro Bottling Co (5-8)
11) Drink Overland Beverage Co's Pure Apple Cider (15-20)
12) Pierce Juice the Best of the Grade (5-8)
13) Drink Riceutrine/Moreland & Myers Dist. Phone Osage 7043 (5-8)
14) Reif's Special "A Pure Liquid Food" "The Peer of All Soft Drinks" (25-30)
15) Soterian Ginger Ale/Drink Sulpho-Saline for the Stomach (10-12)
16) Westport Carbonating Works Master Bottlers H.P.M. 1916 K. C. Mo. (5-8)

B-23
1) Abner-Drury (AD Logo) Ginger Ale (20-25)

2) You pay drink Ale 81 "A Late One" (Spinner) (10-12)
3) Anton Bottling Co. Hannibal, Mo. (10-12)
4) Drink Anton's So-Da-Licious (10-12)
5) Arnold Sodas (5-8)
6) Arrowhead Pale Dry Ginger Ale (5-8)
7) Baxter Springs Bottling Works (5-8)
8) Drink Big Lu it's made for you All Flavors (St Louis, Mo) (10-12)
9) Drink Bone-Dry/Moreland & Myers, Dist. Phone 7043 (15-20)
10) Drink Buster Beverages Buster Bottling Company Macon, Ga. (15-20)
11) Butte Bottlers Supply Co. Inc. Wholesale & Retail Bottlers Supplies Phone 2622 116 S. Main St. Butte, Montana (15-20)
12) Drink Canadian Club Dry Ginger Ale Dist. by Coca-Cola (Block) Bot'lg. Co., Wichita (40-50)
13) Chero-Cola Bottling Company Albemarle, N. C. (30-35)
14) Cleary's Bottling Works Shenandoah, Pa./The Sanitary Plant (5-8)
15) Clicquot Club Ginger Ale (2 Var (A) 'Ginger Ale' Lower Case Letters Var (B) 'Ginger Ale' Upper Case Letters) (5-8)
16) Drink Club Royal Carbonated Beverages (5-8)
17) Ashburn Bottling Co. Coca-Cola (Script) (40-50)
18) Coca-Cola (Script) Bottling Co. You Pay (Spinner) (75-100)
19) Coca-Cola (Script) (40-50)
20) Drink Coca-Cola (Script)/Same (40-50)
21) Drink Coca-Cola (Script) in Bottles (40-50)
22) Weldon Coca-Cola (Script) Bottling Wks. Inc., Weldon, No. Car. (40-50)
23) Drink Coney Island (5-8)
24) Crystal Springs Bottling Works Sheboygan, Wis. (5-8)
25) Drink "One and Only One" Dr. Brown's/Celery Tonic (10-12)
26) Drink Eagle Brand fine Beverages (5-8)
27) Edelweiss Products/Green River (5-8)
28) Flock's Carbonated Beverages (5-8)
29) Goetz Co. Gozo/The most delicious Cereal Beverage (15-20)
30) Goetz Co. St. Joseph, Mo. Gozo/The most delicious Cereal Beverage (15-20)
31) Golden Grain Juice Co. Minneapolis (5-8)
32) Drink Grafs "The Best What Gives" (5-8)
33) Griesedieck Bev. Co. St. Louis Buy Hek (15-20)
34) Drink Hillemann's Beverages (5-8)
35) Irondequoit Ginger Ale/Irondequoit Mineral Water (5-8)
36) Kayo Bottling Works Deerfield, Wis. "Kayo" the real Chocolate Drink (5-8)
37) Kies Bottling Works Ph 60 Owego, N. Y. (5-8)
38) Lang's Ginger Ale Arabia Dry (10-12)
39) Lang's Ginger Ale Hyan Dry (10-12)
40) Minnehaha Pale Beverages Minneapolis U. S. A. (10-12)
41) Minnehaha Pale Root Beer Minneapolis U. S. A. (10-12)
42) Minnehaha Pale Special Minneapolis U. S. A. (10-12)
43) Moellering Beverages (5-8)
44) Munson Beverages are Sweetened with Pure Cane Sugar (5-8)
45) Old English Ginger Ale (5-8)
46) Overland Beverage Company Nampa, Idaho (15-20)
47) Penn Beverage Co. Philadelphia Penn Special (10-12)
48) Picher Bottling Co. Picher, Okla. (5-8)
49) Polar Ginger Ale/Same (5-8)
50) Drink Rock-Arc (5-8)
51) Saegertown Ginger Ale (5-8)
52) The C. Z. Seelig Co. Beverages & Cigars (5-8)
53) Drink Silver King Ginger Ale & Sparkling Water (5-8)
54) Here is to your Health Silver Springs Beverages Silver Springs Co. Madison, Wis. (5-8)
55) Spark-Lin-Ale the Perfect Ginger Ale Martins Ferry, Ohio (10-12)
56) Supreme Carbonated Beverages (5-8)
57) Supreme Carbonated Beverages/Carlyle Bottling Works Carlyle Illinois (5-8)
58) Sy-Ro the greatest Beverage, Sy-Ro Co. Methuen, Mass. (5-8)
59) Drink Torah (5-8)
60) Drink "Utica Club Ginger Ale" (10-12)
61) Weisbrod & Hess Philadelphia/Drink Peacock Beverages (15-20)

B-24
1) Berkeley Club Ginger Ale America's Best (3-5)
2) Coca-Cola (Script) (30-35)
3) Coca-Cola (Script) Bottling Co. Springfield, Mo. (40-50)
4) Drink Coca-Cola (Script) (30-35)
5) Drink Coca-Cola (Script) in Bottles (2 Var (A) Large Letters (B) Small Letters) (30-35)
6) Drink Coca-Cola (Script) in Bottles Hopkinsville, Ky. (2 Var (A) Large Letters (B) Small Letters) (30-35)
7) Dr. Pepper (40-50)
8) Ask for Fleck's Quality Beverages Since 1856 (3-5)
9) Lotz Dry Ginger Ale Binghamton, N. Y. (3-5)
10) Mission Bottling Co. Gilroy, Calif./Same (15-20)
11) Drink Morning Glory Whole Tomato Beverage (3-5)
12) Drink Mundorff's Beverages (3-5)
13) Rock Spring Water Ginger Ale (3-5)
14) Ask for Simpson Spring Beverages (3-5)

B-25
1) Drink Hyball Ginger Ale All Ginger Mfg. by Sethness Co. - Chicago, Ill.-/True Fruit Concord Grape Soda (15-20)

B-27
1) Lone Star Health Drink Fergus Beverage Co. (FB Co. Logo) (25-30)

B-29
1) Coca-Cola (Script) in Bottles/Drink Goldelle Ginger Ale (25-30)
2) Coca-Cola (Script) in Bottles/When Thirsty Try a Bottle (25-30)
3) La Plata Bottling Works, Durango, Colo. (5-8)
4) The J.B. St. Clair Muscatine Bottling Works, Muscatine, Iowa. (5-8)

B-30
1) Arcana Beverages Phone 4-2541 Williams & Buchele Peoria, Ill. (10-12)
2) Coca-Cola (Script) Bot. Wks. Murfreesboro, Tenn. Phone 60. Coal Phone 31 (50-60)
3) Drink Coca-Cola (Script) Bethlehem Bottling Works, Inc. (50-60)
4) Drink Coca-Cola (Script) in Bottles (50-60)
5) Drink Coca-Cola (Script) Coca-Cola (Script) Bottling Works, Incorporated Bethlehem, Pa. (50-60)
6) Crescent Star Pale Dry Ginger Ale (10-12)
7) Drink Dr. Brown's "One and Only One"/Celery Tonic (15-20)
8) Eagle Soft Drink Co. So. Milwaukee Phone 27-W (10-12)
9) Holland Dry and Light Rock Ginger Ale (10-12)
10) Husting's Soft Drinks Phone Grand 844 (10-12)
11) Kirsch's Beverages (10-12)
12) Lipsey's Products Co. Chicago U. S. A. the World's Greatest Tonic (10-12)
13) Lambert's Nehi Bottling Company Phone 780 (25-30)
14) Drink Oertel's Carbonated Beverages (25-30)
15) Wentz Orange Crush Co. Phone Hemlock 6886 (25-30)
16) Ozaukee Springs Bottling Co. Port Washington, Wis. Phone 52 (10-12)
17) Compliments of Raleigh Pepsi-Cola (Block) Bottling Co. (60-75)
18) Schmeltzer Bros. Soft Drinks are good and good for you Pottsville, Pa. (10-12)
19) R.G. Sinclair Bottler Galesburg, Ill. (10-12)
20) For Health's Sake drink So Good Ciardi & Co. Dover, N. J. (10-12)
21) Tip Top Bottling Co. (St Louis, Mo) (10-12)
22) Zeisler's Bottling Works Phone 350 (St Charles, Mo) (10-12)

B-31
1) Bellingham Bottling Works Bellingham, Wash. (30-35)

B-32
1) Drink Abendschan Bros. Soda Water Lamar, Colo. (20-25)
2) Drink Coca-Cola (Script)/Bottled in Charleston, S. C. (75-100)
3) Manhattan Coca-Cola (Block) Bottling Co./Wholesale Candy Beverages (75-100)

4) John Graf Co./Grafs Beverages the best what gives (15-20)
5) John Graf Co. the Genuine Ginger Ale/Jamaica (15-20)
6) Mt. Zircon Spring Water Co. Rumford, Maine/Mt. Zircon Ginger Champagne (15-20)
7) Superior Ginger Ale none better/Jazz & Jes-So for Thirst? (20-25)
8) Ten Penny Dry (15-20)
9) Ute Chief Manitou Ginger Ale/Ute Chief Manitou Mineral Water (20-25)

B-34
1) "Everybody's Drinken It" Lemon-Kola (20-25)

B-35
1) Butte Bottlers Supply 112 So. Main Phone 2522 (15-20)
2) Coca-Cola (Script) Bottling Works Wooster, O./Emil C. Arff, Prop. Phone 12422 (40-50)
3) Great Falls Bottlers Supply Co. a Complete Line of Bottlers Supplies 107-109 4th St. So. Phone 9997 (15-20)
4) Hollywood Dry Pale Ginger Ale (10-12)
5) Ask for Kist Mixers (8-10)
6) Original "Manitou" Beverages/Sparkling Water Lime Rickey Ginger Ale (Pale Dry) (8-10)
7) "Mixes Well" The Windsor Dry Ginger Ale Co. Toledo, O. (8-10)

B-36
1) White Owl Mixing Ginger Ale

B-40
1) Nu-Icy flavor you can't forget (Fatter Curved Bottle) (12-15)
2) Nu-Grape a flavor you cant forget (Fatter Curved Bottle) (12-15)
3) Pepsi-Cola (Script) (Pepsi-Cola 5 Times) (Bottle)/"America's Biggest Value" (12-15)
4) Pepsi=Cola (Script) Refreshing Healthful Pepsi=Cola Famous for Over 30 Years a Sparkling Bracing Beverage (Bottle)/"America's Biggest Nickel's Worth" (12-15)

B-41
1) Silver Springs Beverages Madison, Wis. (10-12)

B-42
1) Chero-Cola there's none so good 5c (15-20)
2) Drink Chero-Cola there's none so good 5c/If Lost-Finder Please Return to Chero-Cola. Bot. Co. (15-20)
3) Drink Coca-Cola (Script) in Bottles/Delicious and Refreshing (35-40)
4) Double Eagle Ginger Beer is Absolutely Pure/Double Eagle Ginger Beer Registered 8 oz. (Bottle) (25-30)
5) Compliments of Key-Stone Spring, East Poland, Me. E.H. Pratt, Prop. (Left-Handed) (12-15)
6) Drink "London Dry" Pale Ginger Ale (8-10)
7) Milwaukee Home Beverage Sup. Co. 4021 St. Claire Ave. M. Miller, Prop. (8-10)
8) Monarch Beverage Co. Chicago Chi-Dry Pale Ginger Ale (8-10)
9) Saegertown (8-10)

B-48
1) Compliments of Centennial Bottling Wks. Coshocton, Ohio (12-15)

B-49
1) Compliments John Harvilla Minersville/Merry Xmas Happy New Year 1928-29 (15-20)

B-53
1) Fort Dodge Bottling Works, Phone 174/We sell Sterilized Drinking Water. (12-15)

B-65
1) Compliments of Natural Dry Corp. Rochester, N. Y./Above all drink Natural Dry. (10-12)

B-75
1) Country Club Pale Ginger Ale Newton, Mass. (25-30)

B-501
1) Buffalo Rock Ginger Ale (15-20)

B-502
1) Nesbitt's (10-12)

B-503
1) Alexander Bottling Co. "Better Bottled Beverages" Falls City, Nebraska (20-25)
2) Open your Bottle of Hollywood Dry Pale Ginger Ale Bottled in Bond (20-25)

B-504
1) Original "Manitou" Sparkling Water and Pale Dry Ginger Ale (25-30)

B-505
1) Apollinaris (12-15)

C-3
1) The Berlin Bottling Works (10-12)
2) Chi-Dry Pale Ginger Ale Monarch Beverage Co. Chicago (10-12)

C-5
1) Pablo made by Pabst Milwaukee/Pablo the Happy Hoppy Drink (5-8)

C-6
1) Clicquot Club Ginger Ale aged 6 mos. (Baby Holding Bottle) (5-8)

C-7
1) "Canada Dry" the Champagne of Ginger Ales (2 Var (A) Spinner Dot (B) Raised Ridge) (3-5)
2) Diamond Ginger Ale the best since 1865/Same (3-5)
3) Mission Dry/Same (3-5)
4) Utica Club Pilsener-Wuerzburger it's in the taste-Pale Dry Ginger Ale/Same (5-8)

C-9
1) Aren Mineral Spring Water Co. (3-5)
2) Buck the Beer-Y Beverage (3-5)
3) C and C Ginger Ale (3-5)
4) "Canada Dry"/The Champagne of Ginger Ales (Spinner) (5-8)
5) Canoc Ginger Ale (Spinner) (3-5)
6) Enno Sander (St Louis, Mo) (3-5)
7) Grafs the best what gives (3-5)
8) Husting's Soft-Drinks (Spinner) (3-5)
9) Drink Moxie (Spinner) (20-25)
10) Orange Fizz Silver King Ale (3-5)
11) Saratoga Vichy Water/(Sv Logo) (Spinner) (3-5)
12) White Rock (Spinner) (3-5)

C-10
1) Drink Big-Ben quality Beverages (3-5)
2) Bruckner Beverages Inc. New York City (3-5)
3) Drink Grafs Beverages Phone Mitchell 3500/Carbonated Beverages "The Best Since 1873" (3-5)
4) Drink Grafs Beverages Phone Orchard 8800/Carbonated Beverages "The Best Since 1873" (3-5)
5) Grafs the best what gives (3-5)

C-11
1) Atlanta Ice & Bottling Co. Veribest & Royal Beverage (15-20)
2) Drink Big Ben Beverages (3-5)
3) Drink Big Ben quality Beverages (10-12)
4) Big Chief Bottling Co. formerly The Whistle Bottling Co. Denver, Colo. (10-12)

5) Drink Bon Ton quality Bottled Beverages Phone Monroe 4988 (3-5)
6) Drink bottled Coca-Cola (Script)/B.P.O.E. (Head of Elk) (40-50)
7) Drink Coca-Cola (Script)/B.P.O.E. (Head of Elk) (40-50)
8) Drink Coca-Cola (Script) in Sterilized Bottles (40-50)
9) Confain Bottling Works Williamsport, Pa. (3-5)
10) Dupo Bottling Works Dupo, Ill. (3-5)
11) Glen Rock Bottling Works Phone-Maj.405 Waukegan, Ill. (3-5)
12) Drink Grafs Beverages Phone Mitchell 3500/Carbonated Beverages "The Best Since 1873" (3-5)
13) Drink Grafs Beverages Phone Orchard 8800/The best what gives White Soda Ginger Ales (3-5)
14) Hydrox Ginger Ale Pale Extra Dry/Hydrox Beverages Every Drop Pure Phone—Calumet 5500 (3-5)
15) Drink Hygrade Products Lindell 3331 (St Louis, Mo) (3-5)
16) Husting's Carbonated Beverages/Same (3-5)
17) Imperial Pale Dry Ginger Ale Oakland, Cal. (3-5)
18) Jakes Purity-Brand Beverages Warren, Ohio (3-5)
19) New Century Beverage Co Pale Dry Niagara Ginger Ale (3-5)
20) Radio Club Pale Dry Ginger Ale Bostelmann Chicago (3-5)
21) Roxo (5-8)
22) Valley Park Bottling Co. Phone V. P. 56 Valley Park Mo. (3-5)
23) Westphal Ginger Ale-Root Beer Phones Euclid 252 Forest 2337 (3-5)
24) You will like White-Wood Ginger-Ale Root Beer/Compliments of Liggett Drug Stores Inc. (3-5)

C-12
1) Buffalo Rock Ginger Ale (5-8)
2) Canada Dry (1-2)
3) Canada Dry/Same (1-2)
4) Clicquot Club (Pronounced Kleeko) Beverages (3-5)
5) Cloverdale Soft Drinks/Same (3-5)
6) Coca-Cola (Script) 'Drink of the "Fans"' (in Ball Bat) 'League' (in Baseball) (75-100)
7) Confair's (Bottle) (3-5)
8) High Rock (3-5)
9) Enjoy Kist Beverages (3-5)
10) Krim's "Pale Dry" (3-5)
11) London Dry Ginger Ale Co. Wilmington, Del. (3-5)
12) Mercer Beverages (3-5)
13) The Minnehaha Co. Spring Water/Silver Fizz (5-8)
14) Drink Mission Beverages (3-5)
15) Morgan's Ginger Ale (Bottle)/Chickering 4-3464 (3-5)
16) Drink Nesbitts (5-8)
17) Pepsi (Block) (12-15)
18) Schille's Bottled Beverages Columbus, O. (3-5)
19) 7 Up demand the original (5-8)
20) Drink Spur a Cola Beverage (3-5)
21) Spur it's a finer Cola/Same (3-5)
22) Drink Squirt/Same (3-5)
23) Tumble Brook Beverages Hartford Conn. (3-5)

C-13
1) America Dry Ginger Ale New York (3-5)
2) Banko's dial 7-3983 (3-5)
3) Barco Brand Ginger Ale (Bottle) Pale Extra Dry/B. A. Railton Co. Chicago-Milwaukee (Bottle) (3-5)
4) Call for Bayer's Beverages (3-5)
5) Pep up with Bayers Beverages Peoples Bottling Co. J.E. 7421 (3-5)
6) Oh Boy Oh Boy Bon-Ton quality Beverages Monroe 4988 (3-5)
7) Cal Cola Cal (Bottle)/Same (3-5)
8) Canada Dry (1-2)
9) Canada Dry Tru-Ade/Sparkling Bond Beverages Phone 2-5147 (5-8)
10) Capitol Beverage Co. drink Smile (3-5)
11) Cloverdale Soft Drinks (3-5)
12) Drink Coca-Cola (Script) in Bottles (40-50)
13) Enjoy Coca-Cola (Script) Trade Mark (10-12)
14) Have a Coke and Smile (10-12)

15) Confair Bottling Co. Williamsport, Pa. (3-5)
16) Country Club Ginger Ale/Country Club Lime and Lithia (3-5)
17) Drink Dr. Pepper (Script) (75-100)
18) Dubois Special Pale Dry Ginger Ale (Bottle) Dubois (On Neck Label)/"Original" drink the best Dubois Beverages Phone 53 (12-15)
19) Faygo Beverages Detroit (3-5)
20) Drink Golden Eagle Beverages (3-5)
21) Grapette Rice Bottling Co. (8-10)
22) Hydrox Beverages every drop pure (3-5)
23) Drink Jack Frost (3-5)
24) Drink Kawrox Products (3-5)
25) Drink the best Long Pine Beverages (3-5)
26) Drink Love's Dream dedicated to the American woman 5c/ The Sun Rise Flavor Co. Tazewell Virginia (25-30)
27) Morgan's Ginger Ale (Bottle)/Cumberland 6-0300 (3-5)
28) Moxie and Virginia Dare Worcester 5-9735 (20-25)
29) Orange Crush (Bottle)/Orange Crush (10-12)
30) Orange Crush/Orange Crush Carbonated Beverage (2 Var (A) Short Bottle (B) Tall Bottle) (10-12)
31) Orange Crush Pure Orange Juice (10-12)
32) Pepsi=Cola (Script) (20-25)
33) Pepsi=Cola (Script) 12 oz 5c (20-25)
34) Qualtop Beverages are Pure Main 66 (3-5)
35) Roxo and Arcadian Beverages (3-5)
36) Saratoga Geyser Water Spa (3-5)
37) Saratoga Vichy (3-5)
38) Fresh up with 7up (in Logo) (5-8)
39) Drink Stoner Bros. Lime Rickey (3-5)
40) Subley Beverage Co. Richmond, Va. (3-5)
41) Drink Sun Punch Phone Riley 1675 (3-5)
42) Drink Tumble Brook Ginger Ale Hartford, Conn. Tel. G-8581 (3-5)
43) "Vic" Beverages R.G.D. Trade Mark/"Vic" Club Soda R.G.D. Trade Mark (3-5)

C-14
1) Canada Dry (1-2)

C-16
1) Bubble Up (in Bubbles) (3-5)
2) Bubble Up (in Bubbles) Wholesome Refreshment (3-5)
3) Frank's it's the best Fruit Beverages (3-5)
4) Green Spot (1-2)
5) Green Spot Fruit Juice Beverages (1-2)
6) Drink O-So Grape Dextro Delicious/Same (3-5)
7) Drink! Squirt (3-5)

C-17
1) Canfield's Beverages (3-5)
2) Collegiate Shirts for the Coke*Set Coke is the Registered Trade Mark of the Coca Cola (Block) Co./Made of a Pacific Fabric (20-25)
3) Crystal Club Beverages/Same (3-5)
4) Frank's it's the best Fruit Beverages (3-5)
5) Great Bear Beverages (3-5)
6) Hall of Waters Beverages Excelsior Springs, Missouri (8-10)
7) La Vida Distinctive Beverages/"They're Naturally Better" (3-5)
8) London Dry the Topper (Pic of man in top hat) of All Drinks (3-5)
9) Drink O-So Grape Dextro Delicious/Same (3-5)
10) Pepsi=Cola (Script) (25-30)
11) Queen-O (3-5)
12) Roma Beverages by Roma since 1907 8 Delicious Flavors (Bottle) (5-8)
13) "Fresh Up" with 7 Up (3-5)
14) Drink! Squirt. (3-5)
15) Squirt Allen Bottling Co. (5-8)
16) Top-Notch Beverages (3-5)
17) Verigoud Soda/Stella Artois (3-5)
18) Virginia Dare Beverages (3-5)
19) Drink Zip Zip for Life (Bottle) (3-5)

C-18
1) Quality Atlantic Beverages Port Chester, N. Y. (3-5)
2) Evervess Sparkling Water (3-5)
3) Drink Pepsi-Cola (Script) (15-20)
4) "Fresh Up" with 7 Up (5-8)
5) Towne Club Beverages it's Great Pop (3-5)
6) Vernor's Ginger Ale 80th Anniversary (5-8)
7) Vernor's Ginger Ale 80th Anniversary (Standing Elf)/Vernor's Ginger Ale Deliciously Different Since 1866 (Elf Pushing Barrel) Flavor Mellowed in Wood 4 years (on end of barrel) (5-8)
8) White Rock Sparkling Beverages (Lady on Rock) (5-8)

C-19
1) Clicquot Club (Pronounced Kleek-O) Beverages (Pic of Eskimo) (5-8)
2) Drink Dad's Old Fashioned Root Beer (12-15)
3) Drink Dr Swetts Root Beer (Dr Swett's Root Beer Bottle Cap) (8-10)
4) Drink Double Cola (5-8)
5) Hires (20-25)
6) Enjoy Kist Beverages (Kist Bottle) (5-8)
7) Drink Nesbitt's (3-5)
8) O-So Beverages drink O-So Beverages (3-5)
9) Drink Pepsi-Cola (Script) (15-20)
10) Drink Squirt (5-8)

C-27
1) Drink Coca-Cola (Script) in Bottles (40-50)
2) Drink Coca-Cola (Script) in Sterilized Bottles (40-50)

C-28
1) Calif. Beverage & Sup. Co. 523 Sixth St. Oakland, Cal. (5-8)

C-31
1) Drink "Bola"/Same (20-25)
2) Enno Sander Seltzer & Soda Co./Same (St Louis, Mo) (5-8)
3) Richfield Club Beverages (5-8)
4) Tommy Green Dry Ginger Ale/Gold Bond Lincoln 1400 (25-30)

C-34
1) Mission Beverages Naturally Good (3-5)
2) Drink Pepsi-Cola (Script) (15-20)
3) Quiky the Grapefruit-Lemon Refresher (3-5)
4) Enjoy Squirt (Squirt Boy) 1959 The Squirt Company (5-8)

C-36
1) Canada Dry/Same (1-2)
2) Drink Bottled Coca-Cola (Block)/Drink Orange Frost (35-40)
3) Edwards Bottling Co. Amarillo, Texas. (3-5)
4) Orange Crush/Orange Crush Kik Cola American Dry Gurds Hires (15-20)
5) Wishing Well Gingerale/Wishing Well Orange (3-5)

C-39
1) Ask for Pure Spring Ginger Ale/Pure Spring Co. Ottawa (8-10)

C-41
1) Canada Dry/Same (1-2)
2) Sunset Club Bottling Co. Oxford 5696/Sunset Club Bottling Co. 8862 Sunset Blvd. Sherman, Calif. (3-5)
3) Sussex Extra Dry Ginger Ale (5-8)

C-501
1) Drink Coca-Cola (Bottle)/Same (8-10)

D-1
1) Hydrox (5-8)

D-3
1) Apollo/Table Waters (5-8)
2) Coca-Cola (Block)/Same (75-100)

3) Goldwell/Apple Juice (5-8)
4) Hay's Lemonade/Same (5-8)

D-6
1) Moxie/Same (2 Var (A) Long Stopper (B) Short Stopper) (12-15)

D-11
1) Apollinaris/Same (12-15)

D-501
1) Hebe Ginger Ale (60-75)

D-502
1) Arrowhead and Puritas Waters (8-10)
2) Silver Springs Water (8-10)
3) Sparkletts drinking Table Beer (8-10)

D-503
1) Club Orange/Same (English Patent No Rd 702661) (8-10)

D-504
1) Coca-Cola (Block)/Same (English Patent No Rd 702661) (50-60)
2) Pepsi-Cola (Block)/Same (English Patent No Rd 702661) (40-50)

D-505
1) Coca-Cola (Block)/Same (English Patent No Rd 811274) (50-60)
2) Corona/Family Drinks (English Patent No Rd 811274) (8-10)

E-1
1) Almanaris Waukesha Water/Super Carbonated Lithiated (3-5)
2) New Home of Bay View Sodas 2975A So. Chase Ave. SH.0803/Same (3-5)
3) Black Bear Beverages it's a bear of a drink/Black Bear Beverages made with Spring Water (3-5)
4) Drink Cleo Cola Vess Beverages/Same (3-5)
5) Drink Dr. Pepper at 10-2-4 O'Clock/Same (35-40)
6) La Vida Beverages deliciously different/La Vida Beverages everybody's choice (3-5)
7) Drink Mission Orange Tel. J-2135/Hy-Grade Beverage Co. Racine, Wis. (3-5)
8) Pepsi Cola (Block) a Nickel Drink-Worth a Dime/Pepsi Cola Distributing Co. Phone Joliet 9421-Joliet, Ill. (35-40)
9) Pepsi=Cola (Script)/"Pepsi-Cola" Bottling Co. Lynchburg (35-40)
10) Pepsi=Cola (Script) Hygrade Soda/Phone Fr.3330-Je.6262 Tower Grove at the Exp. Highway (35-40)
11) Reimer's Beverages Telephone 2-0200 (3-5)
12) Royal Crown Cola Par-T-Pak/Nehi Beverage Co. (10-12)
13) Royal Crown Cola "Tops in Taste"/Same (3-5)
14) Enno Sander Seltzer and Soda Co./Richfield Club Beverages (St Louis, Mo) (3-5)
15) Sanitary Soda Water Co. Phone GR. 3620 (3-5)
16) Drink 7up the "Fresh Up" Drink/7up peps you up 7up cools you off (10-12)
17) Shamrock Brand Soda Water good "Mixer"/Columbia Mineral Water Co. St. Louis Phone Grand 9393 (3-5)
18) Silco Waukesha Water Beverages/Same (3-5)
19) Sparkeeta Beverages made from Sparkletts/Root Beer Table Water Club Soda Lemo-Lime (3-5)
20) Standard Bottling Co. Glacier Club Beverages (3-5)
21) Drink Tip Top Soda Water made of Pure Cane Sugar/Tip Top Bottling Co. Chestnut 1260 1428 N. Jeff. Ave. St. Louis, Mo. (5-8)
22) Drink Tip Top Soda Water made of Pure Cane Sugar Phone Chestnut 1260/Tip Top Bottling Co. 1428 No. Jeff. Ave. St. Louis, Mo. (5-8)
23) Thirsty? Just Whistle Phone Jeff. 0590/Vess Beverages the Best "Mixer" (8-10)

E-2
1) Arnold's Better Grade/Same (10-12)
2) Belfast Brand Ginger Ale/Drink Orange Crush (12-15)
3) Berry Spring Mineral Water Co./Same (3-5)
4) Billy Baxter Club Soda/Billy Baxter Ginger Ale (3-5)
5) Billy Baxter Ginger Ale/B.B. Club Soda Temple Water (3-5)
6) Caproni's Soda Providence, R.I./The Hebe Co. Providence, R.I. (10-12)
7) Cloverdale Ginger Ale Cloverdale Water./Cloverdale Spring Co. Baltimore, Md. (3-5)
8) Conner made Ginger Pure and Wholesome/Conner Bottling Wks. Newfields, N. H. (3-5)
9) Fenway Pale Dry/Golden Dome Beverages (5-8)
10) Kalak Water Co. Brooklyn, N. Y./Strongest Alkaline Water Known (3-5)
11) Maxwell Pale Dry/Star Beverages Philadelphia, Pa. (10-12)
12) Maydale Beverages Maynard Mass. Tel90/An investment on good taste (3-5)
13) Drink Moxie Clean/Wholesome Refreshing (10-12)
14) Milton Spring Beverages/Chas. C. Copeland Co. Milton Mass. (3-5)
15) Ochee Spring Water Company/High Class Beverages (3-5)
16) Pureoxia Ginger Ale/Same (3-5)
17) Seltzer's Ginger Ale/Seltzer & Rydholm Auburn & Portland (5-8)
18) Drink 7up for the 7 Hangovers/Seven-Up for the Stomach Sake (10-12)
19) Sierra Club Ginger Ale/Henry-Brown Co. Glendale, Calif. (5-8)
20) Sierra Club Ginger Ale/Sierra Club Bev. Co. Glendale Calif. (5-8)
21) Simpson Spring Beverages/Same (3-5)
22) University Club Ginger Ale/Dennis Bot'g Works Ellsworth, Me. (3-5)
23) Vernor's Ginger Ale Detroit, Mich. (5-8)
24) Warwick Club Ginger Ale/Same (5-8)

E-3
1) Drink Booth's Beverages try Booth's Cola/Same (5-8)
2) Cope's quality Beverages (3-5)
3) Drink Dr. Pepper at 10, 2 & 4 O'Clock/Drink a bite to eat at 10, 2 & 4 O'Clock (3-5)
4) Drink Dr. Pepper Energy Up/Drink a bite to eat at 10, 2 & 4 O'Clock (5-8)
5) Drink Dr. Pepper at 10, 2 & 4 O'Clock/Same (5-8)
6) Kalak Water Co. of New York, Inc./A delicious Alkaline Mineral Water (5-8)
7) Pepsi-Cola Hygrade Sodas/Same (25-30)
8) Drink 7up all ways 7up blends best/7up quenches thirst all ages like 7up (10-12)
9) Silver Brook Beverages (3-5)
10) Compliment Stoner's Ginger Ale (3-5)
11) Tip Top Soda All Flavors/Same (5-8)

E-4
1) Arcadia Dry Ginger Ale Sparkling Water/Vernor's Ginger Ale (10-12)
2) Barkley's Beverages/Phone Uniontown 371 (3-5)
3) Drink Batchelor's bottled Sodas/"Keep Me Busy" (3-5)
4) Beaufont Dry Ginger Ale/Climax Dry Ginger Ale (5-8)
5) Belfast Dry Ginger Ale/Belfast Sparkling Water (5-8)
6) Belfast Ginger Ale/Belfast Sparkling Water (5-8)
7) Belfast Ginger Ale Doug. 0547/New Century Bottling Co. (5-8)
8) Berghoff Extra Dry Ginger Ale/Drink Berghoff Fort Wayne, Ind. (10-12)
9) Drink Big Boy Beverages/Same (3-5)
10) Drink Bireley's/Non-Carbonated Beverages (3-5)
11) Bobby Burns Ginger Ale/Blue Wing Beverages (3-5)
12) Bright Spot Bottling Co. Milwaukee/Delicious Sodas (3-5)
13) Bruckner's Beverages/U-No-Us (3-5)
14) Chi-Dry Pale Ginger Ale/Monarch Beverage Co. Phone Canal 6500 (3-5)

15) Chicago Beverage Co. Phone Rockwell 5010/De Luxe a Pure Beverage (3-5)
16) Climax Dry Ginger Ale/Drink Tru-Ade (10-12)
17) Club Royal Beverages/H. G. Degenring (3-5)
18) Club Royal Beverages/Same (3-5)
19) Coca-Cola (Script)/Same (40-50)
20) Coca-Cola (Block) Bottling Co. Dubuque/Same (40-50)
21) Drink Coca-Cola (Script)/Delicious-Refreshing (50-60)
22) Drink Coca-Cola (Script)/In Sterilized Bottles (50-60)
23) Oklahoma Coca-Cola (Script) Bottling Co./Same (40-50)
24) Milwaukee Coca-Cola (Script) Bottling Co./615 Cherry Street Marquette 0974 (40-50)
25) Coleman's Ginger Ale/Noted for its Flavor (3-5)
26) Crystal Rock Beverage Co./Reading-Lancaster (3-5)
27) Crystal Rock Water Co., Inc./Owners of Penn Bottling Works (3-5)
28) Crystal Soda Water Co./425 Franklin Ave. Scranton, Pa. (5-8)
29) Double Eagle Ginger Beer/Double Eagle Bottling Co. (Screwdriver Tip) (3-5)
30) Dr. Brown's Celery Tonic/Schultz sparkling Beverages (2 Var (A) Round Top (B) Squared Top) (3-5)
31) Drink Dr. Pepper (Script)/Good for Life (60-75)
32) Duffy's Delicious Drinks/Phone Tabor 6259 (2 Var (A) Screwdriver Tip (B) No Screwdriver Tip) (3-5)
33) Eagle Soft Drink Co. Phone 27/Drink Eagle Ginger Ale (3-5)
34) Epping's Drinks since 1863/Same (3-5)
35) Fox Snappy Drinks/Fox Lime Rickey Fox Ginger Ale (3-5)
36) Fox Snappy Drinks/Same (3-5)
37) Fritz Soda Water Co./Phone HE. 0575 (3-5)
38) Gideon Stolz Co. Salem, Ore./Drink G-S Bottled Beverages (3-5)
39) Golden Drops/Two Rivers Beverage Co. Two Rivers, Wis. (5-8)
40) Golden Dwarf/Ginger Ale (Screwdriver Tip) (8-10)
41) Drink Golden Star Ginger Ale/Golden Star Bottling Works (5-8)
42) Demand Grafs Beverages/The best what gives (8-10)
43) Graham's "Better Beverages"/Same (3-5)
44) The Grand-Pop Bottling Co. Phones Cherry 0727 & Parkway 4835/Distinguish the best from the rest (3-5)
45) Green Mountain Ginger Ale Co./Phone 3894 Albert Croux (3-5)
46) N.G. Gurnsey & Co. Keene, N. H./Quality Beverages (3-5)
47) Herman's Bottling Works, Inc./Telephone Locust 5189 (8-10)
48) Hi-Dry Pale Ginger Ale/Monarch Beverage Co. Phone Canal 6500 (3-5)
49) Hoffman Beverages/Same (3-5)
50) Husting's Beverages/Same (3-5)
51) Hyklas Dry Ginger Ale The Distillata Company/Makes you glad you're thirsty (3-5)
52) Imperial Beverage Co./Same (3-5)
53) Indian Maid Ginger Ale/Gluek's Pilsener Pale (5-8)
54) K & F Bottling Co. 5415-17 Haverford Ave./Kamp Fire Beverages (3-5)
55) Kick's Beverages/Same (3-5)
56) Kohlman's quality Beverages/Kohlman's Beverages Phone J. 2193 (3-5)
57) Drink Klee's Sodas/Klee's Orange Klee's Grape (5-8)
58) Lafayette Beverages Inc. (3-5)
59) Lake Region Beverage Co./Same (3-5)
60) Lakeside Sodas/Same (3-5)
61) Lane's Cloudy Orangeade/Compliments Lane's Bottling Works (3-5)
62) Original Manitou/Natural Gas Carbonation makes it better naturally (5-8)
63) Mavis Pale Dry Ginger Ale/Mavis Bottling Co. (3-5)
64) McCarter's Pale Dry Ginger Ale/McCarter's Bottling Co. Philadelphia (5-8)
65) Mehler's Beverages/Same (3-5)
66) Meyer's quality Beverages/Meyer's Lime Rickey (3-5)
67) Meyer's quality Beverages/Same (3-5)
68) Meyer's quality Beverages San Francisco, Calif./Same (3-5)

69) Mohawk Beverages/For Particular People (3-5)
70) Monroe Bottling Works/Beverages (3-5)
71) Drink Moxie/Same (8-10)
72) Drink Moxie/Drink Pureoxia (8-10)
73) Drink Nehi/Meehan Bros. 400 W. Tus. Ave. Barberton, O. (15-20)
74) Massillon Nehi Co./227 Third St. N. W. Phone 7937 (15-20)
75) Nehi Bottling Co./Same (12-15)
76) Nehi Bottling Co. Gar. 8158/Same (12-15)
77) H. C. Nennich 2007-09 N. Hancock St./Beverage Specialist (5-8)
78) Nevin-Frank Co. Butte, Montana/Beverages (10-12)
79) New Century Lime Rickey/Doug. 0547 (5-8)
80) Drink Nic Nac 5c/Drink Jackson Brew 5c (15-20)
81) Norka Beverages (3-5)
82) Prague Nu-Icy Bottling Works/Dial 6-5312 Binghampton (5-8)
83) Nu-On Products Co. 1012 Mission St. San Francisco/Bottlers Supplies (3-5)
84) Oakland Club Lime Rickey Doug. 0547/Pioneer Beverages Ltd. (10-12)
85) Drink Oertel's Carbonated Beverages/Drink Oertel's Real Lager (10-12)
86) Drink Orange Crush it's Real Orange Juice/Say it by it's full name to avoid substitutions (15-20)
87) Orange-Crush/Pepsi=Cola (Script) (30-35)
88) Orange Crush Doug. 0547/New Century Lime Rickey Doug. 0547 (10-12)
89) Orange Crush, Nehi Ozarka Water/Eagle Bottling Co. 1903 Cherry-HA.5131 (12-15)
90) Orange Crush PIED. 0674/S & S Lime Rickey PIED. 0674 (10-12)
91) Seal Rock Orange Crush Co./Spring Water used Exclusively (10-12)
92) Drink Pep/Albert's Products Co. (3-5)
93) Drink Pepsi=Cola (Block) in Bottles/Oertels Carbonated Beverages (30-35)
94) Drink Pepsi=Cola (Script)/Same (15-20)
95) Pepsi-Cola (15-20)
96) Pepsi-Cola (Block) Bottling Co./Arrow Beer (20-25)
97) Pete's Peppy Pop/Sunset-Orange-Kist (5-8)
98) Poudre Valley Bot. Wks./Phone 1134 (3-5)
99) Queen City Beverages/For Particular People (3-5)
100) Drink Rader's Root Beer/"A Drink of Merit" (3-5)
101) S & S Ginger Ale/Imperial Beverage Co. (3-5)
102) Saegertown Old Style Ginger Ale/Aristocrat Extra Dry Ginger Ale (5-8)
103) Schille's Grape/Peter Schille 121 E. Main, Columbus, O. (8-10)
104) Schneider's Grand Prize and Ginger Ale/Brooklyn, N. Y. (10-12)
105) Schneider's Grand Prize Ginger Ale/171-183 Stockholm St. Brooklyn, N. Y. (10-12)
106) Schneider's Grand Prize Ginger Ale/Phone Foxcroft 4-8440-1-2 Brooklyn, N. Y. (10-12)
107) Seven Up—- Moxie/Lambert Distributing Co. (5-8)
108) Shogo Lithia Springs Co./Quality Beverages (3-5)
109) Silver King Brewed Dry Ginger Ale/Silver King Sparkling Water (3-5)
110) Silver Plume Beverages/Phones: Austin 2782 Euclid 4555 (3-5)
111) Tacoma Dry Ginger Ale/The Prince of Ales (3-5)
112) Drink Temple Hill Dry Ginger Ale/Baker Bottling Works, Inc. (5-8)
113) Drink Try-Me/Same (8-10)
114) Drink Wee/Havana Bottling Works (5-8)
115) Whistle Bottling Co. 807 Franklin Ave., Youngstown, O./ Everything in Soft Drinks (10-12)
116) Whistle Bottling Co. Los Angeles/Same (10-12)

E-5
1) American Soda Water Co. 661-67 South 11th St. Newark 3, N. J. (American Flag) Bigelow 3-5555-5537 (3-5)

2) Bartle's Bartle's (3-5)

3) Bellingham Beverage Phone 401 (3-5)

4) Canada Dry Products Budweiser-Fort Pitt -666- Castle Distributing Co. 206 S. Jefferson St. (10-12)

5) Cheer Up Cheer Up (in Bottle) Ferd. Winkler Bottling Co. 121 S. First St. Belleville, Ill. Phone 730 (10-12)

6) (Coca-Cola Bottle) Avenue Grocery Meats-Poultry-Beverages Sample L-9 (40-50)

7) Drink Coca-Cola (Script) in Bottles Serves Hospitality in the Home (40-50)

8) Compliments Tell City Coca-Cola (Script) Bottling Co., Inc. (Coca-Cola Bottle) (40-50)

9) Enjoy Coca-Cola (Script) (40-50)

10) Dad's Root Beer (10-12)

11) Drink Dad's Old Fashioned Root Beer Dad's Root Beer Bottling Co. 1202 N. 2nd Street Stevens Point, Wis. Tel. 2009 (10-12)

12) Compliments The Dalles Soda Works, Inc. Your Favorite Beverages 800 East Second St. The Dalles, Oregon Phone 2875 (5-8)

13) Dr. Pepper (In Logo) Beckley, WV (60-75)

14) Wake Up Your Taste Dr. Pepper Lenoir City (60-75)

15) Easton Distributing Co. Ale—Beer—Soft Drinks Ballantine's-Bavarian 2118 Liberty St., Easton, Pa. Phone 7963 (10-12)

16) High Hat Beverages Krystal Bottlers', Inc. 111-113-115 So. 1st Ave. Sioux Falls, S.D. (5-8)

17) Ju-C-Orange specify Krim Pale Dry (5-8)

18) Enjoy Kist Beverages Colonial Bottling Works 348-350 East Penn St. Norristown, Pa. (5-8)

19) Enjoy Kist Beverages Hettinger Kist Bottling Company Hettinger, North Dakota (5-8)

20) Enjoy Kist Beverages (Kist Beverages in Logo) (5-8)

21) Enjoy Kist Beverages Old Faithful Beverage Co., Inc. Idaho Falls, Idaho (5-8)

22) Enjoy Kist Beverages Seven Up Bottling Company, Inc. 309 South Victoria Pueblo, Colorado (5-8)

23) Kist Bottling Co. Telephone 3622 124 Fourth St. Rome, N. Y. (5-8)

24) Mission Orange Bottling Co. 109 South "A" Street McAlester, Okla. Phone 683 Pop Kola (5-8)

25) Greetings from Nehi Bottling Co. Newport News, Va. Bottlers of Royal Crown Cola (15-20)

26) Nehi Bottling Co. Wilmington, N. C. Phone 2340 Royal Crown (Bottle) (20-25)

27) Nesbitt Bottling Co. Frank Wurnig "Fine Beers and Beverages" Phone 25 Winner, S.D. (15-20)

28) Tickle your Tongue with O-SO Grape Rich 1 Dextrose O-SO Grape Bottling Co. 1202 N. 2nd Street Stevens Point, Wis. Tel. 2009 (5-8)

29) Orange-Crush (Crushito on Top of Man) (35-40)

30) Bottlers of Pepsi-Cola (Block) – Squirt "Elk Spring" Elk Spring Beverage Company Wakefield, Mass. Tel. Cyrs. 9-1433 – 9-3441 (25-30)

31) Distributor Pepsi-Cola (Block), Cloverdale Soft Drinks B.H. Koch Lewisburg, Pa. Phone 5-7111 (25-30)

32) Drink Pepsi=Cola everyday Pepsi-Cola Dist. Co. Hutchinson, Kans. (25-30)

33) (Pepsi-Cola Bottle) Pepsi Cola (Script) Bottling Co. Columbus, Miss. Sample No.9 (25-30)

34) (Pepsi-Cola Bottle) (7up Bottle) The Maple City Ice Co. quality Beverages (40-50)

35) (Pepsi-Cola Bottle Cap) Carl W. Albrecht Beverage Distributor 3407 Duquesne Ave. West Mifflin Boro Ho. 1-8620 (25-30)

36) (Pepsi-Cola Bottle Cap) Pepsi-Cola (Block) Bottling Company of Clarksdale 312 Sunflower PH. 1110 (25-30)

37) Pepsi=Cola (Script) (25-30)

38) Pepsi=Cola (Script) Bottling Co. Dial CI 3-3691 207-209 N. Main St. Petersburg, W.Va. (25-30)

39) Pepsi=Cola (Script) Haaser's Produce Distributors of Beer and Beverages Main 1898 Fremont, O. (25-30)

40) The Pop Shoppe (5-8)

41) Minars 7 Up Bottling Co. Fergus Falls, Minn. (7 Up Bottle) (10-12)

42) Seven Up Bottling Co. Fresh Up with-7 Up Watertown, Wis. Janesville, Wis. (10-12)

43) You like it 7up (in Logo) it likes you Fred Winkler Bottling Co. Phone 730 (10-12)

44) Zip Co. Phone Humboldt 4100 Chicago an Excellent Drink (7 Up Bottle) Straight or Mixed (10-12)

45) Enjoy Sun Crest Beverages (5-8)

46) Enjoy Sun Crest Beverages (5-8)

47) Drink Sun Spot "Bottled Sunshine" (15-20)

48) Valley Park Bottling Co. Valley Park, Missouri Phone Valley Park-56 (5-8)

E-6

1) Belfast Dry Ginger Ale/Belfast Sparkling Water (3-5)

2) Bobbie Ale Soda Water/Golden Drops White Cap (3-5)

3) Bourbon (Pale Dry) Ginger Ale/The Grand-Pop Bottling Co. Phone Cherry 0727 (3-5)

4) Dai-Lee Beverage Quincy, Ill. (3-5)

5) Dr. Nut World Bottling Co. (15-20)

6) Faygo Beverages Detroit, Mich./Faygo Beverages Feigenson Bros. Co. (3-5)

7) Gordon Bottling Works Cobleskill, N. Y. (3-5)

8) Manhattan Bottling Works Phone West 206 (3-5)

9) Mascola Bottling Wks. "Top Notch Beverages" (3-5)

10) Nehi Bottling Co. Lynchburg, Va. (15-20)

11) Nehi Bottling Co. Poughkeepsie, N. Y./Royal Crown Cola Nehi & Par-T-Pak (15-20)

12) Nevin-Frank Co. Butte, Montana (10-12)

13) Harding's Pepsi-Cola (Block)/Same (20-25)

14) Silver Springs Ginger Ale/Same (3-5)

15) Sterling Spring Water Co. (3-5)

16) Drink Supreme Sodas/Supreme Bottling Co. Waukesha (3-5)

17) "Top Notch Beverages" Mascola Bottling Wks. (3-5)

18) Union Soda Water Co. St. Louis, Missouri (8-10)

19) Ute Chief Manitou Mineral Water (5-8)

20) Virginia Dare Sodas Wyandotte Beverage Co./Same (3-5)

E-7

1) Atlantic Beverage Co. Queen Cola Petersburg, Va. (12-15)

2) Bagdad Ginger Ale/Belmont "#" Select (5-8)

3) The Buckeye Producing Co Toledo, Ohio/Green Seal Beverages (12-15)

4) Coca-Cola (Block) Bottling Co. Warren, Ohio (30-35)

5) Coca-Cola (Script) in Bottles/Delicious Refreshing (10-12)

6) Drink "Howdy" Woodriver Bottling Works Phone 303r (5-8)

7) Majestic Ginger Ale (5-8)

8) Manhattan Bottling Works Phone West 206 (3-5)

9) The Mougey Ice & Beverage Co./Wooster, O. Phone 186 (10-12)

10) Say Nehi the taste tells (15-20)

11) Old Scotch Ginger Ale (5-8)

12) Orange-Crush Phone 4-1277 (10-12)

13) Pepper's Ginger Ale Ashland, Pa. (5-8)

14) Prima Company Beverages Chicago, Phone Lincoln 4302 (3-5)

15) Thirsty? Just Whistle Phone Jefferson 0590 (10-12)

16) Wagner's Bottling Works Phone Tri-City 154 (5-8)

17) Drink Was-Cott Ginger Ale/Same (10-12)

E-8

1) Berry Spring Pale Dry/Berry Spring Orange Dry (5-8)

2) Chelmsford Ginger Ale/Chelmsford Orangeale (5-8)

3) Chero-Cola 5c/Same (20-25)

4) Coca-Cola (Script) in Bottles/Delicious Refreshing (30-35)

5) Coca-Cola (Block) Bottling Company/Minneapolis Atlantic 2700 (40-50)

6) Diamond Ginger Ale/Same (5-8)

7) Excelsior Bottling Works/Schenectady NY (5-8)

8) Drink Gin-Cera 5c "It Gingers You Up" (12-15)

9) Drink Gin-Cera 5c "It Gingers You Up"/"Drink Gin-Cera in Bottles" (12-15)

10) John Harvilla Minersville, Pa./Soft Drinks Beer & Porter (10-12)

11) Hermann's Ginger Ale is Famous/Manf'g by A.G. Hermann Washington, D.C. (15-20)

12) Drink Hires in Bottles/Same (20-25)
13) Original "Manitou" Ginger Champagne/Original "Manitou" table water (10-12)
14) Drink Moxie drink Moxie/Same (8-10)
15) Drink Moxie drink Moxie/Drink Pureoxia drink Pureoxia (8-10)
16) Nutro Ginger Ale/Same (5-8)
17) Pepsi-Cola (Block) Co Charlotte, N. C./Same (40-50)
18) Reif's Special/Same (15-20)
19) Standard Bottling Co Denver Colo/Same (8-10)
20) Sussex Ginger Ale/Same (5-8)
21) Whistle Bott Co Denver (12-15)

E-9
1) American Bottling Co./Pure Sodas Grand Forks N.D. (5-8)
2) Anaconda Products/Anaconda, Montana (12-15)
3) Atlantic Btg. Wks. Best Quality./Same (5-8)
4) Avon Springs Bottling Wks./Pure Sodas Beer-Ale-Porter (5-8)
5) Bernard Botg. Wks. Marine, Ill./Quality Soda in Sterilized Bottles (5-8)
6) Drink Buck "First For Thirst"/National Beverage Company, Chicago. (5-8)
7) Canada Dry Canada Dry/Same (3-5)
8) Drink Caton Ale Pale Dry Golden/Same (5-8)
9) Drink Chero Cola none so good/Chero Cola Botg. Co. Greenville, S. C. (15-20)
10) Christo-Colo Christo-Colo/Same (Richmond, Va) (8-10)
11) Citra-Cola. Citra-Cola/Same (8-10)
12) Clicquot Club Ginger Ale/Same (5-8)
13) Coca Cola (Block) Botg. Co. Beatrice, Nebr./Same (35-40)
14) Refreshing Drink Coca-Cola (Block)/Invigorating Drink Coca-Cola (Block) (40-50)
15) Cooks Mineral Water/The Water of Quality (5-8)
16) Crystal Soda Water Co. Scranton, Pa./Same (5-8)
17) Deborah Ginger Ale/Deborah Root Beer (5-8)
18) Electrified Ginger Ale/Electrified Beverages (5-8)
19) J.C. Fullerton, Fairfax, Minn./Pure Soft Drinks, Ciders, Pop, Etc. (5-8)
20) Golden Pheasant Ginger Ale & Sodas/Pelham Club Cream City Prod. Co. (5-8)
21) Drink Gosman's Ginger Ale./Baltimore, Maryland. (3-5)
22) Grafs (3-5)
23) Graino a Real Beverage/Grain Juice Co. Dallas, Texas. (5-8)
24) Drink "Grapico" naturally good./J. Grossman's Sons New Orleans, La. (8-10)
25) Drink Indian Club Ginger Ale/Same (5-8)
26) Drink King Cola./Virginia Bev. Corp. Salem, Va. (5-8)
27) Drink King Cola the Royal Drink./Same (5-8)
28) Kiss Kola Mfg. Co. High Point./Drink Kiss Kola. (12-15)
29) Lime Cola Co. Portsmouth, Va./It's Good Phone 93 (12-15)
30) Mecklenburg Spgs., Chase City, Va./Calcium Water Nature's Remedy (12-15)
31) Mint Cola, a Drink Without a Kick/Same (5-8)
32) Drink Moxie Clean/Wholesome Refreshing (5-8)
33) Original "Manitou" Ginger Champagne./Original "Manitou" Table Water. (5-8)
34) Original "Manitou" Sparkling Water/Same (5-8)
35) Ocola the Improved./Western Ohio Bottling Works. (5-8)
36) Ora-Ade Coca-Cola Dry Ginger Ale/Pachal's quality Beverages (15-20)
37) Drink Ori-Ole Ginger Ale/Greater Richmond Bottling Works (15-20)
38) The Owens Spring Water Company/Sodas and Ciders Glenwood, Minn. (5-8)
39) Palmer Brand High Grade Soda/The S. C. Palmer Co. Washington D.C. (10-12)
40) Drink Pepsi-Cola (Block) Healthful/Drink Pepsi-Cola (Block) Invigorating (35-40)
41) Pepsi-Cola (Block) Bottling Works/T.W. Thrash, Propr. Tarboro, N. C. (40-50)
42) Pepsi Cola (Block) most delicious./Pepsi Cola (Block) very healthful. (35-40)
43) Drink Phillips Bros. Champion Ginger Ale/A Knockout for

Thirst (5-8)
44) Drink Phillips Bros. Champion Ginger Ale/An Extra Glass in Every Bottle (5-8)
45) Poland Water Poland Water/H. Ricker & Sons South Poland, Me. (5-8)
46) Drink Pyramid Beverages/Same (5-8)
47) Rock Creek Ginger Ale/Same (5-8)
48) Saratoga Quevic Spring Water./Quevic Ginger Ale. Quevic Root Beer. (2 Var (A) Large Letters (B) Small Letters) (5-8)
49) Drink Satanet, it's Good./Same (5-8)
50) Shawmut Beverages/McCarthy & Son Sherborn Mass. (5-8)
51) Simpson Spring Beverages/Same (5-8)
52) Drink Spar-Ko Best by Test/Bottled in All Flavors (5-8)
53) Drink Taka-Kola./Same (5-8)
54) Ute Chief Manitou Ginger Ale/Ute Chief Manitou Mineral Water (5-8)
55) Virginia Etna Virginia Etna/Same (5-8)
56) Warwick Club Ginger Ale/Warwick Bot'g. Wks. Artic, R.I. (5-8)
57) "Thirsty ? Just Whistle"/Same (10-12)

E-11
1) A.B.C.B. Washington 6, D.C./Bottled Soft Drinks good and good for you (5-8)
2) Big-Giant Cola 16 oz. Bigger'n Better/Same (5-8)
3) Have a Coke drink Coca-Cola (Script)/Same (30-35)
4) It's Cott to be good/Same (5-8)
5) D&Z Bottling Co. tel. EU 8-8871/Delicious and Zestful True Fruit Beverages (5-8)
6) Dr Pepper the Friendly "Pepper-Upper"/Same (15-20)
7) Frostie Root Beer/Same (8-10)
8) Lotta Cola 16 oz. Lotta Cola 16 oz./Same (8-10)
9) Nesbitt's of California/Made from Real Oranges (5-8)
10) Nesbitt's Nesbitt's/Same (5-8)
11) Drink Pepsi Cola (Script) drink Pepsi Cola (Script)/Drink Pepsi-Cola (Script) drink Pepsi-Cola (Script) (10-12)
12) Drink Phillips Bros. Champion Ginger Ale/Drink Ke-La drink Ke-La (5-8)
13) Drink Phillips Bros. Champion Ginger Ale/An Extra Glass in Every Bottle (5-8)
14) Popular Club Ginger Ale/Same (5-8)
15) Quiky Grapefruit-Lemon Refresher/Same (5-8)
16) "Fresh Up" with Seven-Up/Same (5-8)
17) Enjoy Squirt never an after-thirst/Same (5-8)

E-13
1) Drink Coca Cola (Script) in Bottles/Same (1-3)
2) Have a Coke Drink Coca-Cola (Script)/Same (1-3)
3) Drink Double-Cola/Same (2-4)
4) Drink Nesbitts drink Nesbitts/Same (2-4)
5) Fresh Up with Seven-Up/Same (2-4)

E-14
1) Drink Abeles Clearock Beverages/Same (2-4)
2) Anderson Beverages Famous for Quality (2-4)
3) Drink B-1 it's Viteminized/Same (2-4)
4) Drink B-1 Lemon-Lime more zip in every sip! (2-4)
5) Drink Barq's it's Good/Same (2-4)
6) Drink Barq's Wholesome Beverages/Same (2-4)
7) Belfast Dry Ginger Ale/Belfast Sparkling Water (2-4)
8) Belfast Ginger Ale/Belfast Sparkling Water (2-4)
9) Big-Giant Cola 16 oz. Bigger'n Better/Same (2-4)
10) Big Shot Beverages Jefferson Bottling Co. (3-5)
11) Bireley's Beverages it's Now Carbonated (2-4)
12) Bireley's Orange Drink (2-4)
13) Bireley's Orange Drink/Same(2-4)
14) Blue Anchor Beverages/Same (2-4)
15) Bobbie Ale Soda Water/Golden Drops White Cap (2-4)
16) Booth's Beverages Booth's Beverages/Same (3-5)
17) Bubble Up Bubble Up/Same (2-4)
18) Drink Bubble Up/Same (2-4)
19) Bull's Head Ginger Ale/Bryant quality Beverages (5-8)
20) Canada Dry Canada Dry/Same (2-4)

21) Canada Dry of Atlantic City (3-5)
22) Canada Dry quality Beverages/Same (2-4)
23) Drink "Canada Dry"/Same (2-4)
24) Carter's Beverages (2-4)
25) Cheer Up Cheer Up/The Sparkling Refresher (2-4)
26) City Bottling Works Delicious Beverages (3-5)
27) Clicquot Club Beverages (2-4)
28) Cloverdale Ginger Ale/Cloverdale Soft Drinks (2-4)
29) Coca-Cola (Script) Coca Cola (Script) (3-5
30) Coca Cola (Script) Coca Cola (Script)/Same (3-5)
31) Enjoy Coca Cola (Script) it's the real thing (2-4)
32) Have a Coke Drink Coca-Cola (Script) (2-4)
33) Have a Coke Drink Coca-Cola (Script)/Same (2-4)
34) Have a Coke Drink Coca-Cola (Script)/It's the real thing enjoy Coca Cola (Script) (2-4)
35) Pocatello Coca-Cola (Script) Bottling Co. Inc. P.O. Box 1128 Pocatello, Idaho (20-25)
36) Cola Moca adventure in good taste/Same (2-4)
37) Cott quality Beverages (2-4)
38) It's Cott To be Good/Same (2-4)
39) Country Club Ginger Ale (2-4)
40) Crystal Beverages Mt. Carmel, Pa./Same (2-4)
41) Drink Dad's Root Beer/Same (5-8)
42) Dakota-Kist Btl'g Co. Hatton, N.D. (3-5)
43) Dexcola Abco/Same (2-4)
44) Diamond Ginger Ale/Same (2-4)
45) "Diamond Quality Beverages America's Finest"/Same (2-4)
46) Drink Double-Cola/Same (2-4)
47) Drink Double-Cola the Flavor's Double!/Same (2-4)
48) Double Eagle Ginger Beer/Double Eagle Beverages (2-4)
49) Drink Dr. Pepper at 10, 2 & 4 O'Clock/Drink a bite to eat at 10, 2 & 4 O'Clock (2 Var (A) Dr Pepper Block (B) Dr Pepper Script) (8-10)
50) Dr. Pepper Botg. Co. Logan W.Va./Same (15-20)
51) Dr. Pepper Botg. Co. Pensacola Fla./Same (15-20)
52) Dr. Pepper Distinctly Different/Same (3-5)
53) Dr. Pepper Dr. Pepper/The Friendly "Pepper-Upper." (3-5)
54) Dr. Pepper the Friendly "Pepper Upper"/Same (3-5)
55) John G. Epping quality Drinks/Same (2-4)
56) Faygo Beverages Detroit/Same (2-4)
57) Freeman's Beverages (2-4)
58) Fritz quality Beverages since 1873 (3-5)
59) Drink Frostie Old Fashion Root Beer/Same (20-25)
60) Frostie Root Beer/Same (3-5)
61) Golden Pheasant Ginger Ale & Sodas/Cream City Prod. Co. Pelham Club (3-5)
62) Grapeteen the Teen Age Drink/Same (3-5)
63) Courtesy of your Grapette Bottler (10-12)
64) Thirsty or Not! Enjoy..Grapette/Same (5-8)
65) Drink Green Spot (2-4)
66) Drink Green Spot/Cacoosing Dairy (2-4)
67) Greenbrier Ginger Ale/Same (2-4)
68) Harris Sparkling Waters (2-4)
69) Hek Griesedieck Beverage Co. St. Louis (12-15)
70) Harwood Beverages/Battle Creek Michigan (2-4)
71) Drink Hires Root Beer/Same (5-8)
72) Hires Clicquot Club/Grand Rapids Bottling Co. (12-15)
73) Hires Root Beer (3-5)
74) Hires Root Beer/Same (3-5)
75) Hires to you! so refreshing/Same (5-8)
76) Hydrox Beverages every drop pure (2-4)
77) Hydrox Beverages every drop pure/Same (2-4)
78) Island Road Bottling Co. Tastee Club Beverages/Same (2-4)
79) K's Real Fruit Beverages/Same (2-4)
80) Drink Keck's/Same (2-4)
81) Kern's Beverages Fine Natural Flavors (2-4)
82) Mix with Kings Court/Same (2-4)
83) Drink Kist drink Kist/Same (2-4)
84) Kramer Bev. Co. Phone 5-2235 (2-4)
85) Kutztown Bottling Works own made Soft Drinks/Kutztown Bottling Works Distributor of Beer & Porter (5-8)
86) La Salle Beverages/Same (2-4)
87) Drink Lemmy drink Lemmy/Same (2-4)
88) Lively Limes light & lively/Same (2-4)
89) Lively Limes light & refreshing (2-4)
90) Lively Limes light & refreshing/Same (2-4)
91) "Lincoln Bottling Co." "Lincoln Bottling Co."/Same (Bottled Grapette in Newport. OR & Salem, OR) (5-8)
92) Drink the best Lolli Pop (2-4)
93) Lotta Cola 16 oz. Lotta Cola 16 oz./Same (2-4)
94) Lynbrook Beverages/Same (2-4)
95) Old Fashioned Ma's Root Beer/Same (5-8)
96) Mar-Mat Beverages/Refreshing Delicious (2-4)
97) Milton Spring Ginger Ale/Chas. C. Copeland Co., Inc. Milton, Mass. (3-5)
98) Drink Mission enjoy Mission/Same (2-4)
99) Mission Beverages naturally good/Same (2-4)
100) Mission Orange/Same (2-4)
101) Moran's Moran's (Pennsylvania Soda) (2-4)
102) Drink Moxie drink Moxie/Same (5-8)
103) Drink Moxie drink Moxie/Drink Pureoxia drink Pureoxia (5-8)
104) Drink "Mr." Cola for fine flavor/Same (3-5)
105) National Beer Soft Drinks/Same (12-15)
106) Par-T-Pak Nehi R C Cola (10-12)
107) Drink Nesbitt's drink Nesbitt's/Same (2-4)
108) Nesbitt's Nesbitt's/Same (2-4)
109) Nesbitt's of California/Made from real Oranges (2-4)
110) Nesbitt's...the finest Orange/Soft Drink ever made (2-4)
111) Northway Bottling Works, Hamtramck, Mich./Phone Trinity 2-3012 (2-4)
112) O-SO Beverages O-SO Beverages/Same (2-4)
113) Ohio State Beverages Ohio State Beverages (2-4)
114) Drink Pepsi-Cola (Block) (5-8)
115) Drink Pepsi-Cola (Block)/Same (5-8)
116) Drink Pepsi-Cola (Script) drink Pepsi-Cola (Script)/Same (1-3)
117) Drink Pepsi-Cola (Block) Grand-Pop Bottling Co./Same (8-10)
118) Drink Pepsi-Cola (Block) more bounce to the ounce/Same (5-8)
119) Pepsi-Cola (Block) Bottling Co. Lyons, Kansas (12-15)
120) Pepsi Cola (Block) Btlg. Co Memphis, Mo-Keokuk, Ia (8-10)
121) Pepsi-Cola (Block) Cincinnati (5-8)
122) Pepsi-Cola (Block) Memphis, Tenn. (8-10)
123) Pepsi-Cola (Block) Pepsi-Cola (Block) (8-10)
124) Pepsi-Cola (Block) Pepsi-Cola (Block)/Same (8-10)
125) Pepsi pours it on Pepsi Cola/Taste that beats the others cold (8-10)
126) Petermann Beverages/Union City New Jersey (2-4)
127) Drink Phillips Bros. Champion Ginger Ale/An Extra Glass in Every Bottle (2-4)
128) C.F. Plitt & Son quality Beverages/Same (2-4)
129) Poland Spring Ginger Ale/Poland Water Poland Club Soda (2-4)
130) Quiky Grapefruit-Lemon refresher/Same (2-4)
131) Drink Re-O-L\Cola V-8 mixer/Same (3-5)
132) Red Rock Cola/Same (3-5)
133) Red Rock Cola Red Rock Cola/Same (3-5)
134) Regent Beverages (2-4)
135) Regent Beverages fit for a king/Same (2-4)
136) Drink Ritz-E Beverages/Bell Bottling Co. 115 Gano Street Providence, R.I. (2-4)
137) Rock Spring Beverages/J. Ries Btlg. Wrks. Inc. Shakopee, Minn. (2-4)
138) Roselle & Co. Pocatello/Same (Bottled Dr Wells & Roselle Sodas) (2-4)
139) Royal Crown Cola "Best by Taste Test"/Same (2-4)
140) Royal Crown Cola "Better Taste Calls For R C"/Same (2-4)
141) Royal Crown Cola go fresher . . . go RC/Same (2-4)
142) Royal Crown Cola St. Louis, Missouri/Royal Crown Cola Nehi Flavors (8-10)
143) Royal Crown Cola tops in taste/Same (2-4)
144) Drink-Rulon Beverages Drink-Rulon Beverages/Same (2-4)

145) Saratoga Quevic Spring Water./Quevic Ginger Ale. Quevic Root Beer. (2-4)
146) Drink real 7up 7up Company of Buffalo/Same (8-10)
147) Fresh up drink 7 Up/Brooks 7 Up Western Mich. (3-5)
148) "Fresh Up" with Seven-Up (2-4)
149) "Fresh Up" with Seven-Up/Same (2-4)
150) "Fresh Up with" with Seven-Up/Same (2-4)
151) Seven-Up Santa Barbara/:7 Up...Santa Barbara (5-8)
152) "7up" Bottling Co., Inc./You'll like it it likes you (5-8)
153) Silver Springs Ginger Ale (2-4)
154) Silver Springs Ginger Ale/Same (2-4)
155) Simpson Spring Beverages/Same (2-4)
156) Snow Crest Beverages Salem, Mass. (2-4)
157) Society Beverages, Inc. Dayton, Ohio (2-4)
158) Sparkeeta a Sparkletts "Up" Drink/Sparkletts Table Water "California's Finest" (2-4)
159) Drink Sparkling Jump (2-4)
160) "Spur" a Cola Beverage/Same (2-4)
161) Drink Squirt drink Squirt/Same (2-4)
162) Enjoy Squirt never an after-thirst/Same (2-4)
163) Squirt Botg. Co. Manistee Mich./Same (5-8)
164) Star Soda and Ice Cream/K. Takitani Wailuku, Maui (8-10)
165) Suburban Club Bubbles/Same (2-4)
166) "Drink Sun-Ripe" "Not Carbonated" (2-4)
167) 3V Cola Giant 16 oz. Size/Same (2-4)
168) Drink-Tog Drink-Tog/Same (5-8)
169) Tom Tucker Beverages/Same (2-4)
170) Tom Tucker Ginger Ale (2-4)
171) Towne Club Pop Center's (3-5)
172) "Triple XXX" Root Beer/Same (3-5)
173) Drink Tru-Ade a Better Beverage (2-4)
174) Drink Tru-Ade a Better Beverage/Same (2-4)
175) Drink Vana Beverages call Canal 1405 (2-4)
176) Vernor's Ginger Ale Arcadia Dry/Vernor's Ginger Ale Arcadia Water (3-5)
177) Vernor's Ginger Ale Deliciously Different/Same (3-5)
178) Vernor's Ginger Ale San Antonio/Deliciously Different (8-10)
179) Vess Beverages quality Flavors/Same (2-4)
180) Warwick Club Beverages/Same (2-4)
181) Waterloo Beverage 16721 Waterloo Rd. IV. 4474 (2-4)
182) "Drink Waverly Beverages"/Same (2-4)
183) Whelan's Soft Drinks (5-8)
184) Thirsty? Just Whistle/Same (5-8)
185) White Rock Sparkling Beverages (2-4)

E-16
1) Champagne Fizz. the Drink. what is Celery Tonic. (20-25)
2) Western Beverages Co. Alco (20-25)

E-17
1) Elwell's $1000.00 Ginger Ale/Pure Pop Co. Macomb, Ill. (25-30)
2) St. Louis Crystal Water Soda Co./Crystal Sodas Absolutely Pure (25-30)

E-18
1) Hoster-Columbus Gold Top Beverages (25-30)

E-19
1) Drink Orange Crush Krueger's Beer in Cans (40-50)
2) Drink 7-Up Ferd Winkler Bottling Co. Belleville, Ill. (15-20)

E-21
1) Crown Ginger Beer Company/Same (10-12)
2) Pureoxia Ginger Ale/Same (15-20)

E-22
1) "Drink Pachal's Beverages"/(Made in Canada) (10-12)
2) 7-Up quenches thirst drink 7-Up (20-25)

E-24
1) Nevin-Frank Co. Beverages Butte (Black On Green) (35-40)

2) Varsity Dry and Elk Brand Ginger Ale Consumers North Star Bottling Works S. F. (Black On Light Green) (25-30)

E-25
1) One and Only One Dr. Brown's Celery (15-20)
2) Pepsi=Cola Bottling Works Pulaski, Va. (40-50)

E-31
1) Drink White Cap Ginger Ale/Same (12-15)

E-501
1) Bireley's Orangeade Bireley's Orangeade/Same (5-8)
2) Chocolate Dairy Drink/Krim-Ko (5-8)
3) Deep Rock Water Co. (5-8)
4) Ephrata Diamond Spring Water Co./Akron, Pennsylvania (5-8)
5) Green Spot Fruit-Ades/Same (5-8)

F-1
1) Hyan Dry Ginger Ale Lime and Lithia/Lang's A. A. a perfect Brew Malt (20-25)
2) Kist Lime Rickey Klamath Ice. Co. Phone 58 (20-25)

F-2
1) "Drink Bright Spot Sodas" (5-8)
2) Drink Buffalo Lime Rickey/Grape Fruit & Ginger Ale (5-8)
3) Ginger Ale Henry Burkhardt Ginger Ale/Phone Canal 0436 (5-8)
4) Climax Beverages/Same (15-20)
5) California Beverage Co./Drink All American Beverages (5-8)
6) Coca-Cola (Block) Bottling Co./Dyersburg, Tenn. (75-100)
7) Coca-Cola (Block) Bottling Co. Clarksdale, Miss. (75-100)
8) Coca-Cola (Block) Bottling Co. Enid, Okla. (75-100)
9) Sherman Coca-Cola (Script) Bottling Works (Happy Days in bowl of spoon) (125-150)
10) Sherman Coca-Cola (Script) Co. (75-100)
11) Crystal Brand Ginger-ale (5-8)
12) "Crystal Rock" Pale Dry/Same (5-8)
13) Dr Pepper Bottling Co./Arkansas City, Kans. (60-75)
14) Dublin Bay Ginger Ale/Same (5-8)
15) Flynn's-White-Soda (5-8)
16) Gold Seal Pale Dry (in bowl of spoon) When Good Fellows Get Together (5-8)
17) Husting's better Beverages (5-8)
18) Indian Maid Ginger Ale Gluek Brewing Co./Gluek Brewing (15-20)
19) Indian Maid Ginger Ale/Gluek Brewing Company (15-20)
20) Krueger's/Delicious drinks (15-20)
21) Lansford Bottling Works (Bicentennial Celebration 1732-1932 Pic of George Washington in bowl of spoon)/Try a Case of our Dry Ginger Ale (25-30)
22) Drink Lititz Springs Pale Dry/"The Aristocrat of Ginger Ales" (12-15)
23) Orange Crush Bottling Co./Elizabethtown, Pa. (25-30)
24) Pepsi-Cola (30-35)
25) "Fresh Up" with Seven-Up/You like it—— it likes you (20-25)
26) Silco Beverages (5-8)
27) Temple Beverage Co. 3563 Temple St.-Phone Olympia 1214 (5-8)
28) Vol-Pels Beverages (Lion Head in bowl of spoon)/Dry Ginger Ale Lemon Beer Lime Rickey (5-8)
29) White Rock Sparkling Beverages (5-8)
30) Welch's Grape Juice (5-8)

F-3
1) Dr. Pepper the Friendly "Pepper Upper" (75-100)
2) F.J. Ogorchock "Beverages" Phone 619-J Brookville, Pa. (5-8)
3) The Seven-Up Bottling Co. of Ogden Inc. dial 4784 Ogden, Utah 215 25th St. (15-20)

F-4
1) Aren Pale Dry Ginger Ale (in bowl of spoon) (5-8)
2) Arlington Club Pale Dry Ginger Ale F. W. Muller Sons Arlington Heights, Ill. (5-8)

3) Big Bear Soda Millstadt, Illinois (5-8)
4) Blatz Lime Rickey Unexcelled Coverability (12-15)
5) Drink Busch's Special Root Beer John B. Busch Brg. Co. Refreshing and Invigorating (25-30)
6) Compliments Califruit Lime Rickey (5-8)
7) Coca-Cola (Block) Quality Cooler Glascock Bros. Mfg. Co. Muncie, Ind. (75-100)
8) Drink Coca-Cola (Block) a Pure Drink of Natural Flavors (100-125)
9) Drink Coca-Cola (Script) in Bottles (75-100)
10) Cross's Extra Dry Ginger Ale Blend for Liquors (5-8)
11) "A Good Mixer" Delux Cola Atlanta, Ga. (15-20)
12) Duffy's delicious Drinks (5-8)
13) Elkhorn Natural Mineral Water Ginger Ale and Lime Rickey Baker Mineral Springs Co. Baker, Oregon (5-8)
14) A Stirring Message use Glacier Trail Products Hill County Creamery Havre, Mont. (5-8)
15) Gold Seal Pale Extra Dry Ginger Ale Lane's Bottling Works, Inc. a Good Mixer in any Crowd (5-8)
16) Gold Seal Soda Fischer Bros. a Good Stirrer for a Good Mixer (5-8)
17) From One Good Mixer to Another use Goldy Rock Beverages 13 Flavors in Large and Small Bottles "Serving the Public 25 Years" (5-8)
18) Hood River Bottling Works a Complete Line of Beverages Hood River, Oregon (5-8)
19) Hyan Dry Ginger Ale made good-by Ginger! A Lang product (10-12)
20) Drink Naturally Sparkling Idan-Ha Idanha Mineral Water Co. Soda Springs, Idaho (5-8)
21) Insist on Johnson's Lime Rickey-Dry Ginger Ale Superior Calif. Beverage Co. Willows-California-Corning (5-8)
22) Manhattan Bottling Works for Better Mixing & Drinking West 0206 Milwaukee, Wis. (8-10)
23) Milton Spring Beverages Made in the Blue Hills of Milton Charles C. Copeland Co., Inc. (5-8)
24) Lets uncap our Spirits and stir up Business Old Faithful Beverage Co. Idaho Falls, Idaho (5-8)
25) Drink "Pep Up" Big Boy Beverages, Inc. Melrose 2445 (5-8)
26) Pepsi-Cola (Block) Bottling Co., Inc. Princeton, W.Va. (30-35)
27) Pepsi-Cola (Block) Bottling Co. of Waco-Texas (30-35)
28) Compliments of Pepsi-Cola (Block) Bottling Co. Alliance, Nebr. Scottsbluff, Nebr. (Beware: Large Numbers Recently Found) (10-12)
29) Compliments of Seven-Up Bottling Company Springfield, Illinois (20-25)
30) 7-Up a Good Stirrer for a Good Mixer Wood River Bottling Works Phone 18W Wood River, Ill. (20-25)
31) For a Good Mixer Smith and Clody's Extra Dry Ginger Ale (5-8)
32) Drink Squirt courtesy of Bellingham Beverage Co. (10-12)
33) Tip Top Soda Water Tip Top Bottling Co. made of Pure Cane Sugar each Bottle Sterilized (10-12)
34) Vaughan's Ginger Ale (10-12)

F-5

1) Blue Anchor Ginger Ale/John Friedrich 5th & Rising Sun Ave. (10-12)
2) Coca-Cola (Script)/Same (75-100)
3) Coca-Cola (Script) Bottling Co. Bartlesville, Okla./Drink Coca-Cola (Script) in Bottles (75-100)
4) Drink Coca-Cola (Script) in Bottles/Same (75-100)
5) Drink Coca-Cola (Script) in Bottles/Phone Coatesville 507 (75-100)
6) Drink Coca-Cola (Script) in Bottles/Phone Woon: 4010 Batchelor's-Ginger Ale (75-100)
7) Drink Coca-Cola (Script) in Sterilized Bottles/Chesterman Co. (75-100)
8) Drink Coca-Cola (Script) in Sterilized Bottles/Coca-Cola (Script) Phone 289 (75-100)
9) Dubuque Coca-Cola (Script) Bottling Co. Phone 884/Drink Coca-Cola (Script) in Bottles (75-100)
10) Magnolia Coca-Cola (Script) Bottling Co. El Paso, Texas/Drink Coca-Cola (Script) in Sterilized Bottles (75-100)

11) Milwaukee Coca-Cola (Script) Bottling Co. Phone Grand 906/Drink Coca-Cola (Script) in Bottles (75-100)
12) Milwaukee Coca-Cola (Script) Bottling Co. Phone Grand 906-909/Keep a Case in the Home (100-125)
13) Drink Dr. Pepper/Little Rock Bottling Co. Phone 4-1469 (75-100)
14) Drink Dr. Pepper in Bottles/Dr. Pepper Bottling Co. (75-100)
15) Drink Dr. Pepper in Bottles/Nehi Bottling Co. Phone 2-1686 (75-100)
16) Drink Dr. Pepper in Bottles/Union Bottling Works Phone Preston 0366 (75-100)
17) Drink Klassy brand Beverages/Klassy Products, Inc. Phone 302-46 (5-8)
18) Drink Lithia Soda Water/Lithia Bottling Co. Phone 339. (8-10)
19) Drink Montana Dry Ginger Ale (8-10)
20) 5c Moxie 5c the best Drink in the World/Always ask for Kramer's better Beverages (40-50)
21) Mountain Valley Mineral Water Ginger Ale/The Denver Ice and Cold Storage Company Phone Main 8368 (8-10)
22) Drink Richter's Beverages/Phone 2-2611 Fresno (15-20)
23) Rochester Bottling Co./Quality Beverages 6-8 7th St., N. W. (12-15)
24) Drink Whistle/Wenner's Beverages -dial 4215- (25-30)
25) Thirsty? Just Whistle/Arizona Whistle Bot. Works (25-30)

F-6

1) For better Health drink Alkalaris/Phone Belmont 1478 (8-10)
2) Arrowhead Ginger Ale/Same (8-10)
3) Drink Becco-Nourishing as Beer/Becker Products Co. Ogden, Utah (15-20)
4) Becker Products Co. Ogden, Utah/Same (10-12)
5) Bethesda Pale Dry Ginger Ale (8-10)
6) "Canada Dry" Pale Ginger Ale/McLaughlin's "Belfast Style" Ginger Ale (5-8)
7) "Drink Cascade Ginger Ale"/Same (5-8)
8) Chewaukla Mineral Springs Co. Chicago, Ill./From Chewaukla Springs Hot Springs, Arkansas (5-8)
9) "Cherry Blossoms"/"A Blooming Good Drink" (5-8)
10) Chero-Cola/Same (35-40)
11) -Coca-Cola- (Block)/Lawrence Bottling -& Mfg. Co.- (75-100)
12) Coca-Cola (Block) Bottling Works –Waynesboro, Pa.-/Same (75-100)
13) The Coca-Cola (Script) Bottling Co. –Wichita Kansas.-/Manufacturers of High Grade Carbonated Beverages. (75-100)
14) Coleman's Ginger Ale/Noted for its Flavor (8-10)
15) Dry Rock Pale Ginger Ale/Altmann' Phone 21755 Syracuse, N. Y. (8-10)
16) Why not order a Case of Hill's High Grade Beverages Framingham Bottling Co. Phone 843 W/Hang me up in the Kitchen (8-10)
17) Drink Hires in Bottles/Same (35-40)
18) Hund & Eger Bottling Co. Pabst Beer Agents/Pure Soda Water in Sterilized Bottles (35-40)
19) Jack Sprat Brand/Same (5-8)
20) London Dry Ginger Ale/London Life Malt best by test (15-20)
21) Manhattan Pepsin Ginger Ale—Phone West 206 -/Merely a matter of good taste. (8-10)
22) McHugh & Moran bottlers of Schlitz Beer/Manf's. of Soft Drinks. (20-25)
23) Miller's Pale Dry Ginger Ale/Rochester Soda Water Co., Inc. (8-10)
24) Miller's Pale Dry Ginger Ale/#777 (8-10)
25) Mt. Pleasant Bottling Works/Phone 53 (10-12)
26) N. Y. Bottling Work's Carbonated Beverages/Phone 2-4611 A. Cornrich (8-10)
27) Orange-Crush Bottling Co. Statesville, N. C./Orange-Crush Bottling Co.—Statesville, N. C. – (20-25)
28) Roxo Water & Ginger Ale/Phone Broadway 5030 (5-8)
29) -You like it- Schmeltzer's Ginger Ale -It's Great-/Pottsville, Pa. (5-8)
30) Shipley's Bottling Works/Frederick, Maryland (5-8)
31) "Drink Smile"/Smile of the Orange. (5-8)
32) "Drink Smile"/Orange Smile Sirup Co. (5-8)

33) Smith & Clody/Ginger Beer and Soda Waters. (10-12)
34) "3-C Nectar" the Drink of the Gods/Contains no Habit Forming Drugs (30-35)
35) Union Bottling Co. Chattanooga, Tenn./Home Bottling Supplies (20-25)
36) Alois Vana, Inc. Manufacturers Carbonated Beverages/1835-37 Fisk. St., Tel. Canal 1405/1406 (5-8)
37) Drink Whistle-Hires Root Beer Keep Cool-/Bangor Bottling Co. McAloon & Geagan, Props. (20-25)
38) Drink Woolner's Beverages Toledo/Same (12-15)

F-7
1) Coca-Cola (Script) Bottling Works Shelbyville, Tenn. (20-25)
2) Drink Coca-Cola (Script) in Bottles 5c Bristol Tenn 1936 (12-15)
3) 7 Up (15-20)

F-8
1) Enjoy Coca-Cola (Script)/Same/Same/Same (15-20)

F-9
1) Coca-Cola Bottling Co. Terre Haute, In. (125-150)
2) Drink/Coca-Cola (Block)/in Bottles/Leaksville, N. C. (125-150)
3) Fremont Beverage Co./Phone 24, Fremont, Neb./Drink Fremo/The Perfect Beverage (50-60)
4) Imperial Ginger Ale/Erie Pure Ice Co./Imperial Ginger Ale/Erie Pure Ice Co. (35-40)
5) Silver City Beer & Ice Co./Coal-Wood-Soda Water Budweiser-Hay & Grain/Roofing Paper-Beaver Board Roofing Paint-Celotex/Phone 10 (75-100)
6) Chas. Westerholm Co./Red Seal/Ginger Ale & Iron brew/Phone Monroe 802 (35-40)

F-13
1) Drink Becco Nourishing as Beer Becker Products Co. Ogden, Utah (50-60)

F-15
1) Save 15 Crowns from Arrowhead Pale Dry Ginger Ale and receive Mixing Spoon Free (12-15)
2) Coca-Cola (Block) Bottling Works of Greenwood, Miss. (60-75)
3) Seven-Up Bottling Co. Springfield, Illinois fresh up with Seven-Up (20-25)
4) The quality Beverage Seven-Up Bottling Co. Springfield, Illinois (7-Up Logo in bowl of spoon) (20-25)
5) You like it 7up it likes you (20-25)
6) Tip Top Soda Water Tip Top Bottling Co. made of Pure Cane Sugar each Bottle Sterilized (20-25)

F-18
1) Afri-Kola Co. Atlanta. (15-20)
2) Gold Coin Beverages/S. F. Avery—Tel. 919—(15-20)
3) Hund & Eger Bottling Co. Pabst Beer Agents/Pure Soda Waters in Sterilized Bottles. (50-60)
4) Judd the Julep Man Julep is not a Pop/Saginaw, Mich. (15-20)

F-21
1) Califruit Lime Rickey Distributed by Coca Cola (Block) Bottling Company Billings, Montana (125-150)

F-23
1) Barco (in Seal) Pale Extra Dry Ginger Ale B. A. Railton Co. Quality Products B. A. Railton Co. Chicago & Milwaukee (25-30)
2) Serve Popular Club Ginger Ale Co. (25-30)
3) Silver Club Ginger Ale Co. Ginger Ale Sparkling Water Lime Rickey Club Soda (25-30)

F-24
1) Columbia Ginger Ale Beacon Rock Lithia Water Camden Bottling Co. Camden, N. J. both phones 253 (15-20)
2) Coca Cola (Script) tastes best ice cold (5-8)
3) Drink Coca Cola (Script) in Bottles Delicious-Refreshing (5-8)
4) Hoffman Beverages Pale Dry Ginger Ale Cream Soda Coco

Cream Root Beer Birch Beer Fruity Ginger Ale Lemon Soda Orange Soda Raspberry Beverage Cherry Beverage Grape Beverage Sarsaparilla (15-20)
5) Drink Nehi in your Favorite Flavor (25-30)

F-25
1) Johnstones Original Orange Julep if you like Oranges you will like Orange Jooj it's cloudy Jooj (Logo) That's the Fruit (30-35)

F-27
1) Drink Coca-Cola in Bottles/Baltimore, Maryland (2 Var (A) Coca-Cola (Block) (B) Coca-Cola (Script) (75-100)
2) Drink Coca-Cola (Script) in Bottles/Home Service Inc. (75-100)
3) The Coca-Cola (Script) Bottling Co./Buy Coca-Cola (Block) by the Case (75-100)
4) The Coca-Cola (Script) Bottling Co. "Every Bottle Sterilized"/Buy Coca-Cola (Script) "Better in Bottles" (75-100)
5) Drink Lime Cola and Enjoy Living/Same (25-35)
6) Nehi Bottling Co. Sherman, Tex./Same (40-50)
7) Orange Crush/Covington Maid Ice Cream (35-40)
8) Polar Ginger Ale/Bieber-Polar Co. (15-20)
9) Roseville Ice & Beverage Co. Phone 211/Same (15-20)

F-29
1) Coca-Cola (Script) Hund & Eger Just to Stir up a Little Business (125-150)
2) Coca-Cola (Script) Bottling Co.-Superior, Nebr. (125-150)
3) Hyklas Dry Ginger Ale (20-25)
4) Drink the Best Silver Plume Pale Dry Ginger Ale (in bowl of spoon) Bruhnke Bros. Phones: Austin 2782-Euclid 4555 (20-25)

F-501
1) Compliments of Orange Crush Bottling Works La Crosse, Wis. (60-75)

F-502
1) National Nugrape Company (75-100)

F-503
1) "Malted Grape Nuts Chocolate Flavored"/"A Delicious Food Drink" (10-12)

F-504
1) Drink Red Rock Cola/Same (35-40)

F-505
1) Cigars-Stogies-Pipes Ginger Ale/W.H. Strauss & Co. Johnstown-Altoona (20-25)

F-506
1) Gardner Bros. Ice Cream Ice—Coca Cola (Block) (150-200)

F-507
1) Coca-Cola (Block) Bottling Co. Greencastle, In. (200-250)
2) Gardner Bros. Ice Cream Ice—Coca-Cola (Block) (150-200)

F-508
1) Drink Coca-Cola (Block) in Bottles (150-200)

F-509
1) Golden Belt Ginger Ale -Cherry Punch-/Salina Bottling Works (20-25)
2) Suburban Club Ginger Ale/Ginger Mint -Julep- (20-25)

G-1
1) Berkeley Club Ginger Ale one of America's best. (5-8)
2) Coca-Cola (Script) (50-60)
3) Drink Coca-Cola (Script) in Bottles (50-60)
4) Drink Coca-Cola (Script) in Bottles (Bottle) (50-60)
5) Diamond Bottling Works 2146 Florence Ave. Cincinnati. (5-8)
6) Drink Erdman's Beverages Steinsburg, Pa. (5-8)

7) Frank's Pale Dry Ginger Ale it's the best for mixing (Bottle) (3-5)
8) High-N-Dry Ginger Ale "A Drink of Good Taste" (5-8)
9) Morgan Ginger Ale Cumberland 6-0300 (Bottle) (5-8)
10) The Nehi Bottling Co. Phone 467-1500 S. Walnut St. Muncie, Indiana (25-30)
11) Drink Pepsi-Cola (Block) Phone 2-2171 8th & Walnut Sts. Muncie, Ind. (25-30)
12) Pepsi=Cola (Script) A.J. Greenkorn Co. (25-30)
13) Pepsi=Cola (Script) 12 oz. 5c (25-30)
14) 7 Up Ferd Winkler Bottling Co. (Bottle) (15-20)

G-2
1) Diamond Ginger Ale Waterbury, Conn. (3-5)
2) Hawaiian Dry Pale Ginger Ale made where the Ginger grows Rycroft Honolulu (3-5)
3) Royal Crown Cola best by taste-test (3-5)
4) Drink Sun Spot Real Orange Goodness (3-5)

G-3
1) Adlerika Superior to Laxatives (5-8)
2) Three Dandy Mixers Hanfords Club Soda Lime Rickey Ginger Ale (5-8)
3) Kramer's Beverages Atlantic City's own finest in Drinks (5-8)
4) Ripley County Beverage Co. (Inc.) (5-8)
5) Tip Top Soda Water Tip Top Bottling Co. made of Pure Cane Sugar each Bottle Sterilized (10-12)

G-4
1) Drink Barq's (3-5)
2) Buck Beverages first for taste (3-5)
3) Drink Cascade Ginger Ale (5-8)
4) Coca-Cola (Script) (10-12)
5) Drink Coca-Cola (Script) (10-12)
6) Drink Coca-Cola (Script) Trade Mark U.S. Pat. off. (5-8)
7) Drink Cuba the Kola Drink (10-12)
8) Double Cola (8-10)
9) Drink Dr. Pepper Good for Life (40-50)
10) Drink Nehi (8-10)
11) Drink Porto Rico Fruit Beverages (5-8)
12) Royal Crown Cola (RC in Logo) (5-8)
13) "Fresh Up" with 7 Up (5-8)

G-5
1) Drink Barma Blatz-Mil. the Unequaled Non Intoxicating Cereal Beverage (15-20)
2) Drink Bludwine (8-10)
3) Buck Beverages "First For Taste" (5-8)
4) Buck First for Thirst (5-8)
5) Drink Cascade Ginger Ale (8-10)
6) Chero-Cola there's none so good (20-25)
7) Chippewa Springs Corporation Chippewa Falls, Wis. (C S C Logo) Purest of all Waters (in circle) (10-12)
8) Coca-Cola (Script) –Ice Christy Ins. Co. Phone-60. Coal-Cement-Sand Phone 31. (50-60)
9) Drink Coca-Cola (Script) Delicious and Refreshing (25-30)
10) Drink Gen-to at Fountains in Bottles 5c (15-20)
11) Drink Nehi (15-20)
12) Pureoxia Ginger Ale made with Distilled Water (15-20)
13) Sheldon Bottling Works Fiebig Bros. Props. Sheldon, Iowa (8-10)
14) Bottler's of Soft Drink and Schlitz Beer Isaac Merkel & Sons Plattsburgh, N. Y. (25-30)
15) Was-Cott Ginger Ale Tazewell M'f'g. Co. made from Mineral Spring Water (15-20)
16) The National Drink Welch's Westfield, N. Y. Opener for Welch's the National Drink (15-20)

G-6
1) Drink Coca-Cola (Script) in Bottles (10-12)
2) It's Cott to be good! (3-5)
3) Drink Vernor's Ginger Ale (3-5)

G-7
1) It's Cott to be good! (3-5)

G-8
1) Bireley's/Bireley's Non-Carbonated Beverages (3-5)
2) Crystal Bottled Waters Co. Phone 264-0221 Phoenix (2-4)
3) Drink Vernor's Ginger Ale (3-5)

G-9
1) Open Cal Ginger Ale (8-10)
2) Pepsi-Cola (Block) (Pepsi-Cola Bottle Cap) (20-25)
3) Served iced Pepsi=Cola buy the 6 bottle carton/Same (20-25)
4) Fresh up with 7 Up (20-25)
5) Silver Foam Ginger Ale (15-20)
6) Drink Sun Crest/Same (15-20)

G-13
1) Buck "First For Thirst" (3-5)
2) Chero-Cola (20-25)
3) Coca-Cola (Script) (20-25)
4) Fox Snappy Drinks (5-8)
5) Grafs the best what gives (5-8)
6) Nevin-Frank Co. (10-12)
7) Original "Manitou" Pale Dry (5-8)
8) Rahr Brewing Co. Soft Drinks (15-20)
9) White Rock (5-8)

G-21
1) C & J Ginger Ale (10-12)
2) Canada Dry Pale Ginger Ale (3-5)
3) Drink Christopher's Orange & Grape Neenah Phone 1431 Ring-1 (8-10)
4) Drink Nehi and Coast Club Ginger Ale (Dry) Nehi Bottling Co. San Jose Columbia 2722 (20-25)
5) Northampton Bottling Works Phone 207 1340 Newport Ave. Northampton, Pa. (12-15)
6) Stephen Yurasits Soft Drink Bottler Phone 386-R Northampton, Pa. (12-15)

G-25
1) Coca-Cola (Block) and Schlitz Hund and Eger St. Joseph, Mo. (75-100)
2) Coca-Cola (Block) Glascock Bros. Mfg. Co. Quality Coolers Muncie, Ind. (75-100)
3) Drink Coca-Cola (Script) in Bottles (75-100)
4) Giering's quality Ginger Ale since 1878 (10-12)
5) Grafs Carbonated Beverage the best since 1873 (15-20)
6) Schultz Sparkling Beverages (15-20)

G-34
1) The Belmont Products Co. Martins Ferry, Ohio Licensed Mfrs. Cup-Topp Ale Dry Ginger Ale (8-10)
2) Cantrell & Cochrane Imperial (Logo) Dry Ginger Ale (8-10)
3) Rothco Pale Dry The Roth & Co. Middletown, O. Mil-Cola for Health (8-10)

G-53
1) Drink Meamber's Beverages (35-40)

G-501
1) Drink Nehi (35-40)
2) Buy-Welch's Grape Juice Preserves and Jellies (10-12)

G-502
1) Sunkist Lemon Soda (10-12)

G-503
1) Drink Coca-Cola (Script)/1959 Sales Meeting (Square Handle) (40-50)

H-1
1) "Ace" Ginger Beer Whistle Bottling Co. (15-20)

2) Eagle Bottling Works 973 Willis East Melrose 2829 (10-12)
3) Erdman Bottling Works Steinsburg, Pa. (5-8)
4) Masterly Dry Pale Ginger Ale Phone 4-0415 Peoria, Ill. (5-8)
5) Nassau Dry Pale Ginger Ale (5-8)
6) Drink Niagara Dry (5-8)
7) Wagner Bottling Works Phone Tri-City 154 Manufacturers of Nehi (Granite City, Ill) (15-20)

H-2
1) Drink Ace Hy Faygo Beverages Cad 3285 (3-5)
2) Ambridge Bottling Works Telephone 360 (3-5)
3) American Soda Water Co. (3-5)
4) Drink Bireley's Non-Carbonated Beverages. (3-5)
5) Drink Blue Anchor Beverages (3-5)
6) Drink Blue Anchor Ginger Ale (3-5)
7) Drink Blue Rock Beverages "In Your Favorite Flavor" (3-5)
8) Buck the preferred Soft Drink "First for Thirst" (3-5)
9) Campari Soda (Script) (3-5)
10) Canada Dry (1-2)
11) Carbon Bottling Works Lehighton, Pa. (3-5)
12) Cerva made in St. Louis (15-20)
13) Chilton Bottling Works Chilton, Wis. (5-8)
14) Coca-Cola (Script) (40-50)
15) Coca-Cola (Script) Bottling Co. Glasgow, Ky. (40-50)
16) Coca-Cola (Script) Bottling Co. La Grange Phone 406 (40-50)
17) Coca-Cola (Script) Bottling Co. Muskogee, Okla. (40-50)
18) Drink Coca-Cola (Script) (40-50)
19) Drink Coca-Cola (Script) Delicious and Refreshing (40-50)
20) Drink Coca-Cola (Script) in Bottles (40-50)
21) Lancaster Coca-Cola (Script) Bottling Wks. 551-553 Spruce St. Lancaster, Pa. (40-50)
22) Laurens Coca-Cola (Script) Bottling Co. Laurens, S. Car. (40-50)
23) Compliments of Lexington Coca-Cola (Script) Bottling Co. (40-50)
24) Roanoke Coca-Cola (Script) Bottling Works Roanoke, Virginia. (40-50)
25) Cornwall Bottling Works Ginger Ale (5-8)
26) Creadon's Ginger Ale (3-5)
27) Crystal Rock Ginger Ale Bottled at the Springs Reading, Pa. (5-8)
28) Crystal Springs Bottling Works Coffeyville, Kansas. (5-8)
29) Drink Dr. Pepper King of Beverages (60-75)
30) Erdman Bottling Works Steinsburg, Pa. (5-8)
31) Drink Gay Ola Gay Ola (Bottle) (12-15)
32) Grafs "The Best What Gives" (3-5)
33) Drink Hires it's always pure (30-35)
34) Idris Lemon Squash (3-5)
35) Jamaica Pale Dry Ginger Ale John Graf Co. (5-8)
36) Kalak the Strongest Alkaline Water of Commerce (3-5)
37) W. Kamm and Son Appleton, Wis. (3-5)
38) Keck's Natural Mineral Water Beverages (3-5)
39) Drink Lewies Beverages L.H. Dunbar Bottling Co. 128 No. Fourth St. Lehighton,—- Pa. (3-5)
40) M & S Orange (3-5)
41) Mountain Valley Mineral Water (3-5)
42) Drink Mugler's Ginger Ale (5-8)
43) National Bottling Co. St. Louis, Mo. (5-8)
44) Drink Nu Icy assorted flavors you can't forget (8-10)
45) Drink Nugrape imitation grape a flavor you can't forget (Bottle) (3-5)
46) Nugrape Soda imitation grape flavor (8-10)
47) Oransoda (3-5)
48) Drink Palm Beverages Palmerton Bottling Works (5-8)
49) Penn's delicious Soft Drinks Reading, Penna. (5-8)
50) Pokegama Springs better Bottled Beverages (3-5)
51) Porto Rico Fruit Beverages Philadelphia, Pa. (5-8)
52) Drink Profile Ginger Ale Joseph Quirin Manchester, N. H. (5-8)
53) Queen-O (3-5)
54) Drink Rahr Brewing Co's Cereal Beverage and Soft Drinks Oshkosh, Wis. (15-20)
55) Drink Rand's Orange Soda (5-8)
56) Drink Red Rock Cola (15-20)

57) S & S Ginger Ale (5-8)
58) Joyce Seven Up Joliet, Illinois (10-12)
59) Silver Rock Ginger Ale P. Setzler & Sons Soda Water Mfg. Co. (5-8)
60) Ask for Simpson Spring Beverages (3-5)
61) Drink Star Sodas (5-8)
62) Insist on Suburban Club "Bubbles" for Fine Drinks (3-5)
63) Sun Crest (Sun Logo) (3-5)
64) Drink Superfine Dry at your Neighborhood Druggist (3-5)
65) Tip Top Bottling Co. (5-8)
66) Was-Cott Ginger Ale North Tazewell, Va. (10-12)
67) Weidenhammer Bottling Works 50 York St. Camden, N. J. (5-8)

H-3
1) Drink Barq's it's Good and Wholesome (3-5)
2) Drink Bireley's Non-Carbonated Beverages. (3-5)
3) C&C Super Beverages (3-5)
4) Canada Dry (1-2)
5) Clicquot Club Bottling Co. Cheyenne, Wyo. (5-8)
6) Green Spot (in Circle) Not-Carbonated Fruit Juice Beverages Pasteurized Green Spot (5-8)
7) Drink Laurentian Dry (3-5)
8) Drink Mission Beverages in all Flavors (3-5)
9) Mission Orange Naturally Good (3-5)
10) Morgan Cumberland 6-0300 (2-4)
11) Drink Nu-Life Grape Big Shot Beverages Jefferson Bottling Co. (5-8)
12) Pepper's Ginger Ale (5-8)
13) Pepsi=Cola (Script) (8-10)
14) Drink Pepsi-Cola (8-10)

H-4
1) Country Club Beverages "Makes Good Drinks Taste Better" (20-25)

H-5
1) Cloverdale Soft Drinks (5-8)
2) Drink Pepsi=Cola (Script)/Same (15-20)

H-7
1) Drink Double Cola (10-12)
2) Grafs Beverages since 1873 (5-8)
3) Drink Pepsi-Cola Bottling Co. Havana, Ill. (40-50)

H-8
1) Pepsi=Cola (Script) Famous for Over 30 years Sparkling Satisfying Pepsi=Cola (Script) an Advertisement Novelty of Pepsi-Cola (Block) Company (15-20)

H-9
1) Just Holler for Polar Sparkling Water Leicester Polar Spring Co. Worcester./Souvenir Grand Council Meeting U.C.T. Providence, R.I. June 4&5, 1909 (30-35)

H-11
1) Grafs Beverages since 1873 (5-8)

I-1
1) "It Hasta Be Shasta" (3-5)
2) "It Hasta Be Shasta"/Mixers low calorie Shasta 8-Flavors in Cans (3-5)

I-4
1) Baby George Juices (3-5)
2) Drink Sambo (3-5)
3) Toddy "Chocolate Malt" (3-5)

I-6
1) For Health enjoy Alymer Tomato Juice (1-2)
2) Drink Mission Beverages/Same (1-2)
3) Sun-Rype/Apple juice (1-2)
4) Toddy "Chocolate Malt" (1-2)

I-7
1) Bruce's Juices Tampa, Florida (Juice Man) (5-8)
2) Dole Pineapple Juice Johnny Pineapple (Pineapple Man) (5-8)
3) Drink IGA Juices (5-8)
4) Dr Phillips Orlando, Fla. Pure Orange-Grapefruit and Blended Juices (5-8)
5) Drink Won-Up (5-8)

I-11
1) Canada Dry (1-2)
2) Canada Dry/Same (1-2)
3) Join the Clicquot Club (Eskimo) (1-2)
4) Drink Coca-Cola (Script)/Same (2-4)
5) Drink Coca-Cola (Script)/Enjoy Coca-Cola (Script) (2-4)
6) Enjoy Coca-Cola (Script) (2-4)
7) Cragmont (1-2)
8) Drink Double-Cola/Same (2-4)
9) Oil City Beverage Co. (2-4)
10) Drink Pepsi-Cola (Script) (2-4)
11) Drink Pepsi-Cola (Script)/Same (2-4)
12) Royal Crown Cola/Same (1-2)
13) Sego Liquid Diet Food (1-2)
14) ...It hasta be Shasta (1-2)
15) "It Hasta be Shasta!"/Same (1-2)
16) "It Hasta Be Shasta!"/Shasta Mixers 8 Flavors in Cans (1-2)
17) Towne Club (1-2)
18) Drink Vernors/Complimentary not to be Sold (1-2)
19) Vess Sodas in Cans in Bottles (1-2)

I-12
1) Drink Coca-Cola (Script)/Have a Coke (2-4)
2) Hoffman Sparkling Beverages/Same (1-2)
3) Drink Pepsi-Cola/Same (2-4)
4) Pepsi-Cola (Script) Same (2-4)
5) "Fresh Up" with Seven-Up/7 Up you like It..it likes you! (2-4)
6) Drink Vernors/Complimentary not to be Sold (1-2)

I-13
1) A & W Root Beer (12-15)
2) Bev-Rich Premium Soda in Cans (1-2)
3) Brookside Beverage Co. Clifton-Bloomington N. J. 472-6900/Same (1-2)
4) Canada Dry (1-2)
5) Drink Coca-Cola (Script) (2-4)
6) Drink Coca-Cola (Script)/Have a Coke (2-4)
7) Heinz Tomato Juice the Pick of the crop/Jus De tomato Heinz le choix la Recolte (1-2)
8) Royal Crown Cola (in Logo) (1-2)
9) "Fresh Up" with Seven-Up/7 Up you like it..it likes you! (2-4)

I-16
1) Drink Coca-Cola (Script)/Have a Coke (2-4)
2) Drink Coca-Cola (Script)/Same (2-4)
3) Dr. Pepper/The Friendly "Pepper Upper" (2-4)
4) Drink Dr. Pepper (in Logo)/Distinctively Different (2-4)
5) Drink Double-Cola/Same (2-4)
6) Hires Root Beer/Same (2-4)
7) Nesbitt's/Same (1-2)
8) Nesbitt's of California/Made from Real Oranges (1-2)
9) Drink Pepsi-Cola (2-4)
10) Drink Pepsi-Cola/Glaser Beverages (3-5)
11) Drink Pepsi-Cola (Script)/Drink Pepsi Cola (Script) (2-4)
12) Royal Crown Cola (Crown) (1-2)
13) "Fresh Up" with Seven Up/You like it 7 Up it likes you! (1-2)

I-17
1) Drink Coca-Cola (Script) (Ro-Loc Process) (30-35)
2) Frank's it's the Best Quality Beverages (1-2)
3) Hires Root Beer/Same (2-4)
4) King Beverage Co./R.L. 6-2172 Round Lake, Ill. (1-2)
5) Anyway you get Kist it's Delicious/Enjoy Kist Beverages (1-2)
6) Royal Crown Cola/Same (1-2)

7) "It Hasta Be Shasta"/Mixers Low Calorie Shasta 8-Flavors in Cans (1-2)
8) Drink Shurfine Soda/Compliments of your Friendly Shurfine Retailer (1-2)

I-19
1) Drink Pepsi-Cola (5-8)

I-20
1) Tru-Treat Grapefruit Drink (5-8)

I-23
1) In Alaska it hasta be Shasta (5-8)

I-27
1) Canada Dry/Same (5-8)
2) Drink Coca-Cola (Script)/Have a Coke (15-20)
3) Drink Dr. Pepper/Distinctively Different (15-20)
4) Frostie Root Beer/Same (5-8)
5) Drink Pepsi-Cola (Script) (10-12)
6) 7 Up (in Logo)/"Fresh Up" with Seven-Up (5-8)

I-501
1) Bubble Up (in Logo) (5-8)
2) Donald Duck Soft Drinks in Cans (5-8)

I-502
1) Opener for Cans of Coca-Cola (Block) Syrup (20-25)

J-5
1) Kayo Chocolate (1-2)
2) Kayo Chocolate/Chocolate Products Co. (1-2)
3) Orange Crush Co./Same (5-8)

J-6
1) Kayo Chocolate (1-2)
2) Drink Sambo (2-4)

J-9
1) Royal Crown Cola in cans and bottles (2-4)

J-11
1) Can-A-Pop (2-4)
2) It's Cott to be good! Manchester, N. H. (1-2)
3) Drink Grafs Canned Beverages/Same (1-2)
4) "Use Libby's Famous Juices"/Same (1-2)
5) Drink Mission Beverages/Same (1-2)
6) Royal Crown Cola best by taste-test/Same (3-5)
7) "It Hasta Be Shasta" (1-2)
8) "It Hasta Be Shasta"/Shasta Mixers Low Calorie 5 Flavors in Cans (1-2)
9) Shasta mixers low calorie 6 flavors in cans (1-2)
10) Sun-Rype (1-2)
11) Sun-Rype/Apple Juice (2-4)

L-1
1) Pepsi/Pepsi-Cola (on Bottle Cap)/Pepsi (35-40)

L-2
1) Drink Jackson's Napa Soda (75-100)

M-1
1) Keep in Step with Major Cola in Bottles at Founts/Same (35-40)

M-2
1) Bola ('The Cleveland Sandusky Co. Bola Bola' On Bottle)/Bola a Delicious Cereal Drink (75-100)
2) Say! Drink Hires its Pure (100-125)
3) Pureoxia Ginger Ale (on Bottle Pureoxia Ginger Ale Distilled Water made from Distilled Water The Pureoxia Co. Boston, Mass.) (40-50)

M-3
1) Dr. Pepper good for life/At 10, 2 and 4 O'Clock/Drink a bite to eat (Red) (75-100)
2) London Dry Ginger Ale/A San Miguel product/A San Miguel Product (Red/Ott) (60-75)
3) Drink Moxie 100%/Frank Archer invites you to visit Moxieland/The home of Moxie (Red) (2 Var (A) Frank Archer Slanted Letters (B) Frank Archer Straight Letters) (40-50)

M-6
1) Banko's Beverages (12-15)

M-9
1) Enjoy Bubble Up (5-8)

M-19
1) Coca-Cola (Script) (On Small Bottle attached to Opener) (60-75)
2) Drink Coca-Cola (Script)/Same (175-200)
3) Pepsi=Cola/Same (Beware: Opener has been Reproduced) (40-50)
4) 7 Up/Fresh Up (Brass) (15-20)
5) 7 Up/"Fresh Up" (Chrome) (15-20)
6) Tom Joyce 7 Up (25-30)

M-20
1) Drink J.J. Flynn & Co's Quality Line of Soda Waters White Label Ginger Ale Everybody's Favorite Quincy, Ill. (25-30)

M-21
1) Pureoxia (Sterling) (35-40)

M-23
1) Drink Coca-Cola (Script) Trade Mark/Same (Red) (25-30)
2) Have a Coke (Block) Trade Mark/Same (Black) (25-30)
3) Drink Pepsi-Cola (Script) (Black) (20-25)

M-29
1) Coca-Cola (Script) Coca-Cola (Block) Bottling Company of Waynesburg Waynesburg, Penn. Robert A. Lee Phone 250 (25-30)
2) Budweiser-Highlander-Burgie-Pepsi Cola-Squirt-Flavors Roundup Bottling Co. Phone 63 Dell and Jim-Owners Roundup, Montana (15-20)
3) (Pepsi in Bottle Cap) Pepsi-Cola Bottling Co. 1500 East Main St. Flat River, Mo. Ge1-2140 (Man Having a Cookout) (15-20)
4) Pepsi-Cola Compliments of Pepsi-Cola Bottling Co. Flat River, Mo. Ge1-2140 H.H. Peterson, Pres. (15-20)
5) Say "Pepsi, Please!" Pepsi-Cola (Block) Bottling Co. Memphis, Tenn. (15-20)

M-30
1) Clicquot Club Quality since 1881 Clicquot Club Bottling Co. 938 Phillips Street Missoula, Montana (15-20)
2) Compliments of Wisconsin Dells Coca-Cola (Script) Bottling Corp. dial (608) 254-8400 Wisconsin Dells, Wisc. (15-20)
3) Thomasville Coca-Cola (Script) Bottling Company (25-30)
4) Crescent Bottling Co. "Your Friendly Liquor Dealer" 28 oz. & 12 oz. No Deposit Soda Bottles 25th & River Ave. Camden, N. J. WO 4-2268 (5-8)
5) Drink Frostie Root Beer you'll love it! (15-20)
6) Grafs Soda Pop & Pabst Blue Ribbon Beer Solon Springs Dist. Co. (10-12)
7) Liberty Bell Bottling Co. Importing Distributor for Complete Line of Soft Drinks Rheingold-Iron City-National Bohemian-Colt 45 and Other Popular Brands 24 hour Ice Vendor Drive-in and Delivery Service 1857 So. 5th St. Allentown, Pa. Phone 797-2035 (15-20)
8) Marvel's Old Fashion Root Beer you'll love it's Creamy Flavor Marvel's Beverages "The Eastern Shore's Oldest Bottling Company" (15-20)
9) Oil City Beverage Co., Inc. Ph. 645-5271 119 State St. Oil City, Pa. 1971 (5-8)
10) Pepsi-Cola Dr Pepper 7 Up Hendrix Bottling Co. Bottlers of Dr. Pepper-Pepsi-Cola-7 Up Mattoon, Ill. (15-20)

11) Pepsi-Cola Pepsi-Cola Bottling Co. (15-20)
12) Pepsi-Cola Pepsi-Cola Bottling Co. Flat River, Mo. Phone 431-2140 (15-20)
13) Pepsi Pepsi-Cola Bottling Co. 1500 East Main St. Flat River, Mo. Phone 431-2140 (15-20)
14) Royal Crown Cola Royal Crown Bottling Co. Decatur, Alabama (20-25)
15) 7 Up (Pic of Super Chef) (10-12)
16) 7 Up Seven Up Boise, Idaho Retail Price 49¢ (10-12)
17) 7 Up The Uncola. Seven Up Bottling Co. 2939 Academy Way Sacramento, Calif. 95815 Phone 929-7777 (10-12)

M-33
1) Coca-Cola (Script) Trade Mark is Coke Trade Mark (25-30)

M-39
1) "Don't Blow Your Top" open Zeisler Soda (St Charles, Mo) (10-12)

M-40
1) Coca-Cola (Script) teaches 16,000,000 Readers Monthly through Better Homes & Gardens (25-30)

M-45
1) John Graf Co./Jamaica Pale Dry Ginger Ale (10-12)

M-51
1) Ale 81 it glorifies (in Bottle Cap) Ale-8-One Bottling Co. Carol Rd.-Ph. 744-3484 Winchester, Kentucky (5-8)
2) Cott Quality Beverages Metri/Cola Big 16 Oz. Size the Diet Cola (5-8)
3) "To a Valued Friend & Customer of" John Huber your Coca-Cola (Script) Orange-Crush Salesman Ph. Ex 7-2343 Colfax (10-12)
4) Drink Kist Beverages (5-8)
5) Pepsi-Cola (Block) Distributor A. L. Wilkerson Phone Sav. 2-3042 (10-12)
6) Enjoy Sun Crest Beverages (5-8)

M-54
1) Coca-Cola (Script) (all Steel Handle) (12-15)
2) Coca-Cola (Script) (on Small Bottle attached to plastic handle) (15-20)

M-60
1) B-1 Lemon Lime Soda (10-12)

M-69
1) Seasons Greetings St. James Dr. Pepper Co. Sun-Drop Golden Cola Hamm's Beer (60-75)

M-83
1) Enjoy Coca Cola (Script) (10-12)
2) Let your Pepsi-Cola Taste decide 376-3113 take the Pepsi Challenge! Dick Harding (10-12)
3) Don Smith Distributing Co. call Lennox 9-3005 for your Soda Freeburg, Illinois (3-5)

M-85
1) Drink Coca-Cola (Script) Reg. U.S. Pat. Off. (20-25)
2) 7up (in Logo)/Seven-Up Bottling Company 701 W. 3rd St. Tulsa, Oklahoma Lu 7-7247 (15-20)

M-100
1) Enjoy Coca-Cola (Script) Trade Mark (10-12)
2) Kelford Coca-Cola (Block) Bottling Co. Inc. Kelford, N. C. (10-12)
3) A-Treat S. Stover Beverages 10th St. Telford Pa Phone 723-4576 the Answer to your Entertaining Needs (5-8)

M-120
1) Coca-Cola (Script) in 12 Oz. Bottles (75-100)

M-501
1) Drink Coca-Cola (Script) Reg. U.S. Pat. Off. (5-8)

M-502
1) Coca-Cola (Script) (25-30)

M-503
1) Coca-Cola (Script)/Coca-Cola (Script) (in Red Circle) (60-75)

M-504
1) Coca-Cola (Script) (on Coca-Cola Bottle) (35-40)
2) Coca-Cola (Script) (on Coca-Cola Cup) (35-40)
3) Coca-Cola (Script) (on Coca-Cola Glass) (35-40)
4) Coca-Cola (Script) (on Coca-Cola Logo) (35-40)

M-505
1) Drink Coca-Cola (Script) (25-30)

M-506
1) Enjoy Coke (25-30)

M-507
1) Canfield's (15-20)

M-508
1) Compliments of Platterville Bottling -Works-Roseleip & Shepherd Props. (15-20)

M-509
1) C&C Drink Super C&C/Same (60-75)

N-3
1) Enjoy Coca-Cola (Script) (25-30)

N-4
1) Boston Drug & Beverage Corp./Tel. Liberty 0656 (35-40)
2) Coca-Cola (Script) the pause that refreshes/Same (250-300)
3) Drink Jumbo a Super Cola/Same (35-40)
4) Drink Nugrape/Same (35-40)
5) National Nu Grape Co./Atlanta, Ga. (35-40)
6) Drink Pop Kola/Drink Tick Tock Atlanta Bottling Works (35-40)
7) Drink Pop Kola/The Braser Company Chattanooga, Tenn. (35-40)
8) Rock Spring/(Crest Logo) (35-40)
9) Sun Crest more flavor for your money/Same (20-25)

N-5
1) Coca-Cola (Script)/Same (200-225)
2) Double-Cola/A Great Drink (100-125)
3) Compt's West End Brg. Co./Utica Club its in the taste Pilsener Wuerzburger—Ginger Ale (100-125)

N-7
1) St. Joseph Soda & Seltzer Works, St. Joseph, Mo. (35-40)

N-8
1) Virginia Etna Roanoke, Va. New York natural water Carbonated Ginger Ale (35-40)

N-9
1) Anderson's Beverages famous for quality (3-5)
2) To be used for Beverly Club and Arrowhead Ginger Ales (5-8)
3) Birch Beer (5-8)
4) Black Bear Beverages Healthful-Refreshing call SH. 7570 (3-5)
5) Blue Rock Beverages Fairview, Montana (5-8)
6) Brookdale Beverages Mfg. of Sparkling Beverages Edison 8-9175 ask for Brookdale by Name (5-8)
7) Burkhardt's 4% the Perfect Mixer (10-12)
8) Calso water the Perfect Neutralizer (3-5)
9) Compliments of A. Cerra Bottling Works Carbondale, Pa. Phone 987 (3-5)
10) Clicquot Club Ginger Ale-White Soda Sparkling Water Mester Bottling Co. Dial 2-8818 (5-8)
11) Climax Beverages (10-12)
12) Climax Pale Dry Ginger Ale (10-12)

13) Clipper Club Soda completely Carbonated for Prompt Service call Princeton 8192 (5-8)
14) Coca-Cola (Script) Delicious Refreshing (75-100)
15) Coca-Cola (Script) Sheridan Springs Quality Beverages Phone 118 Lake Geneva, Wis. (75-100)
16) Drink Coca-Cola (Script) and Gold Seal Ginger Ale (75-100)
17) Crystal Beverages Mt. Carmel, Pa. (5-8)
18) Diekman's Ginger Ale Phone 209 (3-5)
19) Doerner's Beverages (3-5)
20) Serve Eagle Beverages 27 Emma St. Phone 6.2732 (3-5)
21) Ed's Soda Bar Westphalia, Michigan (3-5)
22) "English Club Beverages" Mfg. by The George H. Mitchell Co. Waterville, Maine (5-8)
23) Drink Faygo Beverages (3-5)
24) Drink Fox Head Beverages made with Waukesha Spring Water (5-8)
25) Fox Head Waukesha Sparkling Water Carbonated Beverages (Pic of Fox Head) (5-8)
26) -Galler's—Beverages—a Real Mixer- Phone Hoboken 3-1167 (3-5)
27) Golden Age Beverage Co. (3-5)
28) Drink a Hershey all flavors (3-5)
29) Hood River Bottling Works Complete Line of Beverages Phone 4552 Hood River, Oregon (3-5)
30) Husemann Bottling Works Red Bud, Ill. Phone 134 (3-5)
31) Hydrox Beverages made from Pure Fruit Flavors (3-5)
32) Enjoy Kist Beverages dial 7-4711 Binghamton, N. Y. (3-5)
33) Koldrok Club Soda Higher Carbonation (3-5)
34) Koldrok Pale Dry Ginger Ale Superior Quality (3-5)
35) Lotz Dry Ginger Ale Binghamton, N. Y. (5-8)
36) Mercer Beverages (3-5)
37) "Merri" Bigger Bottles better Beverages O.Neill, Nebr. (3-5)
38) Drink Mission Beverages (3-5)
39) Moxie and Virginia Dare Worcester Dial 5-9735 (15-20)
40) Nehi Bottling Co. Mfrs. of Gold Seal Hi Ball Soda Belleville, Ill. (25-30)
41) Nehi Bottling Co. Mfrs. of Gold Seal Hi Ball Soda Royal Crown Cola Belleville, Ill. (25-30)
42) Nelson's Club Ginger Ale (5-8)
43) New Yorker Beverages (5-8)
44) New Yorker Ginger Ale (5-8)
45) Owl's Head Ginger Ale Hatfield & Bell, Inc. (5-8)
46) Bottled by Pepsi-Cola (Block) Bottling Co. Protect your Mixed Drinks use Clicquot Mixers (40-50)
47) Drink Pepsi=Cola (Script) (40-50)
48) Drink Pepsi=Cola (Script) Phone 2674 W (40-50)
49) Livermore Beverages Pepsi=Cola (Script) Stamford 5-1196 (40-50)
50) Pepsi-Cola (Block) (40-50)
51) Phillips Bros. Champion Ginger Ale (5-8)
52) Compliments Schmeltzer Bros. 53 Years of Service 1883-1936 (5-8)
53) Confair Beverage Co. 7up Jack Frost (10-12)
54) Confairs Beverages 7up Berwick, Pa. (10-12)
55) Joyce Seven Up Joliet, Ill. (10-12)
56) Joyce 7up Inc. Joliet Ill. (10-12)
57) 4% Scheu's 4% "The Perfect Mixer" Phone-Plaza 6481 (5-8)
58) Sheffield Bottling Co. Philadelphia 40, Pa. Baldwin 9-0848 (5-8)
59) Shep's Beverages Pittston, Pa. Phone OL 4-2841 (5-8)
60) Birch Beer (5-8)
61) Use Shivar Ginger Ale Lime Rickey Sparkling Water Quarts-Pints-Splits (5-8)
62) Silver State Carbonated Beverages Reno (3-5)
63) Smile of Delight drink Sunny Kid Beverages made Famous by the Public CL 8585 (3-5)
64) Tom Tucker Ginger Ale (5-8)
65) Top Hat Citrus Soda an Ideal Drink a Perfect Mixer (5-8)
66) Vess Beverages Belleville Bottling Co. Full Quart 10c (5-8)
67) Waukesha Waters, Inc. "Almanaris" "Poland" (2 W in Circle) Del. 1616 buy only the best "Apollinaris" "Mountain Valley" (5-8)

68) Irene Rich says to Reduce eat Sensibly drink Welch's Grape Juice (3-5)

69) Pinney Beverage Co. White Rock Water Becker's Beer Budweiser Beer Salt Lake City, Utah (25-30)

70) Winnebago Bottling Co. Carbonated Beverages Winneconne, Wisconsin (3-5)

71) Wittmann's Beverages Rich. Hill 2-0352 (3-5)

N-10

1) Drink Blue Ridge True Fruit Beverages (St Louis, Mo) (5-8)

2) Christin Ginger Ale (5-8)

3) Cornrich's (5-8)

4) Drink Cornrich's Beverages (5-8)

5) Drink Country Club Ginger Ale (10-12)

6) J.G. Fox & Co. "Fox" Snappy Drinks (5-8)

7) Imperial Beverages (5-8)

8) Mountain Valley Mineral Water from Hot Springs, Ark. (5-8)

9) Schultz Sparkling Beverages (5-8)

10) Drink Tip-Top Soda Water (10-12)

N-11

1) Ask your Grocer for Belfast Dry-Ginger Ale-or call Doug. 0547 – 0548 (5-8)

2) Coca-Cola (Script) Christy & Huggins Co. Murfreesboro, Tenn. (175-200)

3) Drink Coca-Cola (Script) Coca-Cola (Script) Bottling Co. Waterloo, Iowa (175-200)

4) Drink Falstaff Pale Dry Ginger Ale and Lemon Soda (15-20)

5) Drink Howdy John H. Hoke Lebanon, Pa. (5-8)

6) Original "Manitou" Pale Dry Ginger Ale and Sparkling Water (10-12)

7) Original "Manitou" Pale Dry Ginger Ale Ginger Champagne Sparkling Water (10-12)

8) "Since 1878" Sal-U-Taris Scotch Soda for your High-Ball (5-8)

9) Buy Silco Beverages (5-8)

N-20

1) Birk Brothers Brewing Co. Superb and Goldeck Beverages/ Birk's Root Beer Phone Lincoln 495 (20-25)

2) Birk Brothers Company Superb & Goldeck Beverages/Birk's Root Beer Phone Lincoln 495 (20-25)

3) Butte Bottlers' Supply Co. 115 S. Main St. Phone 549j/ Bottlers' supplies malt & hops (20-25)

4) Drink Ceco/The Delightful Cola Drink (20-25)

5) Drink Coca-Cola (Script) in Bottles/Coca-Cola (Script) Bottling Works Pulaski, Tenn. (200-250)

6) John L. Getz & Son 258 West King St./Soft Drinks, Syrups, and Crushed Fruits (20-25)

7) Hoster-Columbus Company Inc. Columbus, Ohio/Bruin Non Intoxicating a Cereal Beverage (30-35)

N-22

1) Coca-Cola (Script) Grand Forks Bottling Co. Phone 409 Grand Forks, N.D. Seasons Greetings (125-150)

2) Drink The Kurth Company's Beverages good to the Last Drop Sold Everywhere (60-75)

3) Reno Brewing Co., Inc. New Style Lager Canadian Club Dry Ginger Ale all flavors Soda Water Reno,—Nevada (60-75)

N-24

1) Big Boy 12 oz. T. M. Reg. Per Quality Extra Beverages Tel: 1616/Tops-Sparkling Water Tel: 1616 (St Charles, Mo) (15-20)

2) Felix Dry Ginger Felix Orange Dry/Felix Grape Fruit Dry Felix Club Soda (15-20)

N-26

1) Celebrating our 50th Anniversary Washington Coca-Cola (Block) Bottling Company Washington, Georgia (100-125)

2) K. & C. Beverage Co. Phone 321 142 E. 7th Ave.-Tarentum, Pa. (10-12)

3) For the best Drink White Rock Sparkling Beverages 2140 W. Fillmore-Alpine 2-6293 (10-12)

N-29

1) Coca-Cola (Script) (100-125)

2) Drink Coca-Cola (Script) every Bottle Sterilized Bottled by Starr Brothers Phone 2-0147 Akron, O. Sample No. 26 (100-125)

3) When you drink a Dr. Pepper Good for Life you drink a bite to eat (100-125)

4) Nehi Bottling Co. Culpeper, Va. (Royal Crown Royal Crown Cola on Bottle) (35-40)

5) Drink Polar Ginger Ale Very Refreshing (No. 1144 Combination Bullet Pencil & Opener) (15-20)

N-38

1) Old Colony & Grapette Madison Bottling Works (20-25)

N-42

1) Cott quality Beverages Manchester, N. H./(Pic of a Fish) (20-25)

N-43

1) Coca Cola (Block) Bottling Co./Sample No. 1100 (60-75)

2) Coca Cola (Block) Bottling Co. Kansas City, Mo. (60-75)

N-44

1) Coca-Cola (Script) Bottling Company./(Coca-Cola (Script) On Bottle) when thirsty try a bottle (150-175)

N-56

1) Drink Coca-Cola (Script) (15-20)

2) Enjoy Coca Cola (Script) (15-20)

3) Double-Cola (10-12)

4) Dr Pepper (15-20)

5) Nugrape (10-12)

6) Drink Pepsi-Cola (15-20)

7) Me and My RC (8-10)

N-62

1) Coca-Cola (Block) and Schlitz Hund and Eger St. Joseph, Mo. (75-100)

2) Hund and Eger (20-25)

3) Nehi Par-T-Pak 7 Up Phone 7-7521 (40-50)

N-67

1) Distributors of Schmidt's Beer Compliments of Palmyra Beverages Mfg. of Kist Beverages (40-50)

N-79

1) An Advertising Novelty of The Pepsi-Cola Company Evervess Sparkling Water (20-25)

N-84

1) Coca-Cola (Script) Bottling Works Nashville, Tennessee (30-35)

N-85

1) Drink Nehi 5c quality Beverages/Drink Nehi in all Popular Flavors take a good look at the Bottle be sure its Nehi (Metal Handles) (75-100)

N-501

1) Drink Chero-Cola there's none better 5c (50-60)

2) Drink Chero-Cola there's none so good 5c (50-60)

N-502

1) Drink Chero-Cola there's none so good 5c (50-60)

N-503

1) Pureoxia Ginger Ale (60-75)

N-504

1) Drink Coca-Cola (Script) in Bottles/Delicious and Refreshing (100-125)

N-505
1) Compliments of Coca-Cola (Script) Bottling Works Nashville, Tenn. (Coca-Cola (Script) on Bottle) (50-60)

N-506
1) 50th Anniversary Coca-Cola (Script) in Bottles (50-60)
2) 50th Anniversary Coca-Cola (Script) 1900 1950 (50-60)

N-507
1) Drink Coca-Cola (Script) or Be Smart (Sliding Window Ad) (125-150)

N-508
1) Drink Coca-Cola (Script) Reg. U.S. Pat. off./Enjoy Coca-Cola (Script) Trade-Mark (R in Circle) (3 Var (A) Coca-Cola in Logo Smooth Handles (B) No Logo Smooth Handles (C) No Logo Grilled Handles) (50-60)
2) Drink Coca-Cola (Script) Reg. U.S. Pat. off./Spring Sales Meeting 1955 (50-60)

N-509
1) The Coca-Cola (Script) Bottling Co./Delicious and Refreshing (40-50)

N-510
1) Drink Coca-Cola (Script) in Bottles Delicious and Refreshing (60-75)

N-511
1) Drink Coca-Cola (Script) in Bottles (300-350)

N-512
1) Royal Crown Cola best by taste-test (20-25)

N-513
1) For your Health and Happiness drink Diet-Rite Cola and R.C. Cola (25-30)

N-514
1) Drink Coca-Cola (Script) (Double Blade Knife/Cap Lifter Blade/Can Opener Blade) (Bone Handles) (250-300)

N-515
1) Drink Coca-Cola (Script) (Double Blade Knife/Cap Lifter Blade/Can Opener Blade) (Composition Handles) (2 Var (A) Short Opener Blade (B) Lone Opener Blade) (250-300)

N-516
1) Coca-Cola (Script) (Coca-Cola (Script) on bottle)/The Coca-Cola (Script) Bottling Co. (Double Blade Knife/Cap Lifter Blade/Rounded Can Opener Blade) (Metal Handles) (250-300)

N-517
1) Coca-Cola (Script) (Coca-Cola (Script) on bottle)/The Coca-Cola (Script) Bottling Co. (Double Blade Knife/Cap Lifter Blade/Two Prong Can Opener Blade) (Metal Handles) (250-300)

N-518
1) Drink Coca-Cola (Script) (Composition Handles) (125-150)

N-519
1) Drink Coca-Cola (Script) in Bottles Greenwood Coca-Cola (Block) Bot. Co (60-75)

N-520
1) Drink Coca-Cola (Script) (20-25)
2) R C Cola (20-25)

N-521
1) Drink Coca-Cola (Script) Reg. U. S. Pat. Off. (30-35)

O-2
1) Drink Cheer-Up a delightful drink a real supercharged beverage (40-50)
2) Drink Coca-Cola (Script) (40-50)
3) Dillon Bottling Works Highlander Schmidt's Dillon Beverages Candy and Tobacco Phone 154-W (12-15)
4) Drink Dr. Nut "It's Delicious!" Floresville-Phone 162 (30-35)
5) Kiel Bottling Works bottlers of Kissy & Mission Beverages Distributors of Heileman's Old Style and Schlitz Beers Phone 29-W Kiel-Wisconsin (30-35)
6) Enjoy Kist Beverages (35-40)
7) Nesbitt (Slice of Orange) (20-25)
8) Enjoy Pepsi=Cola (Script) 5c (40-50)
9) Enjoy Red Rock Cola Copyright 1939 (30-35)
10) Drink Royal Crown Cola best by taste test (40-50)
11) 7up likes you! (30-35)
12) Smile refresh with a smile (Orange Head Man) (20-25)
13) Squeeze (Two Children Hugging) (30-35)
14) Drink Sweet Sixteen Beverages (20-25)
15) Drink Zimba Kola and Nesbitt's Orange (20-25)

O-4
1) Drink Coca-Cola (Script) in Bottles (60-75)
2) York Dr. Pepper Bottling Company York, Nebraska (40-50)
3) Drink Mission Beverages (20-25)
4) Nehi Beverage Phone Ad 4311 (40-50)
5) Nu-Grape Soda imitation Grape flavor (40-50)
6) Pepsi=Cola (Script) 12 oz 5c (60-75)
7) Drink Phillips Bros. Champion Ginger Ale (20-25)
8) Royal Crown Cola (Crown in Circle) (30-35)
9) 7 Up (30-35)
10) Suburban Club Ginger Ale (20-25)
11) Sun Crest (30-35)

O-5
1) Barq's (10-12)
2) Drink Barq's it's good (10-12)
3) Drink Beaufont Ginger Ale Giant Beverages (75-100)
4) Bireley's (10-12)
5) Canada Dry (2 Var (A) Large Letters (B) Small Letters) (5-8)
6) Canning's Beverages (5-8)
7) Climax Beverages (30-35)
8) Drink Coca-Cola (Script) (2-4)
9) Enjoy Coca-Cola (Script) (2-4)
10) Double Cola (10-12)
11) Dr. Pepper (2 Var (A) Block Letters (B) Script Letters) (10-12)
12) Dr. Pepper good for life (15-20)
13) Grapette (15-20)
14) Green Spot (2 Var (A) Spot is Green Painted (B) Spot is Red Painted) (15-20)
15) Drink I-Cee (15-20)
16) Enjoy Ju-C Beverages (5-8)
17) Kist (15-20)
18) "The Liquid" (5-8)
19) "Mr" Cola (10-12)
20) Drink Nehi (60-75)
21) Orange Crush (5-8)
22) Orange Crush Carbonated Beverage (15-20)
23) Pep (5-8)
24) Pepsi-Cola (Script) (5-8)
25) Pepsi=Cola (Script) (10-12)
26) Drink Rock Spring (5-8)
27) Drink Royal Crown Cola (10-12)
28) You like it 7 Up it likes you (5-8)
29) Drink Squirt (Script) (5-8)
30) Squirt (Block) (5-8)
31) Tru-Ade (10-12)
32) White Rock Ginger Ale (5-8)

O-6
1) Catawissa Sparkling Beverages (15-20)
2) Drink Coca-Cola (Script) (75-100)

154

3) Dr. Pepper (Script) (75-100)
4) Frostie Old Fashion Root Beer (35-40)
5) Graf's Carbonated Beverages Since 1873 (35-40)
6) Drink Moran's Beverages (15-20)
7) Royal Crown Cola best by taste-test take Time Out for a "Quick-Up" with (35-40)
8) Seewee Quality Beverages (15-20)
9) 7 Up (30-35)
10) Star and Crescent Beverages (Crescent Logo) Phone 331 Waupun (15-20)

O-8
1) Coca-Cola (Script) (100-125)
2) Coca-Cola (Script) Bottling Co. Linton, Ind. Phone 74 (100-125)
3) Drink Coca-Cola (Script) in Bottles (100-125)
4) Crystal Rock Pale Dry Reading, Pa. (25-30)
5) Drink Mission Beverages (20-25)
6) Drink Nehi (50-60)
7) Drink Poet'y Pop Red Lion Bottling Wks. (30-35)
8) Tip Top Bottling Co. St. Louis, Mo (30-35)

O-10
1) Drink Citizens Soft Drinks buy better Bottle Beverages (75-100)
2) Drink Coca-Cola (Script) in Sterilized Bottles The Coca-Cola (Block) Bottling Co. Chicago, Ill. (100-125)
3) Drink Coca-Cola (Script) in Sterilized Bottles Coca-Cola (Block) Bottling Works Roanoke, Va. (100-125)
4) Suburban Club Ginger Ale Phone Wolfe 3765 (30-35)
5) Drink Try-Me Beverages (30-35)

O-14
1) Sun Crest (30-35)

O-16
1) Drink Cheer Up (20-25)
2) Drink Coca-Cola (Script) (40-50)
3) Royal Crown Cola best by taste-test (20-25)

O-17
1) Coca-Cola Sprite Boy (5-8) (Very Common)

O-18
1) John Arnold's Quality Beverages (75-100)
2) Coca-Cola (Script) (2 Var (A) Marked Protector Mfg. Co. (B) Not Marked Protector Mfg. Co.) (125-150)

O-19
1) Coca-Cola (Script) Bottling Co. San Bernardino Phone 301-82 (75-100)
2) The Eilert Beverage Company (40-50)
3) Drink Ute Chief Manitou Water and Ginger Ale. (40-50)
4) Whistle Bottling Co. Whistle and Other Soft Drinks (40-50)

O-501
1) Drink Coca-Cola (Script) Trade Mark Reg. (150-175)

O-502
1) Drink Coca-Cola (Script) (100-125)

O-503
1) Drink Coca-Cola (Script) (Arrow Pointing to Opener) (150-175)

O-504
1) Drink Coca-Cola (Script) in Bottles (150-175)

O-505
1) Big Bill (20-25)
2) Big Boy (20-25)
3) Coca-Cola (Script) (20-25)
4) Icy-O (20-25)
5) Drink Mavis (20-25)
6) Nehi (30-35)

7) Orange Crush (20-25)
8) Whistle (30-35)

O-506
1) "Fresh Up" with Seven-Up (20-25)

O-507
1) Pepsi=Cola (Script) (30-35)

O-508
1) Drink Pepsi=Cola (Script) (50-60)

O-509
1) Cleo Cola (On Decal) (60-75)
2) Drink Coca-Cola (Script) Delicious and Refreshing (On Decal) (75-100)
3) Dr Pepper (on Decal) (75-100)
4) Orange Crush (On Decal) (40-50)
5) Pepsi=Cola (Script) Refreshing Healthful (On Decal) (60-75)
6) Drink Royal Crown Cola (On Decal) (40-50)
7) 7 Up (On Decal) (40-50)

O-510
1) Coca-Cola (Script) Phone 293 (100-125)
2) 7 Up (35-40)

O-511
1) Coca-Cola (Script) (100-125)

O-512
1) Canfield's (20-25)

O-513
1) Bireley's (20-25)

O-514
1) Minimum Contents 8 Fluid Ozs. Coca-Cola (Script) Reg. U.S. Patent Off. (60-75)
2) Pepsi=Cola (60-75)
3) 7 Up (40-50)

O-515
1) Drink Coca-Cola (Script) (50-60)

O-516
1) Drink Coca-Cola (Script) in Bottles (100-125)
2) White Rock Ginger Ale White Rock (75-100)

O-517
1) Drink Coca-Cola (Script) Trade-Mark (25-30)

O-518
1) Drink Coca-Cola (Script) Delicious Refreshing (on Decal) (75-100)
2) Drink Nehi (on Decal) (60-75)

O-519
1) Drink Coca-Cola (Script) (2 Var (A) Trade Mark (B) No Trade Mark) (40-50)
2) "Fresh Up" with 7up (40-50)

O-520
1) Drink Double Cola (in Circle) (20-25)
2) Hazel Club (15-20)
3) Drink Nesbitts (15-20)
4) "Fresh Up" with Seven-Up 7-Up (20-25)

O-521
1) 7 Up (10-12)

O-522
1) Nehi (40-50)

155

O-523
1) Drink Coca-Cola (125-150)

O-524
1) Compliments Geneva Bottling Works, Inc. PH. Geneva 1100 (40-50)

O-525
1) Drink Coca-Cola (Script) (40-50)

O-526
1) Drink Coca-Cola (Script) (40-50)

P-6
1) Our Specialty "K & K Extra Dry High Ball Ginger Ale" Agents for Atlas bottle Beer The Independent Bottling Works 4423-25 Evans Ave. Chicago Phone Oakland 1826 (30-35)
2) Serve Phillips Bros. Champion Ginger Ale mixes better (15-20)

P-7
1) Coca-Cola (Script) Coca-Cola (Script) Bottling Co. Oklahoma City, Okla. (200-250)
2) Golden West Soda Works Somps & Paillet San Francisco, Cal. (20-25)
3) "Everybody's Drink" Ureeka the Great Saazer Hop Temperance Beverage Ureeka Beverage Co. Boston, Mass. Nourishes the Body Quenches the Thirst on Sale Everywhere (20-25)

P-8
1) Price 25c Manufactured Expressly for Lakewood and Macrisco Beverages/The McCart-Christy Co. Cleveland (20-25)
2) The Welch Grape Juice Westfield, New York/Same (12-15)

P-10
1) Drewry & Sons, St. Paul, Minn./Malt & Carbonated Beverages (30-35)
2) Gold Medal Brand Randall's Grape Juice Ripley, N. Y. USA Home of the Concord Grape Randall's Grape Juice given Highest Award World's Fair (20-25)

P-11
1) Pacific Soda Works/Phone 204 Oregon City, Ore. (60-75)

P-14
1) Drink Coca-Cola (Script) Sample No. 501 (40-50)
2) Compliments of Nehi Bottling Co. Phil Krasnow, Mgr. (35-40)
3) Nu Grape Soda imitation grape flavor (20-25)
4) Drink Pop Kola/Biggest thirst value under the sun (20-25)

P-15
1) Cott quality Beverages Manchester, N. H./It's Cott to be good! (12-15)
2) Compliments of Hornberger's Beverages (12-15)

P-19
1) Drink Bartlett Water Bartlett Springs Co. Props. (10-12)
2) C & J Ginger Ale Beacon Ave Lawrence, Mass. Tel. 7141 (10-12)
3) Compliments of Eagle Bottling Works John H. Anderson, Prop. Tacoma (10-12)
4) Drink Getz's Blue Label Ginger Ale, J.L. Getz & Son, Bottlers, York,—Pa. (10-12)
5) Here it is "Sizz" the One Best Drink Leo Grotte Mfg. Co. (10-12)

P-22
1) James Bros. Mineral Waters Manley/Same (20-25)
2) Kola an Ideal Beverage/Kola Refreshing & Invigorating (20-25)

P-31
1) Compliments of The G. A. Lammers Bottling Co. Denver Colo. (15-20)

P-36
1) Nugrape-Soda imitation grape flavor (30-35)

P-51
1) The Reiners Company Bottlers Huntingdon, PA./Same (15-20)
2) Compliments of Sprague, Warner & Company Richelieu Carbonated Beverages/Same (20-25)

P-53
1) Drink and Enjoy "Greenbrier's" own Ginger Ale and Sparkling Water (15-20)
2) Made for Roberts Fine Beverages 1001 Wilshire Blvd. Santa Monica (12-15)

P-54
1) San Spring Ginger Ale (10-12)
2) Try Scotch Hop Ale a Soda Water Beer. (20-25)

P-58
1) Drink Coca-Cola (Script) (R in Circle) (with Hook to Hang On The Wall) (175-200)

P-60
1) P. & R. Bottling Works A. Werner, Prop. Fine Wines & Liquors, Bottled Beer, Ale & Porter, Soft Drinks & Mineral Waters a Specialty Sixth & Franklin Sts. Reading, Pa. (20-25)
2) Ask for Wiz the Grand Summer Drink Morris Horn & Son Sole Controllers Keystone Cordial Co. 201 South Main St. Wilkes-Barre, Pa. (20-25)

P-69
1) Drink Pepsi=Cola (Script) Delicious Healthful/(Pic of Dwarf Opening a Bottle of Spewing Soda) (Tang marked Dolphin Cutlery New York, Germany) (800-1000)

P-74
1) Drink Bartlett Water Bartlett Springs Co. Prop's. (20-25)

P-79
1) Dr. Pepper King of Beverages Dr. Hoxie Tonic/Same (800-1000)

P-85
1) The Best Ever and Ever the Best Simpson Spring Co.'s Beverages Ginger Ale Co-Clo-Rett Nerve Tonic Three Winners (20-25)

P-88
1) Try Hermann's Root Beer (50-60)

P-90
1) Holdredge Bottling Works Holdredge, Neb./Carbonated Beverages, Supplies, Etc. (20-25)

P-95
1) Seattle Fruit Juice Syrup Co. Bottlers Supplies Free Delivery Phones Main 4618 Main 5211 217 Spring St. 1828 1st Ave. (15-20)

P-104
1) Diet 7 Up (15-20)

P-131
1) 7up (in Logo)/Seven-Up Bottling Company 701 W. 3rd St. Tulsa, Oklahoma Lu 7-7247 (30-35)

P-138
1) Drink Coca-Cola (Script) in Bottles Delicious-Refreshing (40-50)

P-501
1) Pepsi Cola Bottling Co. Charleston, S. Car. J. T. Oglesby, Proprietor (100-125)

P-502
1) Mathews & Watson Phone 174 Ice, Coal & Soda Water (60-75)
2) Ask for Pepsi-Cola (Block) a Nickel Drink Worth a Dime

Associated Enterprises 124 Center St. Phone 205-R Ice & Coal (75-100)

P-503
1) Clicquot Club Ginger Ale Supreme S E C Millis, Mass. (Pic of Eskimo) S E C aged 6 months (2 Var (A) Copper Body (150-200) (B) Enameled Body) (250-300)

P-504
1) Soda & Mineral Water Co. Phone 1140.. Warren, Pa. (12-15)

P-505
1) Apollinaris/Same (125-150)

P-506
1) Suggest the Carioca Cooler (Cuba Libre Plus Lime) made only with Coca-Cola (Block), Lime and Rum Carioca 86 Proof Serve in 10 oz. Collins Glass-Plenty Ice Cia Ron Carioca Destilera, Inc. San Juan, Puerto Rico (60-75)

P-507
1) Coca-Cola (Script) (Coca-Cola (Script) on bottle)/The Coca-Cola (Script) Bottling Co. (Single Blade Knife/Cap Lifter Blade) (Tang marked Coca-Cola Bottling Co. Germany/Kastor & Co.) (600-800)

P-508
1) Original Manitou/The Manitou Mineral Water Co. Manitou, Colo. (50-60)

P-509
1) Drink Camel Soda All Flavors Riverside 1260—616 Blow St.,

St. Louis (40-50)
2) Ben Herr sells White Rock (40-50)

P-510
1) The Coca Cola (Script) Co/Sold in Bottles Everywhere (Tang marked A.W. Wadsworth & Son, Germany) (250-300)

P-511
1) (Coca-Cola Bottle) (150-200)

P-512
1) 7up (in Logo) Seven-Up Bottling Co. E.L. Taylor, Jr. (Tang marked Imperial Prov. R.I. USA) (50-60)

P-513
1) Cantrell & Cochrane's Club Soda/Same (75-100)

P-514
1) Coca-Cola (Script) (Coca-Cola (Script) on Bottle)/The Coca-Cola (Script) Bottling Co. (Double Blade Knife/Cap Lifter-Wire Cutter Blade) (Tang marked Coca-Cola Bottling Co. Germany/Kastor & Co.) (800-1000)

P-515
1) Drink Coca-Cola (Script) in Bottles/Pure as Sunlight (Tang marked Imperial, Providence, Pat. Pen.) (75-100)

R-501
1) 7-Up (10-12)

R-502
1) Comp. of C. Breimeyer (60-75)

RESORCES

BOOKS

Bull, Donald A. *The Ultimate Corkscrew Book*. Atglen, Pennsylvania, USA: Schiffer Publishing Ltd., 1999.

Bull, Donald A. *Bull's Pocket Guide to Corkscrews*. Atglen, Pennsylvania, USA: Schiffer Publishing Ltd., 1999.

Bull, Donald A., and John R. Stanley. *Just For Openers*. Atglen, Pennsylvania, USA: Schiffer Publishing Ltd., 1999.

Bull, Donald, and Manfred Friedrich. *The Register of United States Breweries 1876-1976, Volumes I & II*. Trumbull, Connecticut, USA: Bull, 1976.

Bull, Donald, Manfred Friedrich, and Robert Gottschalk. *American Breweries*. Trumbull, Connecticut, USA: Bullworks, 1984.

Bull, Donald. *A Price Guide to Beer Advertising Openers and Corkscrews*. Trumbull, Connecticut, USA: Bull, 1981.

Bull, Donald. *Beer Advertising Openers—A Pictorial Guide*. Trumbull, Connecticut, USA: Bull, 1978.

Goins, John. *Encyclopedia of Cutlery Markings*. Knoxville, Tennessee: Knife World Publications, 1986.

Kaye, Edward R., and Donald A. Bull. *The Handbook of Beer Advertising Openers and Corkscrews*. Sanibel Island, Florida: Kaye, 1984.

Levine, Bernard. *Levine's Guide to Knives and Their Values*. Iola, Wisconsin: Krause Publications, 1997.

O'Leary, Fred. *Corkscrews: 1000 Patented Ways to Open a Bottle*. Atglen, Pennsylvania, USA: Schiffer Publishing Ltd., 1996.

Petretti, Allan. *Petretti's Soda Pop Collectibles Price Guide The Encyclopedia of Soda-Pop Collectibles*. Antique Trader Books, 1996.

Stanley, John R., Edward R. Kaye, and Donald A. Bull. *The 1999 Handbook of United States Beer Advertising Openers and Corkscrews*. Chapel Hill, North Carolina: John Stanley, 1998.

Van Wieren, Dale P., Donald Bull, Manfred Friedrich, and Robert Gottschalk. *American Breweries II*. West Point, Pennsylvania, USA: Eastern Coast Breweriana Association, 1995.

Newsletters

Bull, Donald. *Just For Openers, Issues 1-20*. Trumbull, Connecticut, USA: Bull, January, 1979 through October, 1983.

Kaye, Edward R. *Just For Openers, Issues 21-40*. Sanibel Island, Florida: Kaye, January, 1984 through October, 1988.

Santen, Art. *Just For Openers, Issues 41-60*. St. Louis, Missouri: Santen, January, 1985 through October, 1993.

Stanley, John R. *Just For Openers, Issues 61-84*. Chapel Hill, North Carolina: Stanley, January, 1994 through October, 1999.

TYPE INDEX